The Woman and the Lyre

The Woman and the Lyre

Women Writers in Classical Greece and Rome

Jane McIntosh Snyder

Southern Illinois University Press
Carbondale and Edwardsville

Copyright © 1989 by the Board of Trustees,
Southern Illinois University

All rights reserved

Printed in the United States of America

Edited by Carol A. Burns

Designed by Joyce Kachergis

Production supervised by Linda Jorgensen-Buhman

92 91 90 89   4 3 2 1

Portions of chapter 5 are reprinted from EGERIA: DIARY OF A PILGRIMAGE, George E. Gingras, Trans. From the Ancient Christian Writers series. © 1970 by Johannes Quasten, Walter J. Burghardt and Thomas Comerford Lawler. Used by permission of Paulist Press.

Illustration on title page adapted from a red-figured kalathoid vase representation of Sappho, Munich 2416.

Library of Congress Cataloging-in-Publication Data

Snyder, Jane McIntosh.
    The woman and the lyre: women writers in classical Greece and
Rome / by Jane McIntosh Snyder.
        p. cm—(Ad feminam)
    Bibliography: p.
    Includes index.
    ISBN 0-8093-1455-X
    1. Classical literature—Women authors—History and criticism.
2. Women and literature—Greece. 3. Women and literature—Rome.
4. Classical literature—Women authors—Translation into English.
5. English literature—Translations from classical languages.
I. Title. II. Series.
PA3067.S69 1989
880'.9'9287—dc19   88–10114
                                                                                       CIP

The paper used in this publication meets the minimum requirements of American National Standard for Information Sciences—Permanence of Paper for Printed Library Materials, ANSI Z39.48-1984. ♾

These women Mt. Helicon and the Macedonian rock of Pieria
    raised—with godlike tongues for songs:
Praxilla, Moero, the voice of Anyte (the female Homer),
    Sappho, the ornament of the fair-tressed Lesbians,
Erinna, Telesilla of wide fame, and you, Korinna,
    singing of the impetuous shield of Athena,
Nossis of womanly tongue, and sweet-sounding Myrtis—
    all of them composers of pages that will last for all time.
Great Heaven created nine Muses, but Earth
    bore these nine, as everlasting delight for mortals.
                              Antipater of Thessaloniki, *Anthologia Palatina*

Contents

Ad Feminam:
Women and Literature

Ad Hominem: to the man; appealing to personal interests, prejudices, or emotions rather than to reason; *an argument ad hominem.*
— *American Heritage Dictionary*

Until quite recently, much literary criticism, like most humanistic studies, has been in some sense constituted out of arguments *ad hominem*. Not only have examinations of literary history tended to address themselves "to the man"—that is, to the identity of what was presumed to be the *man* of letters who created our culture's monuments of unaging intellect—but many aesthetic analyses and evaluations have consciously or unconsciously appealed to the "personal interests, prejudices, or emotions" of male critics and readers. As the title of this series is meant to indicate, the intellectual project called "feminist criticism" has sought to counter the limitations of *ad hominem* thinking about literature by asking a series of questions addressed *ad feminam:* to the woman as both writer and reader of texts.

First, and most crucially, feminist critics ask, What is the relationship between gender and genre, between sexuality and textuality? But in meditating on these issues they raise a number of more specific questions. Does a woman of letters have a literature— a language, a history, a tradition—of her own? Have conventional methods of canon-formation tended to exclude or marginalize female achievements? More generally, do men and women have different modes of literary representation, different definitions of literary production? Do such differences mean that distinctive male- (or female-) authored images of women (or men), as well as distinctly male and female genres, are part of our intellectual heritage? Perhaps most important, are literary differences between men and women essential or accidental, biologically determined or culturally constructed?

Feminist critics have addressed themselves to these problems with increasing sophistication during the last two decades, as they sought to revise, or at times replace, *ad hominem* arguments with *ad feminam* speculations. Whether explicating individual texts, studying the oeuvre of a single author, examining the permutations of a major theme, or charting the contours of a tradition, these theorists and scholars have consistently sought to define literary manifestations of difference and to understand the dynamics that have shaped the accomplishments of literary women.

As a consequence of such work, feminist critics, often employing new modes of analysis, have begun to uncover a neglected female tradition along with a heretofore hidden history of the literary dialogue between men and women. This series is dedicated to publishing books that will use innovative as well as traditional interpretive methods in order to help readers of both sexes achieve a clearer consciousness of that neglected but powerful tradition and a better understanding of that hidden history. Reason tells us, after all, that if, transcending prejudice and special pleading, we speak to, and focus on, the woman as well as the man—if we think *ad feminam* as well as *ad hominem*—we will have a better chance of understanding what constitutes the human.

Sandra M. Gilbert

Preface

This book is intended for anyone who is interested in Western literature and its history, particularly in the voices of women writers of the past. I say "voices" deliberately, for in ancient times oral presentation was the rule. For instance, lyric poetry, in its original sense, was poetry accompanied by the plucking of the strings of a lyre, the instrument associated with Apollo, god of music and poetry. Ancient writing was intended not for solitary enjoyment but for public occasions—dinner parties, ceremonies, celebrations. Instead of reading silently to oneself, one listened to poetry or prose sung or recited aloud. The poet's actual voice was an intrinsic element of the art.

Unfortunately, the voices from antiquity have to a great extent been silenced, for many works by both women and men have been lost over the centuries. The reader will note that every one of the writers discussed in this book is represented today only by a small portion of what she actually wrote. Often the poems that have come down to us are short excerpts quoted by grammarians to illustrate the poet's diction or syntax. Others are in the form of tattered fragments rescued from scraps of papyri. (For a lively account of the papyrus discoveries at Oxyrhynchus in Egypt in the 1890s, see Leo Deuel, "Pearls from Rubbish Heaps: Grenfell and Hunt," in *Testaments of Time: The Search for Lost Manuscripts and Records* [New York: Knopf, 1965], 132–49.) In some cases, nothing remains of the work but a reported title or two. A translator's remark on Sappho applies to other writers of the ancient world as well: "One seems to be hearing faint snatches of a human voice, coming up through a vast chasm of deep silence" (Suzy Q. Groden, *The Poems of Sappho*

[Indianapolis: Bobbs-Merrill, 1966], xiii). Much has been irretrievably lost, but I hope that with the help of this book and the work of other scholars from which it draws, the reader can hear at least the echoes of women's voices speaking to us through the silence of two millennia.

I have tried to let these women speak for themselves by including as much translation from their remaining words as is feasible in a short survey; the translations are my own unless otherwise specified. Detailed explications of the sort that a professional classicist might expect will not be found here, but ample references to fuller discussions are given in the notes. I have, however, felt it necessary to refute at least some of the arguments found in the scholarly literature that seem to me to represent the kinds of prejudicial attitudes to which women writers of any time or place have usually been subjected: the notion that women's experience is narrow or trivial and therefore automatically inferior as subject matter for literature, the assumption that intensity in a woman writer is a sign of neurotic imbalance, and the idea that women's work should be judged according to some externally imposed standard of propriety instead of according to what the author actually wrote—in short, the denial of the power of the written words of women.

These fragmentary echoes that have come to us across the centuries do carry power, and each writer has her own distinctive voice and vision. Some, like Sappho, may be considered great; others are of only minor stature. Some cannot really be evaluated because so little of their work has survived. All are part of our heritage.

Acknowledgments

I am grateful to The Ohio State University's College of Humanities, to former Dean Diether Haenicke, and to Professor Charles Babcock, Chair, for a sabbatical leave in 1980–81, during which time this project was begun in Ann Arbor, Michigan. Thanks are due as well to the courteous staff of the University of Michigan Libraries and to the Horace H. Rackham program for visiting scholars. I am also indebted to The Ohio State University's Center for Women's Studies for a research grant and to G. Micheal Riley, present dean of The Ohio State University's College of Humanities, for helpful encouragement on numerous occasions and for research funding that enabled me to complete the manuscript.

I also thank the following individuals for various forms of invaluable assistance, support, and inspiration: June Allison, Christy Thatcher Bening, Nadean Bishop, Elaine Fantham, Karen Givler, Christopher Griffin, David Hahm, Judith Hallett, Susan Hartmann, Marianne Johnson, Susan Kemper, Craig McVay, Mildred Munday, Mary Search, Harold Snyder, and Robert Sutton. I am particularly grateful to Helene Foley, Mary R. Lefkowitz, William E. McCulloh, Carl Schlam, and Marilyn B. Skinner for their detailed criticisms of earlier draft portions of the manuscript. Finally, I am indebted to Carol A. Burns of Southern Illinois University Press for her conscientious copyediting and to Marcia A. Dalbey for her unfailing help during the final stages of the preparation of this book.

The Woman and the Lyre

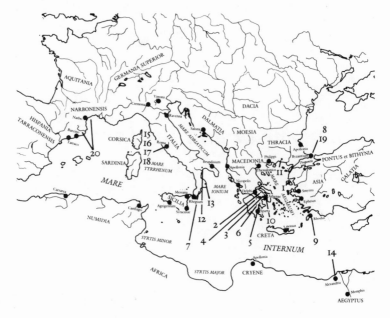

Key to Map

Only those writers whose place of birth or literary activity is relatively certain have been included in the list below.

Number on Map	Writer	Place
1	Sappho	Lesbos
2	Myrtis	Anthedon
3	Korinna	Tanagra
4	Praxilla	Sikyon
5	Telesilla	Argos
6	Anyte	Tegea
7	Nossis	Locri
8	Moero	Byzantium (Constantinople)
9	Erinna	area of Rhodes?
10	Leontion	Athens
11	Hipparchia	Maroneia
12	Theano	Metapontum
13	Myia	Croton
14	Hypatia	Alexandria
15	Cornelia	Rome
16	Hortensia	Rome
17	Sulpicia	Rome
18	Proba	Rome
19	Eudocia	Byzantium (Constantinople)
20	Egeria	Spain/France?

I *Sappho of Lesbos*

The earliest woman writer in Western literature whose work
has—at least in part—survived the passage of time and the willful
attempts to silence the voices of women is also the most famous:
Sappho of Lesbos. Few readers will have heard of Korinna or
Telessila or Erinna or the other writers discussed in this book, but
who has not heard of Sappho, whom Plato hailed as "the tenth
Muse"?[1] Since the time of Plato's elevation of Sappho to the realm
of the Muses, much additional mythology has surrounded her name:
desperate lover of girls, suicidal mistress of a younger man, headmistress of a girls' school, symbol of the Eternal Feminine. Where
is the real Sappho in all of this?

Ancient Biographies of Sappho

While facts about a writer's life are not necessarily reliable keys
to the interpretation of his or her work (indeed, knowledge of the
former can often be more hindrance than help for the latter), human
curiosity—especially about the past—demands the satisfaction of
knowing something of an author's circumstances. In the case of
Sappho, the credible biographical details are overshadowed by an
abundance of obviously legendary inventions, which must, nevertheless, be dealt with at least briefly since their influence on the
modern conception of Sappho has been as profound as it has been
misleading.

Sappho was born towards the end of the seventh century B.C.
during the time known among historians as the Archaic period.
Despite this rather depressing epithet, Sappho's world was char-

acterized by a lively interchange of people, products, and ideas. Greek cities sent out colonists all over the Mediterranean and engaged in active trade with one another and with foreign commercial centers; Greek art and Greek musical instruments of this period show a marked influence of the older cultural centers of the Near East; and Greek people, many of whom lived in isolated areas of the mainland or on islands (as Sappho did), had contact with the world at large through their own travels or through those of their family and friends.[2] It was a time of expansion and sometimes of turmoil, especially as old aristocratic modes of government were challenged by newcomers to the commercial and political arena.

Sappho's birthplace, Lesbos, is the third largest island in the Aegean Sea (665 square miles) and lies only a few miles from the coast of what is now the Turkish mainland, or in Sappho's day, Lydia. Archaeological evidence as well as remarks in the poetry of Sappho and her male contemporary, Alcaeus, shows that this green and fertile island had close commercial and social contacts with her eastern neighbor; it also reveals a long-established tradition of cultural refinement of the sort that could produce not only these two poets but others as well, including such singers as Terpander, of whom little is known, and Arion, whose legendary fame in ancient times was embodied in a charming story of his rescue at sea by a dolphin. Archaeological research on the island has not been as extensive as in some areas of Greece, but discoveries to date suggest that Lesbos was an important center of Greek culture since the time of the Bronze Age many centuries before Sappho.

Our understanding of Sappho might perhaps be deepened if we had the kind of sources of information about the society in which she lived that we do for the writers who worked in fifth-century Athens—extensive inscriptions, the remains of everyday utensils, pictures of daily life on vase paintings, and literary sources encompassing many different aspects of Athenian customs. In contrast, what we know of Archaic Lesbos comes primarily from the fragments of her two most famous poets—Sappho and Alcaeus. Any claims about the social customs of the island in the seventh and sixth centuries not based on these two sources are either mere conjectures or deductions based on knowledge of Greek society in other times and places, which may or may not bear any relationship to the Lesbos of Sappho's day. Nevertheless, Sappho's own accomplishments as a poet, and also the kind of world that she describes, do at least suggest that the women of Lesbos (or at any rate, those of the aristocracy) "enjoyed a freedom found elsewhere only in Sparta and an opportunity for self-development without parallel in Greek history."[3]

What do the ancient biographers have to say of Sappho herself? Here we must be wary of certain recently established characteristics of ancient biographies of writers, especially poets. Such ancient "lives" are generally likely to preserve more fiction than fact, drawing as they do on the authors' own works as though they were autobiographical statements and on unreliable sources such as comedy. In addition, ancient biographies of poets display suspiciously uniform characteristics, often conforming to a pattern involving anecdotes of a miraculous nature, the notion of the isolation of the writer from society (often via exile), and accounts of an unusual or violent manner of death.[4] Keeping these tendencies in mind, we may reduce the possibly accurate biographical data about Sappho to the following details.

Sappho's name, which she herself mentions in the "Hymn to Aphrodite," was, properly, Psappho. Her parents were Skamandronymos and Kleis, of Mytilene on Lesbos, and she had three brothers: Erigyios, about whom nothing is known; Charaxos, who had business connections with Egypt; and Larichos, whose government service on the council (*prytaneion*) in Mytilene suggests that the family was aristocratic. She was married to Kerkylas of Andros, who is never mentioned in any of the extant fragments of her poetry, and she may have had a daughter, named after her own mother (Kleis), who appears to be mentioned in two fragments (the crucial word in one of them, "pais," can mean either "daughter" or simply "child," "girl"). The husband is often assumed by twentieth-century scholars to be fictitious (either, on the one hand, because the homoerotic nature of some of Sappho's poetry is assumed to preclude a husband or, on the other, because she is claimed to be too pure and virginal to have married!); nevertheless, there is no good reason to doubt the report of his existence. Two other details emerge. She was born just at the close of the seventh century, perhaps about 610 B.C., and at some point during a period of political unrest on Lesbos, she is supposed to have taken refuge for a while in faraway Sicily.[5]

Besides these biographical details—all, it must be remembered, drawn from sources much later than Sappho herself and therefore open to question—we have one reference to her among the fragments of poetry written by her contemporary compatriot, Alcaeus: "O weaver of violets, holy, sweet-smiling Sappho. . . . "[6] The first word of the fragment, "ioplok'," is often translated as "lady of the violet hair" on the basis of a later use of the word, but in view of the widespread use of weaving imagery in Greek literature to refer to the creative process of making song, it seems preferable to keep to the literal meaning of the word and suppose that Alcaeus is complimenting Sappho in a metaphorical way on her divine abilities as a poet, not on her hairdo.[7] At any rate, the fragment suggests Alcaeus' admiration and respect for his fellow Lesbian.

Sappho in Ancient Legend

When we leave this bare outline, we quickly find ourselves in the realm of legend. The most famous tale about Sappho, which seems to have gotten its start sometime at least two centuries after her life, concerns her death-leap from the White Rock of Leukas (off the west coast of the Greek mainland) into the sea in pursuit of a handsome ferryman named Phaon, with whom she was supposed to have fallen passionately in love.[8] Now Phaon is clearly a mythological figure; the ancients told stories of his transformation—via the application of a magic salve—from an old man into an attractive youth with whom Aphrodite herself fell in love, subsequently hiding him in a bed of lettuce so that no rival could find him. The leap off Cape Leukas also has mythological analogies; the same story is told, for example, of Aphrodite leaping off the cliffs out of love for another youth, Adonis.[9]

If Sappho mentioned Phaon in her poetry, it was probably in some metaphorical or mythological context (perhaps in connection with the longing for regained youth), which may then eventually have given rise to the pseudobiographical tale of her lover's leap.[10] We first hear of the story in a short fragment from a play by Menander (fourth century B.C.) called *The Leukadia*, in which a speaker contends that Sappho was the first to throw herself off the White Rock of Leukas.[11] It is worth noting that the context of the story's earliest known occurrence is comedy, which seems to be the source (as noted above) for much ancient biographical misinformation. Furthermore, other ancient descriptions indicate that such a plunge off Cape Leukas was a standard metaphor for falling into a swoon, rather than a reference to a literal leap. There is little doubt, then, that the Sappho-Phaon story must be interpreted in the light of its mythological and metaphorical elements.

The most influential version of the Sappho-Phaon story was told in the first century A.D. by the Roman poet Ovid in his *Heroides* 15, a collection of elegiac poems cast in the form of "letters" attributed to various heroines—Medea, Penelope, Dido, and others—all of them mythological except for Sappho. While it is more than likely that Ovid had access to Sappho's own works, the Sappho of this "letter" bears all the marks of a fictionalized heroine created to serve Ovid's own literary purposes, not to supply the reader with carefully researched biographical details. The "letter," a kind of suicide note to Phaon (who has left Sappho for the maidens of Sicily), recalls their lovemaking in explicit detail:

> My love-play delighted you beyond expectation,
>   and the litheness of my rapid movements,
>   and words suited to our sport,
>   and—when the pleasures of us both had been mingled
>   together—
>   the utmost langour in our weary bodies.[12]

Howard Jacobson has aptly summarized the characterization of Sappho in the "letter" as follows: "The real Sappho, with keen esthetic sensibilities and subtle feelings for love and beauty, has degenerated into a grotesque pursuer of material luxury and corporeal lust."[13] He goes on to propose that Ovid presents what is almost a parody of Sappho—not so much to criticize Sappho in any way as to mock the stereotypical lover-poet, as he does so often elsewhere in his elegiacs. In any case, it is clear that Ovid's poem is hardly the place to look for a reliable account of Sappho's life and that despite the enduring fame that it gave to the story of Sappho's love for Phaon, such details must be relegated to the category of legendary invention, not historical fact.

Portraits of Sappho in Ancient Art

Greek art of the sixth and fifth centuries demonstrates the popularity of Sappho as a subject for artistic representation. The four earliest portraits, found on vases produced in the workshops of Athens to satisfy the domestic and foreign markets for decorated clay pots of various sizes and shapes, each bear an inscription identifying the subject as Sappho, though otherwise they show little resemblance to one another. The oldest portrait (c. 510–500 B.C.), of somewhat crude workmanship, shows Sappho alone playing a special long-armed type of lyre known as a barbitos (Goluchow Inv. 32, black-figured hydria now in the National Museum, Warsaw; Para. 246). The same instrument is seen in her hands in a slightly later portrait by the so-called Brygos Painter (c. 480 B.C.)—the artist's appellation deriving from the signature of the potter—in which she stands talking with the poet Alcaeus (Munich 2416, red-figured kalathoid vase, ARV² 385 and 1649, Para. 367). A third portrait, attributed to the Tithonos Painter and also dated to about 480 B.C., depicts Sappho playing the barbitos while she is dancing (Wuppertal 49, red-figured calyx-krater, Norbert Kunisch, *Antike Kunst aus Wuppertaler Privatbesitz*). The fourth representation (440–420 B.C.) shows Sappho in the company of three other women, one of whom extends an ordinary lyre to her as she sits in a chair reading a scroll of poetry, the first word of which appears to be "theoi," "gods" (Athens 1260, red-figured hydria, ARV² 1060, Para. 445). In all of these the emphasis is on Sappho's role as singer and poet.[14]

Sappho continued to be represented by later artists as well; we hear, for example, of a fine bronze statue of her by Silanion, a sculptor of the fourth century B.C., which graced the town hall of Syracuse, Sicily, until it was stolen by a corrupt Roman governor of the first century B.C.—or so Cicero claims in his prosecution speech against the man.[15] Her portrait appears on coins minted in Lesbos as late as the first through third centuries A.D. Some surviving bronze statues and other portraits have been thought to be of Sappho, but without an inscription, definite identification is difficult.

Attitudes toward Sappho

Only in recent years have the fragments of Sappho begun to be read again for what they actually say rather than for what the reader would like them to say. The same scholarly approach that has led to an enlightened understanding of nineteenth- and twentieth-century women poets needs to be applied to women writers of the more distant past. What Adrienne Rich has said of Emily Dickinson, for example, pertains equally well to several of the writers in this book, particularly Sappho: "We will understand Emily Dickinson better, read her poetry more perceptively, when Freudian imputation of scandal and aberrance in women's love for women has been supplanted by a more informed, less misogynistic attitude toward women's experience with each other."[16]

When we examine the scattered comments about Sappho in sources from the Greek, Roman, and Byzantine periods, as well as from the Renaissance and the Victorian ages, we find that—by and large—notions of "scandal and aberrance" in connection with Sappho only begin to emerge after the beginning of the Christian era and seem not to predominate until the Victorian period and its aftermath. To be sure, absence of such notions in some periods seems to be the result of ignorance of some of the aspects of her poetry—due either to mistranslations (involving change of pronouns from "she" to "he," for example) or to a less complete collection of fragments than is now available through modern discoveries. But it is clear that at least for many centuries after her death, Sappho enjoyed immense popularity for the sheer beauty of her language and the directness and power of her expression. A story is preserved—perhaps apocryphal but nevertheless illustrative of Greek attitudes—about the great Athenian statesman Solon (late sixth century B.C.), himself a poet of no mean accomplishment. He was once in his later years particularly taken with a song of Sappho sung by his nephew at a drinking party and immediately asked the young man to teach it to him. When someone inquired why he was so eager to know the song, he replied, "So that having learned it, I may die."[17]

As we have already seen, Sappho was the subject of vase paintings from the sixth and fifth centuries, but from surviving documents from the richest period of Greek literature, the fifth-century Golden Age of Athens, we have only a brief reference to her by the historian Herodotus, who mentions her only in passing in connection with her brother Charaxos.[18] From the fourth century, however, we have evidence that Sappho figured as a character in several comedies besides the play by Menander mentioned above—perhaps in a continuation of the tradition begun at least as early as Aristophanes' *Frogs*, in which the dramatis personae include the tragedians Euripides and Aeschylus. In most cases, only a title ("Sappho") remains, but one fragment includes a dialogue between her and her father in which a riddle format is used to veil contemporary political references, which could no longer be made as openly as they had in the comedy of earlier days.[19] Literary figures, however, particularly dead ones, were fair game, and Sappho's reputation as a master of love poetry (one character says he has learned all the erotic poems of Sappho)[20] no doubt made her the butt of various jokes. In one of the comedies she was apparently cast as the lover of two other literary figures (neither of them her contemporary), the poets Archilochos and Hipponax.[21]

To a fourth-century Athenian, however, perhaps the most remarkable thing about Sappho was that she was a woman. Athenian women were subject to many legal and social strictures—if not to oriental seclusion, as some modern scholars have claimed. The patronizing attitude of Athenian men is well illustrated in a quotation which Aristotle presents in his *Art of Rhetoric* in connection with the universal respect paid to wise people, whatever their presumed drawbacks may be: "The Parians honored Archilochos even though he was sharp-spoken; the Chians Homer, though he was not a citizen of their country; and the Mytilenaeans Sappho, although she was a woman."[22]

In the Roman period, Sappho continued to be known chiefly for her skill as a poet; she was imitated by Catullus and Horace and, as we have seen, used (or abused) by Ovid as the model of the mock-heroic Ovidian lover-poet. A Greek writer (also of the first century B.C.), an obscure elegiac poet named Antipater of Thessaloniki, composed a verse catalog of famous women poets (which appears as the epigraph of this book), of whom only Sappho and Korinna get a whole line to themselves:

> These women Mt. Helicon and the Macedonion rock of Pieria
>   raised—with godlike tongues for songs:
> Praxilla, Moero, the voice of Anyte (the female Homer),
>   Sappho, the ornament of the fair-tressed Lesbians,
> Erinna, Telesilla of wide fame, and you, Korinna,
>   singing of the impetuous shield of Athena,
> Nossis of womanly tongue, and sweet-sounding Myrtis—
>   all of them composers of pages that will last for all time.
> Great Heaven created nine Muses, but Earth
>   bore these nine, as everlasting delight for mortals.[23]

It is primarily in the Christian era that the name of Sappho and even of her birthplace begin to smack of the scandal from which they periodically suffer and recover over the course of the succeeding centuries. Tatian, for example, one of the influential church fathers of the second century A.D., condemns Sappho as a "love-crazy female fornicator who even sings about her own licentiousness."[24] Among pagan writings of the same century, one of Lucian's satires provides a portrait of a "woman from Lesbos" which epitomizes what later becomes a stereotypical notion of scandalous women pretending to be men. The satire involves a dialogue between two prostitutes, one of whom wants to know the details of the other's affair with a woman:

We hear strange things about you Leaina—that the rich woman from Lesbos loves you as though she were a man and that you live together and do heaven knows what with each other. . . . What does the woman want? What do you do when you're together? . . . They say that in Lesbos there are masculine-looking women who refuse to have intercourse with men, but who want to be with women as if they themselves were men.[25]

The other woman responds with a few graphic details of bedroom preliminaries involving not two but three women, and there the dialogue ends. All of the elements often typically connected with Lesbos or Sappho in the Victorian and modern mind are present in Lucian's description: scandal (including the association with prostitution), aberrance, and titillation.

The same notion of scandal found in Tatian and Lucian occurs also in a Byzantine encyclopedic work, the *Suda*, compiled in the tenth century A.D., in which the entry under "Sappho" includes the following biographical comment: "She had three friends and companions, Atthis, Telesippa, and Megara, in connection with whom she had the ill-repute of a shameful friendship."[26]

Although it is clear from such comments as Tatian's and the *Suda*'s that Sappho had fallen into disrepute, there is little evidence for the assertion sometimes made that Sappho's works were systematically burned under Christian emperors such as the fourth-century Theodosius, who concentrated his efforts on the destruction not of pagan books but of pagan sites of worship. One of the papyri containing a fragment from Sappho can be dated to seventh-century Egypt, so we can assume that the poems were still being circulated at least in Egypt at that time; although it is true that there are isolated reports of the burning of pagan libraries, "such destructive fervour was usually reserved for the works of fellow Christians who had deviated into heresy. . . ."[27] A much more serious problem connected with the preservation of Sappho's work (not to mention countless other books of classical literature) seems to have been the decline of learning and scholarship during the sixth through the ninth centuries; Sappho's poems—along with the works of other ancient authors—were destroyed, it would seem, not so often by fire as by neglect.

During the Renaissance Sappho reemerged from a long period of total silence. The treatment of her as a literary figure varied according to the inclinations of different authors, most of whom were acquainted with her chiefly through Ovid's portrait in his *Heroides* and through a few fragments preserved as quotations in the works of Greek and Roman critics and grammarians; as a result, the Renaissance Sappho often bears little resemblance to the poet as she is known today. John Lyly, for example, published a play in 1584 called *Sapho and Phao* in which Sappho is clearly intended as an allegorical representation of Queen Elizabeth, for whom the play was performed. Lyly's Sappho, transformed for the drama into a princess of Syracuse, is described by another character as follows: "Sapho, faire by nature, by birth royall, learned by education, by government politike, rich by peace: insomuch as it is hard to judge, whether she be more beautifull or wise, vertuous or fortunate."[28]

The cast of characters includes—among others—Vulcan, Cupid, Venus, and six ladies of Sappho's court, as well as the handsome ferryman Phaon, who is invited to join the court as a page. By the play's end, Phaon disdains Venus' love for him and leaves Sicily; meanwhile Cupid, too, abandons his mother and joins forces with Sappho, who has fallen out of love with Phaon. There is no reference to anything in the actual fragments of the real Sappho's poetry, and of course no mention is made of any suicide leaps from the Leukadian Rock, since such an allusion would hardly have been appropriate given the obvious parallels between the play's portrayal of Sappho and the Virgin Queen.

In the eighteenth and nineteenth centuries, Sappho's "Hymn to Aphrodite" (the only certainly complete poem of hers extant) was widely translated and influenced poets of various nationalities. Among the published translations of the poem in English, however, a persistent distortion nearly always changed the sex of the beloved mentioned in the prayer from a "she" to a "he," as did Ambrose Philips in 1711, George Herbert in 1717, John Herman Merivale in 1833, Edwin Arnold in 1869, T. W. Higginson in 1871, Moreton John Walhouse in 1877, and J. Addington Symonds in 1893. Moreover, F. T. Palgrave in 1854 managed a version in which pronouns were altogether omitted.[29] Swinburne's paraphrase in 1866 in his "Anactoria" seems to be one of few exceptions here.

Comments about Sappho in the years around the turn of the century range in tone from the floridly worshipful to the primly defensive. An article, "The Sapphic Secret," in the 1894 *Atlantic Monthly* presented Sappho as arch-woman and supergenius:

We need not pause to inquire whether, living in an age of hideous moral laxity, she was a bad or a good woman. Her song is not evil in its substance nor vicious in its essence. Her love-desire is that of a burning, music-charmed genius, full of health and vigor, wandering in the springtime groves of song. . . . Sappho's light is that of absolute, universal womanhood. She knew herself, her sex, and her power; and it is this womanly knowledge, informed with a genius never yet surpassed, that brims her words with imperishable fascination.[30]

Another approach concentrated on the notion, evidently derived from a comment in the tenth-century *Suda* about her *mathetriai,* (pupils), that she was the head of a girls' school and as such must have been a model of purity: "Her position at the head of her school . . . attests the fact of the esteem which she enjoyed. There has never been an age of the world when society was so corrupt that young women would be sent from a distance to study under a teacher who had a sullied reputation."[31] A similar effort to imbue Sappho with Victorian respectability centered on the equally insupportable fancy of the great classical scholar Wilamowitz that she was the official religious leader of a cult of female worshippers devoted to Aphrodite.[32] Sappho as Everywoman, as headmistress, as priestess—such notions may strike the late twentieth-century reader who studies the fragments of her poetry as absurd, but the tenacity of some of these ideas is astounding; even in the new (1970) edition of the *Oxford Classical Dictionary,* Sappho is described as "the centre of some kind of θίασος [religious guild] which honoured Aphrodite and the Muses and had young girls for its members." There is simply no evidence for this notion in either the fragments themselves or in the ancient biographical material.

In more recent years, the "gentlemanly" approach to Sappho has involved defensiveness of a different sort. Hints of scandal and aberrance lie not far below the surface of pleas that the reader observe the proprieties of discretion: "Whatever the intimacies of her life may have been—and it may be suggested that there are limits beyond which it is as impertinent to inquire into the private lives of eminent people of the past as of eminent people who are alive—it is clear that in her own day in Lesbos her repute was unblemished."[33] Similarly, Sappho was defended from charges of scandal on the grounds that she only inclined to scandalous thoughts, not scandalous deeds: "To the . . . question . . . whether evidence for practice as well as inclination is to be found in the fragments of Sappho's poetry, a negative answer must be returned."[34] If by "evidence for practice" the author meant explicit description of sexual activity, such descriptions are noticeably rare in Greek lyric poetry of all kinds; Greek attitudes were such that the most graphic portrayals of sex are found not in love poetry but in satire and comedy.

Still another approach summoned Sappho's poetic genius itself to bear witness against implied charges of scandal and aberrance: "It is against the nature of things that a woman who has given herself up to unnatural and inordinate practices . . . should be able to write in perfect obedience to the laws of vocal harmony, imaginative portrayal, and arrangement of the details of thought. . . ."[35] The speciousness of such logic requires no further comment.

Not until the 1970s did scholars and popular critics alike begin to approach Sappho's poetry with the kind of forthrightness and objectivity that Adrienne Rich advocates in connection with Emily Dickinson. Although some of the scholarly articles about Sappho still reveal the influence of Victorian attitudes, many represent a fresh look at the fragments on their own terms. And although some feminists and lesbian feminists are perhaps overzealous in claiming Sappho as their champion, others present Sappho in a realistic and balanced light. As Klaich remarks: "Sappho was a poet who loved women. She was not a lesbian who wrote poetry."[36]

A thorough study of the reactions to Sappho's poetry over the course of the nearly twenty-five centuries since she lived and wrote would require a book-length treatment in itself.[37] More will be said about a few of these views in the following discussions of the most important fragments of Sappho's poetry.

The Poetry of Sappho

Nearly all of the surviving fragments of poems by Sappho contain major gaps within the text or are merely short excerpts (a line or two) from a longer piece, facts which are often obscured by translators who fail to include ellipses to show where the text is incomplete. The Greekless reader might erroneously assume, on the basis of such translations, that Sappho was noted for brief epigrams, whereas in fact she usually preferred a form composed of several four-line stanzas.

A large number of the approximately two hundred fragments attributed to Sappho consist of only one or two words. Only those fragments that are long enough to convey some intelligible sense (forty altogether) are translated and discussed here. I have divided these fragments into six groups: poems addressed to Aphrodite, love poetry, poems concerning friends and rituals, poems dealing with mythological themes, wedding songs, and miscellaneous fragments on various subjects.

Poems Addressed to Aphrodite

The following poem, usually called the "Hymn to Aphrodite," is written in imitation of the standard form of a Greek prayer, in which the deity is first addressed and identified, reminded of a past relationship with the speaker, and then called upon to perform some service, in this case to aid in the fulfillment of some unspecified pursuit by Sappho on the battlefield of love.

I

O immortal Aphrodite of the many-colored throne,
child of Zeus, weaver of wiles, I beseech you,
do not overwhelm me in my heart
with anguish and pain, O Mistress,

But come hither, if ever at another time
hearing my cries from afar
you heeded them, and leaving the home of your father
came, yoking your golden

Chariot: beautiful, swift sparrows
drew you above the black earth
whirling their wings thick and fast,
from heaven's ether through mid-air.

Suddenly they had arrived; but you, O Blessed Lady,
with a smile on your immortal face,
asked what I had suffered again and
why I was calling again

And what I was most wanting to happen for me
in my frenzied heart: "Whom again shall I persuade
to come back into friendship with you? Who,
O Sappho, does you injustice?

"For if indeed she flees, soon will she pursue,
and though she receives not your gifts, she will give them,
and if she loves not now, soon she will love,
even against her will."

Come to me now also, release me from
harsh cares; accomplish as many things as my heart desires
to accomplish; and you yourself
be my fellow soldier.[38]

One of the characteristics of Sappho as a writer is her ability to
adapt traditional forms (such as the prayer) to suit her own purposes. In the case of the "Hymn to Aphrodite," the goddess' presence is made remarkably vivid through the central description—
which occupies all but the first and last stanzas of the poem—of
her "epiphany" at some time in the past. The report of the goddess'
words within the description, first indirectly and then directly
(through quotation) not only pays tribute to Aphrodite's wonderful
power but also implies, through the repetition of the word "again,"
that she has exerted that power on Sappho's behalf many times in
the still more distant past. Oddly, then, the poem continually moves
backwards into the past, and yet the vividness of the description
evokes the image of the goddess as a real force in the immediate
present, who is being called upon to assist Sappho now. Whether
the piece was actually offered up as a prayer is dubious, especially
in view of the artfulness in emphasizing the past relationship by
making it occupy the bulk of the poem, but we can be certain, on
the basis of the treatment of the gods in Archaic literature and art,
that Aphrodite is no literary nicety, no symbol of some abstract
notion of love: she is a real and potent force in Sappho's world.
While we need not approach the poem with the sort of literal-
mindedness that would assume that it refers to an actual day in the
poet's life, the sheer power of the description, with the emphasis
on the swiftness of Aphrodite's descent, precludes the recent assumptions that the goddess is merely Sappho's projection of herself

or that the poet is using the figure of Aphrodite as a device for lighthearted self-mockery.[39] Aphrodite's smile (in the fourth stanza) is the smile of power and benevolence and serenity (like the so-called Archaic smile on statues of the period), not of humor or amusement or derision.

Much as been written on whether the goddess' past service centered on problems of unrequited love or estrangement or infidelity. But as far as the poem itself is concerned, the question is moot; the emphasis is not on the nature of the discrepancy between Sappho and her woman friend but on Aphrodite's absolute power to transform the situation: to change flight into pursuit, refusal into desire, rejection into love.

2

> Hither to me from Crete, to this holy
> temple, where your lovely grove
> of apple trees is, and the altars
> smoke with frankincense.
>
> Herein cold water rushes through
> apple boughs, and the whole place is shaded
> with roses, and sleep comes down
> from rustling leaves.
>
> Herein a meadow where horses graze
> blooms with spring flowers, and the winds
> blow gently. . .
>
> Here, O Cyprian, taking [garlands],
> in golden cups gently pour forth
> nectar mingled together with our
> festivities. . . .

Like the "Hymn to Aphrodite," 2 is also cast in the form of a request that Aphrodite—here called "Cyprian" after her birthplace, Cyprus—come from afar and make herself present. This time, however, the request is tied to description not of a past assistance but of a present ritual, whose setting at springtime in a temple in the middle of a meadow becomes the focus of the extant portion of the poem. The piece is delightfully sensual, appealing at once to our sense of sight (the temple and its altars, the grove of apple trees), smell (the frankincense), touch (the coldness of the water, the coolness of the shade), and sound (the rushing of water, the rustling of leaves, the whispering of the breeze). The effect is hypnotic; Sappho transports the listener (we must remember that these poems were meant to be heard, not read) to a place where the magic of sleep descends from the rustling leaves of trees, the sound of which is echoed through the preponderance of *s* sounds in the original Greek. Unfortunately the fragment breaks off just as the speaker invites the goddess to join in the ritual, about which we have no further details. We can safely assume that the description reflects some sort of experience involving a communal rite in honor of the goddess, but to suppose that Sappho is speaking in the role of an official priestess of Aphrodite, as some have done, is going too far, since nothing in the language of the fragment compels such an interpretation.

5

O [Cyprian] and Nereids, grant
that my brother come hither unharmed
and that as many things as he wishes in his heart to come
   about
are all brought to pass,

And that he atones for all his former errors,
and is a joy to his [friends],
a [pain] to his enemies; but for us
let there be no misery.

May he wish to do honor to his sister
. . . painful suffering . . . of the citizens . . .
. . . Cyprian . . .

Fragment 5 is another prayer to Aphrodite (if the Greek text has been correctly restored) together with the daughters of Nereus (the Old Man of the Sea); it represents an example of a common genre in ancient poetry, the *propempticon* or "send-off" poem written as a wish for the safe return of a friend or relative who is going on a journey. In this instance, Sappho prays on behalf of her brother, most likely Charaxos, who, as we can surmise from the fifth-century Herodotus, had commercial interests at Naukratis in the Nile Delta of Egypt and thus occasion for frequent sea travel.[40] According to Herodotus, Charaxos paid a large sum of money to purchase the freedom of a courtesan in Egypt by the name of Rhodopis, a deed for which Sappho later ridiculed him in one of her poems. Although in general we must be careful not to assume that Sappho's poems (anymore than anyone else's) are factual accounts, in this case the genre and the historical information about the brother suggest that this piece may have been occasioned by a specific event in the poet's life.

Aphrodite was not the only deity to whom Sappho addressed prayers. Readers of the complete body of fragments will find her appealing to the Muses, to Eros, and to Hera, whose worship she connects in one fragment (17) with that of Zeus and Dionysus in what appears to be a trinity of deities especially emphasized in Lesbos.[41] All of these fragments reveal the same characteristics observed in the "Hymn to Aphrodite": sincerity of belief and the complete absence of satirical treatment or symbolic usage so common in portrayals of the gods in works by later Greek and Roman authors such as Euripides or Ovid.

Love Poetry

Longer Fragments

31

He seems to me to be like the gods
—whatever man sits opposite you
and close by hears you
talking sweetly

And laughing charmingly; which
makes the heart within my breast take flight;
for the instant I look upon you, I cannot anymore
speak one word,

But in silence my tongue is broken, a fine
fire at once runs under my skin,
with my eyes I see not one thing, my ears
buzz,

Cold sweat covers me, trembling
seizes my whole body, I am more moist than grass;
I seem to be little short
of dying. . . .

But all must be ventured. . . .

Fragment 31 was a famous poem in the ancient world; any Latin student who has gone far enough beyond elementary grammar to read the lyrics of Catullus will recognize it as the model on which the Roman poet based his own version (poem 51) beginning "Ille mi par esse deo videtur" ("That man seems to me to be equal to a god"). Sappho's poem seems to have been far better understood by Catullus and by the ancient literary critic who preserved it for us (pseudo-Longinus in his essay, *On the Sublime*) than it has been in the twentieth century. Catullus' poem, though perhaps less forceful than Sappho's, is clearly a description of the physical and emotional responses experienced by the speaker in reaction to the woman he loves (loss of speech, a burning sensation, etc.). "Longinus" admired Sappho's poem because he thought it was a superb description of the symptoms experienced by a person who is madly in love.[42] He confines his remarks to praise of her selection and arrangement of details, with no comment on who the man of the first line might be or what his relationship with the woman is.

The man of the opening line has been magnified in importance ever since the publication in 1913 of a book on Sappho by the German scholar Wilamowitz. He was an enormously influential scholar, and rightly so, but his blindness with respect to Sappho has profoundly distorted the modern view of her and particularly of this poem. To paraphrase his interpretation: The woman sits opposite a man and jokes and laughs with him. Who can he be other than her bridegroom? The wedding guests enter, and Sappho takes up the barbitos and sings a song similar to the ones she has composed for the weddings of so many of her pupils. This time she sings of her passionate love for the bride. But, contrary to the remark in the *Suda* about Sappho's 'shameful friendships,' this love is completely honorable because she is not embarrassed to mention it openly and because she sings of it in the context of a wedding.[43] So Wilamowitz "proves"—by mere assertion—that 31 is a wedding song! And thus Sappho's homoeroticism is diluted and placed into a context which offers no offense to Victorian morality. (Interestingly, homoeroticism in male Greek writers like Solon or Theognis does not seem to have provoked the same kind of prudishness among Victorian scholars.)

The absurdity of Wilamowitz' explanation of 31 has been amply noted in recent years and the obvious pointed out—that a wedding song must have chiefly to do with the bride and groom, not with the speaker's passion for one of them.[44] Yet the wedding-song theory persists. Treu, for example (following Snell), thinks the poem is "in all probability" a wedding song, albeit of a "personal" nature, since it begins with a praise of the "groom"; Frankel likewise dubs the poem a "personal" marriage song; and in an interesting recent twist on the theme, McEvilley proposes that the poem is an intentional distortion of the genre, in which Sappho wants the audience to think at first that they are about to hear a marriage song, which she then transforms, in a deliberate upsetting of the audience's expectations, into a description of her own inner feelings.[45]

One of the reasons that the wedding-song theory has continued to enjoy so much acceptance is that some scholars felt it necessary to explain the man of the opening line. As recently as 1977, an attempt was made to suggest that the man is the object of attention not only of the presumed "bride," but even of the speaker of the poem: "Two girls grow up together or they become friends early in their lives. What happens if some day one of them is attracted to a man and must as a result desert her friend? What happens if both girls realize they love the same man but one of them succeeds in winning him?"[46] Few scholars seem to be aware—as Catullus and "Longinus" were—that the man (*whatever* man) is simply not important in the poem except as part of the background for the poem's setting and as a foil for the exposition of the speaker's feelings. He is calmly "godlike" in response to the woman's sweet talk and charming laugh, whereas the speaker, in the same situation, is instantly struck dumb.

Some critics, while not necessarily subscribing to the wedding-song theory, nevertheless continue to attribute undue importance to the man by assuming that the poem is about jealousy. This interpretation, which rests on the supposition that the "which" of the first line of stanza 2 refers to the sight of the man and woman together, is contradicted by the third line of the stanza ("for the instant I look upon you . . . ," the "you" in the Greek clearly being singular). Also the remainder of the fragment clearly indicates that the speaker is describing her reaction upon seeing the woman. Hence the "which" in question must refer to the woman's talk and laughter, not to the sight of some tête-à-tête that provokes in the speaker an attack of jealousy, or even more absurdly, a homosexual "anxiety attack."[47] The heart of the poem is a description not of jealousy or anxiety but of overwhelming passion.

We might also usefully take note of the female language of the song. For example, the emphasis in the description of the woman is on her activity, not on specific physical characteristics (height, hair color, etc.). Instead, the speaker focuses on the woman's speaking and laughing, much in the same way that the narrator of 16 (see below) calls to her mind Anaktoria's "lovely walk and the bright sparkle of her face." In addition, the detailed, introspective picture of the narrator's feelings on seeing and hearing the beloved woman, concludes—just before the narrator's illusion of near-death—with a comparison drawn from nature. The speaker is "chlorotera de poias," "paler" or "moister" than grass. (The phrase is usually translated as "greener than grass" by those who want to read the poem as one about envy and jealousy.) In Greek the adjective *chloros* is often used of young shoots, and also describes wood, honey, and the pale yellow-green band in the spectrum of a rainbow. Thus the word is connected with youth and life—not the death seemingly experienced by the speaker in the very next line. The death is only apparent, as emphasized in the opening word of line 16, "I seem. . . ." Far from being an absurd exaggeration, as many have taken the phrase, "chlorotera de poias" anchors the speaker's experience firmly in the natural world, a world of freshness, growth, and moisture. Just as nature quickens with the advent of spring, so the speaker quickens even as she seems to die.[48]

16

Some say that the most beautiful thing
upon the black earth is an army of horsemen;
others, of infantry, still others, of ships;
but I say it is what one loves.

It is completely easy to make this
intelligible to everyone; for the woman
who far surpassed all mortals in beauty,
Helen, left her most brave husband

And sailed off to Troy, nor did she
remember at all her child
or her dear parents; but [the Cyprian]
led her away. . . .

[All of which] has now reminded me
of Anaktoria, who is not here.

Her lovely walk and the bright sparkle of her face
I would rather look upon than
all the Lydian chariots
and full-armed infantry.   *[This may be the end of the poem.]*

Fragment 16, whose cyclical structure through the military references at the beginning and end of the fragment suggests that it
may be a nearly complete poem, illustrates Sappho's ability to in-
terweave the personal with the mythological, as well as the abstract
with the concrete. The underlying form of the piece is one found
in many Greek and Roman poems: the catalog, or more specifically,
the priamel, in which a list of items is presented, followed by a
concluding statement which somehow ties the items together.[49] In
this instance, three items are presented as potentially "the most
beautiful thing upon the black earth"; then all are rejected in favor
of the speaker's assertion that the most beautiful thing is "what one
loves." This generalization is then illustrated both through the allusion to Helen, who left her home in Sparta to accompany the
object of her desire, Paris, back to Troy, and through the speaker's
similar longing for the one she loves, Anaktoria.

The poem's conclusion, with its return to military imagery and
the implicit comparison between Anaktoria's appearance and the

splendor of the military display, strikes at least one critic as "a little fanciful."[50] But physical beauty is elsewhere in Archaic poetry expressed in terms of motion and brightness (as in Alkman's poems) rather than mere static shape. The military imagery of the poem reinforces Sappho's definition of Anaktoria's beauty; it is the movement of her body and the brightness of her facial expression that the speaker calls to her mind, not static qualities like shape or size or coloring. Thus there is nothing particularly odd in the speaker's statement that she would much prefer to behold Anaktoria's "lovely walk" and "bright sparkle" than watch the movement of troops and the gleam of their weaponry. In effect, the poem both accepts and rejects the splendor of military might; it is beautiful—but it is nothing when set against the splendor of the person one loves.

Some scholars have searched for stark logic in the poem's examples and, finding it wanting, have criticized the song as too loosely tied together. After all, they say, how does the fact that Helen left her husband and child and went off to Troy prove the narrator's thesis that what is most beautiful is what one loves?[51] If we look for association of ideas and images, rather than strict logic, however, we can see the poem as highly coherent. The emphasis of the song is on the concept of "kalliston" (line 3)—the power of whatever is "most beautiful," and Helen, as the most beautiful woman in the world, is the supreme exemplum of "kallos" (line 7, the corresponding line in the next stanza). Although the gap in the text of stanza 4 prevents us from seeing the exact connection, it appears to be the thought of Helen that reminds the narrator of the absent Anaktoria (lines 15–16). Even if Helen represents par excellence what is "most beautiful," to the narrator the most beautiful thing in the world is the sight of Anaktoria. And again through association and implication, the epic-scale naval expedition and displays of military might connected with the abduction of Helen pale in significance to the splendor of one face—the face that by the narrator's standard is the most beautiful.

Thus the myth of Helen, while it does not "prove" the thesis of the song, incorporates all of the elements of the catalog—ships, foot soldiers, cavalry, and an object of love, Helen herself—and at the same time provides the poem with a foil for the speaker's own redefinition of "to kalliston." The most beautiful thing in the world is not Helen, but Anaktoria, who represents for the narrator "what one loves." Beauty is defined not in a cosmic way in mythical terms, but in a particular way in terms of a single individual's perception. Through that perception, the myth of Helen has been transformed, for Helen is no longer a passive object of others' attentions. Like the narrator, who actively seeks the sight of Anaktoria, Helen evidently chooses to leave behind her husband and forget her child and parents. Just as the narrator seeks Anaktoria, so Helen here seeks her voyage to Troy to be with Paris.[52]

94

. . . .
"Honestly, I wish I were dead!"
Weeping many tears she left me,

Saying this as well:
"Oh, what dreadful things have happened to us,
Sappho! I don't want to leave you!"

I answered her:
"Go with my blessings, and remember me,
for you know how we cherished you.

"But if you have [forgotten], I want
to remind you . . .
of the beautiful things that happened to us:

"Close by my side you put around yourself
[many wreaths] of violets and roses and saffron. . . .

"And many woven garlands
made from flowers . . .
around your tender neck,

"And . . . with costly royal
myrrh . . .
you anointed . . . ,

"And on a soft bed
. . . tender . . .
you satisfied your desire. . . .

"Nor was there any . . .
nor any holy . . .
from which we were away,

. . . nor grove. . . ."

Fragment 94, although badly mutilated, contains enough detail to reveal the more calmly sensual side of Sappho's poetry. Known to modern readers only since its publication at the turn of the century, it is a description of past intimacy recalled—rather than passion experienced in the present tense, as in 31, previously discussed. Like 31, however, this piece was also subjected to Wilamowitz' purifying interpretations, though fortunately with less impact on succeeding views of the fragment than in the case of his so-called marriage song. Wilamowitz read the poem as follows (to paraphrase his German). Sappho will perform the song for her pupils, to tell them how her feelings are hurt when her pupils go off into the world and forget their teacher. The poem reveals to us what her circle of girls delighted in—picking flowers, dressing up, and sleeping sweetly when they were tired out from dancing. Sappho's school trained aristocratic girls in the value of good manners. No doubt the food was plentiful, though I have no proof of that.[53]

Despite the very sensual language and setting of the poem (the garlands, the anointing of bodies with perfumed oil, cushions, a bed, etc.), Wilamowitz chose to render the obvious sexual undertones of "exies potho[n]" ("you satisfied your desire") with the bland phrase, "you stilled your need for rest," a need that he takes to have been brought on by excessive dancing. (Notice that what is left of the poem itself makes no mention at all of dancing, much less of plentiful food.) The other fragments in which Sappho uses the word *pothos* (desire) establish clearly that the word is erotic.

More recent interpretations generally acknowledge the sensual aspect of the poem even if the subject matter is sometimes played down with descriptions such as a "long list of girlish pleasures."[54] But some scholars seem to have pursued Wilamowitz' notion of "hurt feelings" by assigning the opening line of the fragment (at least one line is missing from the poem's beginning) to the speaker. Since quotation marks were not used in ancient Greek texts, the line could be assigned either to the speaker or to the other woman. Scholars who attribute the line to the speaker see the whole piece as a sort of confessional lament of an anguished Sappho who wishes she were dead. Burnett has recently shown in detail that it is more reasonable to assume that the first extant line should be assigned to the departed friend, whose youthful tendency towards exaggerated language reveals an "affectionately melodramatic" kind of person whose "raw emotion" is set against Sappho's own "perfected meditation." As Burnett demonstrates, Sappho's memory of the bed of lovemaking and of fulfilled desire "has taken from blunt objects and fleeting sensations their enduring essence."[55] The poem, then, is hardly a "confession," but rather a recapturing of past pleasures through memory, by which the "dreadful things" mentioned by the girl—that is, the impending separation—are transformed into Sappho's "beautiful things" beginning in stanza 4.

The imagery in the second half of the fragment is worthy of May Sarton: violets, roses, and saffron (a type of crocus with purple flowers). The female associations of flowers in Sappho's poetry are well established through references in other fragments to a woman who is like a mountain hyancinth trampled by shepherds (105c), the roses around Aphrodite's temple (2), the many-flowered fields in Lydia where Atthis' departed friend roams (96, line 11), the wreaths of flowers worn by the yellow-haired girl of 98, and the golden flowers connected with Kleis (132). The predominance of such flower imagery in Sappho is all the more striking when we note its rarity in her compatriot, Alcaeus, whose favorite imagery involves the sea. The anthological list here in Sappho 94 is filled out by further references to natural beauty in the form of myrrh, a resin produced by certain trees and shrubs, and the grove alluded to (line 27) as the fragment breaks off. Just as the departed woman in 96 (another poem concerned with the theme of separation, discussed below) is described through a simile involving the moon, flowery fields, the sea, and dew, so here the past relationship between the two women is depicted through recollection and recreation of their mutual enjoyment of especially sensuous aspects of nature—her flowers and her exotic perfumes. Like 96, this fragment, too, is primarily concerned with private human emotions set within the context of selected aspects of the natural environment.

Shorter Fragments

47

Eros shook my heart, like the wind
assailing the oaks on a mountain.

51

I do not know what to do; my mind is split.

49

I loved you, Atthis, once long ago. . . .
You seemed to me to be a small and graceless child.

48

You came, you did [well?], and I wanted you;
you made cool my heart, which was burning with desire.

131

Atthis, it has become hateful to you to think
of me; but you fly instead to Andromeda.

130

Eros the loosener of limbs shakes me again—
bitter-sweet, untamable, crawling creature.

126

May you sleep in the bosom of a tender woman friend.

121

But since you are our friend,
seek a younger bed.
For I would not dare
to live with you, since I am older.

120

But I am not someone resentful in
my feelings; I have a gentle heart.

188

Eros, weaver of stories. . .

Here we have a few further hints of Sappho's treatment of love. Eros for her is no mere symbol, no cherubic Cupid, but, like Aphrodite, a potent and real force. He is capable of shaking hearts and loosening limbs, but he can also be a weaver of stories. Perhaps it was this power that Sappho as poet felt the most keenly, whereby through her song she could give voice to the inarticulate emotions of passionate love.

Friends and Rituals

96

. . . [Sardis?]
Often turning her mind here . . .

[She honored you]
like an easily recognized goddess,
she rejoiced especially in your song.

But now she stands out among the Lydian women
as after sunset
the rosy-fingered moon

Surpasses all the stars; the light
spreads over the salty sea
equally as over the many-flowered fields.

And the dew grows beautifully liquid
and roses and tender chervil
flourish, and flowery honey-lotus.

But she, roaming about far and wide,
remembers gentle Atthis with desire;
her tender heart is surely heavy [because of your fate].
. . . to come. . .

Fragment 96, like 94, stresses the power of memory to assuage the pain of lovers' separation; the narrator consoles her friend Atthis by remembering the departed woman's admiration for Atthis and by portraying her as also engaged in the act of remembering. The extended simile in the middle section of the fragment, in which the narrator compares the departed woman to the moon, almost becomes part of the setting of the poem; as McEvilley observes, "The reader is left with the impression that the distant girl, wandering up and down, and Sappho and Atthis thinking of her, are described on the actual moonlit night of the simile."[56]

154

The moon gleamed in its fullness,
and as the women stood around the altar. . . .

160

Now these things will I sing beautifully
to my women-friends.

56

I do not think there will be at any time
a woman who looks on the light of the sun
with wisdom such as yours. . . .

81b

O Dika, put lovely garlands on your tresses,
binding together shoots of dill in your tender hands.
For the blessed Graces favor more the well-flowered,
but turn away the ungarlanded.

156

[A woman] by far more sweet-melodied than a harp,
more golden than gold . . .

155

I'm overjoyed to say farewell to you, Miss Overlord.

The short fragments in this group are tantalizing in their incompleteness. What happened as the moon gleamed and the women stood around the altar? What did the singer sing to her women friends? We cannot tell, but it is clear that these fragments, too, reveal an interconnectedness between friendship and rituals which involve song, remembrance, and nature. All is not sweetness and moonlight, however; Sappho can display a stinging wit, as in 155 when she puns on the name of a departing woman whom the speaker finds overbearing. But the general impression left by these fragments is of the harmony of women's experience with one another.

Mythological Themes

44

[The Wedding of Hektor and Andromache]

Cyprus . . .
The herald came,
Idaeus . . . swift messenger
[who said]:
" . . . and of the rest of Asia . . . the fame is undying.
Hektor and his companions are bringing a
      quick-glancing girl
from holy Thebes and the river Plakia—
tender Andromache—in ships upon the salty
sea; many golden bracelets and purple garments
. . . many-colored adornments,
countless silver cups and ivory."
So he spoke. Quickly [Hektor's] dear father leaped
      up;
the word went out over the broad-plained city to his
      friends.
At once the sons of Ilos yoked mules
to the well-wheeled chariots. The whole throng
of women and . . . of maidens . . . .
But apart, the daughters of Priam . . .
and unmarried men yoked horses to the chariots,
and greatly . . .
. . . charioteers . . .
. . . like to the gods . . .
. . . holy . . .
set forth . . . to Ilium
and the sweet-melodied aulos [and kitharis] were
      mingled,
and the noise of castanets. . . . Then the maidens
sang a holy song; the divine echo reached the sky . . .
and everywhere along the road . . .
libation vessels . . . ,
myrrh and cassia and frankincense were mingled.
But the women, as many as were older, cried out,
and all the men shouted a high-pitched lovely song,
calling upon Paean, the far-shooting and well-lyred;
they sang of Hektor and Andromache, like to the gods.

142

Leto and Niobe were very dear friends. . . .

These fragments show that Sappho's poetry also included traditional mythological themes such as the stories of the marriage of Hektor and Andromache at Troy and of the unfortunate fate of Niobe, whose rash boast that she was superior in childbearing to the goddess Leto caused the death of her children and her own transformation into a weeping mountain. The papyrus in which 44 ("The Wedding of Hektor and Andromache") is preserved says that this poem was the last one in Book 2 of the works of Sappho as collected and edited by the Hellenistic scholars at Alexandria. Since the poems were grouped together into nine books on the basis of meter, we can assume that the other poems in Book 2 were written in similar rhythms—the dactylic meters of which one type in particular was used in epic poetry like Homer's *Iliad* and *Odyssey*—and may also have dealt with themes drawn from epic subject matter.[57] The language of the Hektor and Andromache fragment is characterized by Homeric epithets ("far-shooting" Apollo, "well-wheeled" chariots, etc.), which are noticeably absent from Sappho's more personal poetry.

Fragments from Wedding Songs

111

Raise high the roof-beams!
Sing the Hymeneal!
Raise it high, O carpenter men!
Sing the Hymeneal!
The bridegroom enters, like to Ares,
by far bigger than a big man.

113

Bridegroom, never will there be another girl like this!

105a

[the bride]
just like a sweet apple which ripens on the uppermost bough,
on the top of the topmost; but the apple-gatherers forgot it,
or rather, they didn't forget it, but they could not reach it. . . .

114

Bride: Maidenhood, maidenhood, where have you gone and
left me?
Maidenhood: No more will I come back to you, no more will
I come back.

110a

[At the wedding]
the door-keeper's feet are seven fathoms long,
and his sandals are made of five ox-hides,
and ten shoemakers worked away to make them.

All of these fragments belong to the genre of the hymeneal, or
marriage song, and many exhibit a lighthearted, even mocking tone
that must have been considered appropriate to the festive occasion:
the groom is like a lumbering Ares; the groom's attendant, the
door keeper, has huge feet; and the bride's departing maidenhood
bids her a final farewell.

The closest analogy to these poems in the surviving body of
Greek literature comes from two centuries later, in the form of
wedding songs incorporated into the comedies of Aristophanes. In
his *Peace*, for example, the protagonist marries the personification
of Peace herself at the end of the play, while the chorus merrily
chants such bawdy lines as:

He is thick and big,
She is sweeter than a fig.[58]

Although we have far too few examples of Sappho's hymeneals
to be sure, it may be that we should see the same kind of good-
humored allusion to the randy condition of the bridegroom in lines
such as "by far bigger than a big man." In any case, while some of
Sappho's wedding songs were lighthearted in one way or another,
others included descriptions of some poignancy, such as that of the
bride likened to a ripening apple so high up on the tree that the
apple pickers have not been able to reach it.

That Sappho did write such songs seems to have puzzled some
modern readers, who find it difficult to reconcile her involvement
in the institution of marriage with the passionate love poetry she
addressed to other women. In the absence of any independent

concrete evidence about the social structures of sixth-century Lesbos, all that can be said with certainty is that for whatever reasons,
Sappho herself evidently did not regard marriage and lesbianism
as mutually exclusive. In Sappho's world, there is room for coex-
istence.[59]

Other Fragments

132

I have a child whose beauty
resembles golden flowers: beloved Kleis,
whom [I would not exchange]
either for all of Lydia or a lovely . . .

98a

. . . for my mother [said that]
in her youth it was indeed a great ornament if someone had
    tresses
wrapped in a purple [band].
But the girl who has hair
brighter than a fiery torch
should wear[?] wreaths
of blooming flowers.
Just now a many-colored
headband from Sardis . . .

98b

For you, Kleis, I have no
many-colored headband, nor
do I know where one will come from.
But for the Mytilenean . . .
. . . these memories of the exile
of the sons of Kleanax . . .
. . . for they wasted away terribly . . .

34

The stars around the beautiful moon
keep hidden their glittering radiance,
whenever in its fullness it shines
[upon] the earth.

102

Sweet mother, I am not able to weave at my loom,
overwhelmed with desire for a youth because of
tender Aphrodite.

146

I have neither bee nor honey. . . .

151

Black sleep [falls upon] the eyes at night. . . .

39

But a many-colored thong
concealed her feet—a beautiful
Lydian work.

55

You will lie dead, nor will there be anyone
remembering you later; for you have no share
in the roses of Pieria, but will roam unseen
in the house of Hades, having flown off among dim
corpses.

147

I say that even later someone will remember us. . . .

This last selection from among the fragments of Sappho's poetry
illustrates the range of her subject matter beyond the categories
already considered. Here we find references to her family (there is
no good reason to doubt the ancient biographical tradition that
Kleis was her daughter, although there is nothing in the Greek of
98b and 132 that would require such an interpretation), to political
events of the times (the end of 98b is thought to allude to a tyrant
of Mytilene by the name of Myrsilus, who is known from Alcaeus'
poetry), and to commonplace motifs such as the charming picture
of the girl at her loom.

We also find here the artist making a claim for her own literary
immortality. In contrast to the person addressed in 55, whose lack
of poetic inspiration (Pieria was the home of the Muses) condemns
her to eternal obscurity, Sappho appears in 147 to be predicting
her own lasting reputation.

The Influence of Sappho on Nineteenth- and Twentieth-Century Literature

The recent resurgence of interest in the poetry of Sappho in the United States is well attested by the abundance of fresh translations that have appeared within the last two decades or so, including the versions by Mary Barnard (1958), Willis Barnstone (1965), Guy Davenport (1965, 1980), Suzy Q. Groden (1966), and David A. Campbell (1982). There is not space here to analyze these and other translations and the impact they have had—along with the Greek text—on modern European and American literature; a few selected examples, however, will give some indication of the range of authors who have drawn, in one way or another, on the poetry of Sappho.[60]

From nineteenth-century England I have already mentioned Swinburne's "Anactoria," a lengthy poem narrated by Sappho as the persona, which contains within it a loose paraphrase of part of the "Hymn to Aphrodite":

> Yet the queen laughed from her sweet heart and said:
> "Even she that flies shall follow for thy sake,
> And she shall give thee gifts that would not take,
> Shall kiss that would not kiss thee" (yea, kiss me).[61]

When "Anactoria" (whose title is borrowed from Sappho's fragment 16) and other pieces by Swinburne first appeared in 1866, they were branded by the critics as libidinous.

In late nineteenth-century France, Pierre Louÿs gained considerable notoriety with the appearance of his *Les Chansons de Bilitis* (1894). He claimed that these poems, only recently excavated at Sappho's tomb, published in Leipzig, and now translated into French for the first time, were the work of one of Sappho's "disciples."[62] Needless to say, his literary pretense did not amuse German scholars such as Wilamowitz, who labeled the *Chansons* "lewd" and "repulsive."[63] Other readers found them charming, but in any case their popularity seems to have been short-lived.

Perhaps the most significant literary influence of Sappho in modern times was in connection with the imagist school of poetry, which reached its height in England and America during the period of 1908–17. The imagist poets—H.D. (Hilda Doolittle), Ezra Pound, Amy Lowell, William Carlos Williams, and others like them—strove to write short, direct pieces clearly focused on a single image. The influence of Greek and Roman lyric—and specifically of Sappho and Catullus—on this group of poets has been amply noted.[64] But one aspect of the influence of Sappho that has perhaps not been remarked on is that the fragmentary state of her poems enhances the concentrated effect of individual images, since the fragments often contain only a very few words apiece: " . . . an exceedingly tender girl plucking flowers . . ." (122), " . . . just now golden-sandalled Dawn . . ." (123), or " . . . like the hyacinth in the mountains which the shepherds trample underfoot, and the purple flower [falls] on the ground . . ." (105c).

H.D. in particular, perhaps because she knew Greek well, reveals the influence of Sappho's lyrics on her own poetry, much of which draws on themes from Greek mythology. Several of her poems take their titles and starting points from fragments of Sappho—though the titles are based on an old numbering system no longer used. For example, H.D.'s poem called "Fragment 113" takes as its point of departure the fragment from Sappho now numbered 146, which reads in its entirety: "I have neither bee nor honey. . . ." (Amusingly, through a grievous misprint in the 1925 edition of H.D.'s poem, the translation of the fragment is rendered as "Neither honey nor tea for me.") H.D. uses Sappho's negatives connected with the images of honey and bee to begin her own poem:

> Not honey,
> not the plunder of the bee
> from meadow or sand-flower
> or mountain bush. . . [65]

Similarly, the beginning of H.D.'s "Fragment Thirty-Six" employs the fragment now numbered 51: "I know not what to do, / my mind is reft." H.D.'s "Fragment Forty" (= 130), "Fragment Forty-One" (= 131), and "Fragment Sixty-Eight" (= 55) are similarly woven from the thread of Sapphic images.

A major concern of women poets of the twentieth century has been a search for their poetic roots, for a sense of continuum and of shared poetic values with other women writers. To cite a recent example, Olga Broumas in her poem "Demeter" names several authors who have been her personal sources of inspiration: "Anne. Sylvia. Virginia. / Adrienne the last, magnificent last" (referring to Sexton, Plath, Woolf, and Rich).[66] Earlier in the century, Amy Lowell expressed this sense of need for a continuum even more vividly through a re-creation, in a long poem called "The Sisters," of her imaginary conversations with Sappho, Elizabeth Barrett Browning, and Emily Dickinson. In Lowell's wish that she could have talked with Sappho, we can perceive the simultaneous sense of isolation and yet also of connection which seems to be the experience of so many poets who are women:

> Ah me! I wish I could have talked to Sapho,
> Surprised her reticences by flinging mine
> Into the wind. This tossing off of garments
> Which cloud the soul is none too easy doing
> With us to-day. But still I think with Sapho
> One might accomplish it, were she in the mood
> To bare her loveliness of words and tell
> The reasons, as she possibly conceived them,
> Of why they are so lovely. Just to know
> How she came at them, just to watch
> The crisp sea sunshine playing on her hair,
> And listen, thinking all the while 'twas she
> Who spoke and that we two were sisters
> Of a strange, isolated little family.[67]

Other twentieth-century women poets who have found in Sappho a poetic "sister" include writers as different from one another as Renée Vivien, Sara Teasdale, and Edna St. Vincent Millay, all of whom felt, in one way or another, a sense of identity with their predecessor from seventh-century B.C. Greece. Today, some twenty-five centuries after Sappho lived and wrote, the emotional intensity expressed so vividly in her poetry still captures the imagination of readers and poets alike. Sappho's prediction in 147 has been fulfilled: "I say that even later someone will remember us."

2 *Women Poets of Fifth-Century Greece*
Myrtis, Korinna, Praxilla, and Telesilla

If there were other women poets during the Archaic period who were active outside the island of Lesbos, they have disappeared virtually without a trace but for one, Megalostrata of Sparta.[1] Archaic Sparta was not only a strong economic and military power (Megalostrata's name, appropriately, means "great-armed") but also an important center for the production of beautiful pottery and bronzes; later Athenian sources are responsible for the biased view of Sparta as nothing but a stern military camp, whence our expressions such as "Spartan diet" or "laconic speech" (Laconia was the district in which Sparta was situated).[2] Sparta's most famous poet was Alkman, whose genius has only recently begun to be fully appreciated. In one of the short fragments from his poems, he praises Megalostrata for her gift from the Muses:

> The fair-tressed Megalostrata, blessed among Maidens, has shown this gift of the sweet Muses.[3]

Although not enough of the text remains to be absolutely sure that the "gift" was the ability to write poetry, if we can trust the preserver of these lines, Athenaeus (who, though he wrote in the second century A.D., relied heavily on earlier sources), Megalostrata was indeed a "poetess" (*poetria*), with whom Alkman was supposed to have fallen passionately in love, attracted by her stimulating conversation.[4] The most interesting aspect of Athenaeus' account (given that the details are probably invented) involves the mention of the woman poet only in relation to her more famous male contemporary and the emphasis on her poetic and intellectual abilities as a means for securing her relationships with men. We shall find similar biases in the biographical remarks about many of the other women writers discussed in this book.

If we are to continue to trace the tenuous links which connect the various members of Amy Lowell's "strange, isolated little family," we must turn ahead to the classical period of Greek literature, which for our purposes may be defined as from about 500 to 350 B.C. or, in other words, from the fifth century to the first half of the fourth century.

However tattered the remains of Sappho's poetry are, at least we have a reasonably good notion of the nature and range of her work; the same cannot be said of the writers considered in the present chapter, of whom only one (Korinna) has had the good fortune to have more than a few lines survive the passage of time and the forces of ignorance. The others are known now only through the preservation of a title or a few scattered words, or through legend. Nevertheless, a careful study of the evidence remaining suggests that while none of these writers achieved the greatness of Sappho, some of them wrote poetry whose loss is to be regretted.

In fifth-century Greece, as in the preceding century, poetry was the chief medium of communication for literary artists—men and women alike. Male writers, at least those who lived in Athens, had access to that most durable of literary genres, the drama, which played a major role in the celebration of state religious festivals held in honor of Dionysos twice each year. Their plays, both comedies and tragedies, which (like those of Shakespeare) were written in a poetic form, were seen by thousands of Athenians at each festival. Prose genres began to flourish at Athens at this time too—including history and philosophy—but as far as we know, none of these was a genre in which Athenian women yet had the opportunity or inclination to write. In fact, the city evidently produced no women writers until the third century B.C., when the philosophical school founded by Epicurus (the Garden) encouraged the full participation of its women members. (More will be said of the Epicureans' enlightened notions in chapter 4.)

The women of the classical era who did write were not Athenians, but lived instead in various towns in mainland Greece, none of which enjoyed the cultural supremacy of Athens. All wrote primarily in the same genre already established as appropriate for women by the reputation of their predecessor, Sappho, namely lyric poetry, and some also wrote short pieces in the dactylic hexameters of the *Iliad* and the *Odyssey*. But whereas Sappho's poetry appears to have been intended primarily for solo performances (that is, one singer accompanied by the lyre), some of these new writers ventured— to judge from the meters they used—into lyrics meant for choral performance by a group of singers, often perhaps in connection with a local religious festival tied to the agricultural calendar or as part of some other town ceremony. Because they wrote for the local audience and were presumably not free to travel easily outside the home district, none of them had a chance to achieve the international reputation earned by the most famous of all choral poets, Pindar (who travelled frequently to write commissioned victory odes in honor of famous athletes), or by his lesser counterparts such as Simonides and Bacchylides.[5] It is not until much later, in the Hellenistic period, that we hear of itinerant women singers and poets, that is to say, of women artists on the international concert circuit.

Myrtis

The earliest woman writer of the classical period of whom we have any trace was in fact supposed by tradition to have been the teacher of Pindar of Thebes. This was Myrtis of Anthedon, a small town in the district of Boeotia, which adjoins Attica to the northwest. Of the works of Myrtis we have not a scrap. Late biographical entries ("Korinna" and "Pindaros" in the *Suda*) make both Pindar and Korinna her pupils. She is called "sweet-sounding" by Antipater of Thessaloniki (in the epigram quoted in chapter 1 cataloging the nine famous women poets) and "clear-voiced" by Korinna (see below). A second-century A.D. travelling rhetorician and Christian apologist, Tatian (whose aversion to Sappho was mentioned in chapter 1), says that a bronze statue of Myrtis was made by one Boïscus, otherwise unknown.[6]

Of Myrtis' poetry, all we know is what can be surmised from a prose paraphrase of one poem. Plutarch (himself a Boeotian) cites Myrtis as his authority for the story of why women were forbidden to set foot in a sacred grove dedicated to a local hero, Eunostos, in the Boeotian town of Tanagra.[7] The gist of the story involves false accusation of rape on the part of a jilted woman, Ochna. Evidently Myrtis' poem related how Ochna, Eunostos' cousin, was rejected in her love for him and in a fit of anger told her brothers that he had raped her, whereupon they slew the boy but were then taken captive by the boy's father. Ochna, pitying the lot of her brothers, confessed her lie; they were allowed to go into exile, and Ochna ended her life via the ancient equivalent of the drug overdose, leaping off a cliff. We have no way of knowing, from this bare prose summary, whether Myrtis' portrayal of the woman was sympathetic, as is, for example, Euripides' depiction of Phaedra's plight in the more familiar version of the false accusation myth in his play, *Hippolytus*. If this piece was typical of the subject matter treated by Myrtis, we can conclude that her chief interests lay in local myths rather than those of a more Panhellenic nature.

Whether or not Myrtis really was the teacher of both Pindar and Korinna (such student-teacher relationships in ancient accounts can be shown in other cases to be sometimes mere fancy on the part of overzealous biographers), she does seem to have been the earliest of the line of lyric poets who emerged from the district of Boeotia.[8] Despite Athenian chauvinist views of Boeotia as a land of country bumpkins, the area was clearly a nurturer of creative artists, at least in the late sixth and early fifth centuries.

Korinna

Life

Fortunately we know a good deal more about the life and work of Korinna, although her dates have been the subject of a lively controversy in the scholarship of the past half-century. According to Pausanias, the second-century A.D. author of a generally reliable guidebook to Greece based on his own travels and on-site investigations, Korinna was the only poet of Tanagra, a Boeotian town a few miles to the east of Pindar's home, Thebes.[9] Except for burial grounds from the Bronze Age many centuries before the classical era, little has been systematically excavated to date, and a recent "rescue dig" carried out before the building of a government airplane factory turned up nothing but Hellenistic tombs, most of which had been robbed. Aside from Pausanias' mention of several public buildings (a theatre, gymnasium, and temples), little is known about Tanagra except that from the seventh century on it was an important center for the mass production of terracotta figurines intended for use as votive offerings and exported all over the Greek world. Evidently the Tanagraean citizenry paid the appropriate honors to their local poet, for Pausanias reports having seen a monument dedicated to her in the town streets (presumably a statue) as well as a painting in the gymnasium that he says showed her putting on the fillet (headband) she won in a poetry contest in Thebes in competition against Pindar. Pausanias accepts the local tradition as fact and goes on to add his personal opinion about Korinna's victory: "It seems to me that she won because of her dialect (she did not sing in Doric, like Pindar, but in a dialect easily comprehensible to the [local judges]), and because she was the fairest in form of women at that time, if one can judge from the likeness [of her in the painting]."[10]

Pausanias seems compelled to explain the reported victory in some terms other than the possible superiority of her entry in the competition. Another, less reliable ancient source, Aelian (third century A.D.), goes even further and claims that Pindar was defeated no fewer than five times by Korinna, all because of "ignorant judges," and that in revenge Pindar labelled her a "sow." H. J. Rose convincingly showed that the latter detail is based on Aelian's foolish misreading of one of Pindar's own poems.[11] The still later Byzantine encyclopedia, the *Suda*, also reports the five victories but without further elaboration. Plutarch's account, on the other hand, transforms the competition into friendly criticism passed on by Korinna to the young Pindar to the effect that he ought to incorporate more myths into his poems. In response, Plutarch claims, Pindar composed a poem in which eight different mythological figures were introduced in six lines, prompting Korinna to laughter and the further advice that one should sow with the hand and not with the whole sack of seed.[12]

Clearly the ancients believed that Korinna and Pindar were contemporaries and, in one sense or another, rivals. The assigning of Korinna to the fifth century went unchallenged until the publication of an article in 1930 by E. Lobel, who claimed that internal evidence within the surviving fragments of Korinna's poetry (including technical matters relating to spelling, meter, etc.) pointed to a third-century date.[13] Briefly put, the chief problem is that while the ancient tradition connects Korinna with fifth-century Pindar, the surviving papyrus of her poetry is written according to the spelling conventions of third-century Boeotia, which were significantly different from those of the fifth century. Was her poetry written in the fifth century and then respelled by copyists in the third so as to make her language more intelligible, or did she live and write in the third century to begin with? Proponents of the early date are not helped by the fact that Korinna is not mentioned in any surviving Greek literature until the first century B.C., in Antipater of Thessaloniki's catalog of the nine mortal Muses.

At present no definitive answer to the question of Korinna's date can be offered. Lobel seems to have won about equal numbers of supporters and detractors, although the predominant trend in the most recent scholarship on the question is to accept the ancients' early date. After all, as others have noted, whereas we have only a small portion left of Korinna's poetry, some of the ancient authors who passed on the tradition probably had access to the complete corpus of her work, and thus they perhaps had a sounder basis for judgment than we do.[14] Furthermore, even though ancient anecdotes connecting important literary or historical figures may sometimes contain slight chronological impossibilities, they usually do not attempt to link figures from two centuries apart. In addition, we have the evidence of an inscribed statuette of Korinna in the Musée Vivenel that is considered by most art historians to have been copied from a statue of the poet said by the Christian father Tatian to have been made by the fourth-century Athenian sculptor Silanion.[15] Although such evidence is by no means conclusive, it does tend to corroborate the ancient tradition whereby Korinna was thought to have been already in existence well before Lobel's date in the third century B.C. In any case, I have chosen here to consider Korinna as a fifth-century poet, on the general principle that ancient traditions, even if not supported by primary sources, should be accepted at least in essence unless sufficient grounds can be cited for mistrusting them.

The Nature of Korinna's Poetry

Whether or not Korinna really was Pindar's rival, what we know of each poet's works indicates a widely discrepant practice in themes and treatment. Although both wrote choral poetry (sung and danced by a choir as part of some festival or celebration), Pindar wrote in the "international" Doric dialect and treated Panhellenic myths, whereas Korinna kept to a literary dialect strongly colored by Boeotian features, apparently focusing on local myths and legends, just as her predecessor Myrtis seems to have done. Besides the longer fragments, we also have some indication of her range of themes from titles preserved by ancient grammarians commenting on some curious feature of her language. (It is to these same grammarians that we owe most of the shorter fragments.) As Korinna herself proclaims in one brief fragment,

664(b) PMG

> But I myself [sing] the excellent deeds
> of male and female heroes.[16]

This proclamation is borne out by the fragments of Korinna's poems as well as by the surviving titles, both of which suggest that her chief subject matter was the telling of Boeotian myths and legends. "Boeotos," for example, must have centered on the hero (a son of Poseidon) after whom the district was named. "Seven Against

Thebes," a theme treated later in Attic drama, probably told the story of the conflict between Polyneices and Eteokles, the sons (and brothers!) of Oedipus, over the throne of Thebes. She may also have written poems about Oedipus himself, for a late commentator mentions that she told the story of Oedipus' killing of not only the Sphinx but also the Teumesian Fox, which had the power to escape all hounds.[17] (According to more standard versions of the fox's demise, it was pursued by a hound from which no wild animals could escape, leaving Zeus no choice but to transform them both into stone.) A piece entitled "The Return" seems to have told of an episode in the life of a hero supposed to have been born in Tanagra, the giant hunter Orion, whose constellation is a familiar sight in our winter sky.

Although Korinna must have treated at least a few major mythological figures who are not tied exclusively to Boeotia, the only ones we know of are Iolaos, the nephew and companion of Herakles (also often treated in Pindar's poetry) and Athena. A late source reports that according to Korinna, it was Athena who taught Apollo how to play the aulos (reed pipe).[18] Korinna evidently also wrote a poem called "The Shield of Athena, " whose title appears to be alluded to in Antipater of Thessaloniki's reference to her (in his catalog of the nine mortal Muses) singing of "the impetuous shield of Athena."

The Fragments of Korinna's Poetry

Although Korinna does on occasion speak in the first person, the genre of her poetry (choral songs probably intended for performance at festivals) precludes the possibility of the kind of intimate narrator whom we encountered in some of Sappho's poetry. These poems usually do not represent the inner voice of an individual speaker, but rather the collective voice of the poet and the performers, who join forces to celebrate the local rituals. Whereas Sappho probably sang her poems (or had them sung) to her fellow aristocrats largely in a private context such as parties and weddings, Korinna seems to have been a public poet who wrote for occasions in which the population at large could participate. We must remember that the mythological figures and place-names that she

mentions, although unfamiliar and arcane to us, were in most in-
stances part of the common local heritage.

The first fragment below, contained in a papyrus published in
1907, comes from near the end of a poem that narrates a singing
contest between two Boeotian mountains. Such a topic may seem
odd indeed according to modern literary conventions, but a similar
humanization of the natural landscape in Greek literature can be
found at least two centuries before Korinna's time in Homer's *Iliad*,
where the river Skamandros takes on a human voice and rebukes
Achilles for backing up his waters with piles of Trojan corpses.[19]
The particular folk motif of Korinna's poem, a contest between
two mountains, recurs in modern Greek literature in a nineteenth-
century popular song about a contest between Mount Olympus
and Mount Kissavos.[20] In Korinna's poem, the mountains involved
are Mount Kithairon, on the border between Attica and Boeotia,
and Mount Helicon, in western Boeotia. The fragment opens with
the end of the song sung by one of the competing mountains
(perhaps Kithairon), in which the story is told of how Rhea rescued
her son, the infant Zeus, from the devouring jaws of her husband
Kronos by feeding him a stone instead and hid the infant in a cave
in Crete, where the Kouretes raised a din with their spears and
shields to conceal the baby's crying. The fragment goes on to report
the voting procedure by which the winner of the contest was chosen,
and ends with an account of a temper tantrum thrown by the loser
(the last thirty lines in the papyrus are completely unintelligible):

654.i.12–34 PMG

". . . The Kouretes
hid the very holy infant of the goddess
in a cave, in secret from
crooked-counseled Kronos, at that time when
blessed Rhea stole him

And seized great honor
from the immortal gods." Such things he sang.
Immediately the Muses instructed the Blessed Ones
to cast their pebbles—secret ballots—
into golden-gleaming voting urns.
They all stood up together.

Kithairon seized the larger share of votes.
Swiftly Hermes brought [all] to light,
crying out that he had seized
lovely victory. The Blessed Ones
place a crown [upon his head]
and adorned him; his heart was filled with joy.

But the other one, Helicon,
gripped by dreadful pain,
[tore out] a bare boulder;
the mountain [yielded]; piteously
[he groaned] and from on high hurled
it [downward], [breaking it] into
a thousand tiny stones. . . .

From various late sources we know that Helicon and Kithairon were thought to be brothers who were rival kings in early Boeotia before they were transformed into mountains. Korinna seems to capitalize on both the human and natural aspects of the two figures. The victor is crowned, just as any ordinary human contestant would be, but the loser is portrayed as a superhuman giant who angrily rips a boulder out of his namesake mountain. The resulting tiny stones are reminiscent of the very instrument of his defeat, the voting pebbles cast by the Muses, who, ironically, often frequented Mount Helicon, famous in Greek mythology as one of their favorite haunts.

The singing-contest fragment is marked by other repeated motifs as well, which help knit together a narrative that is characterized by simple, direct statements without subordination of ideas. The secrecy surrounding Zeus' whereabouts is echoed by the secret ballots used by the Muses, for example; Rhea "seizes" honor from the gods, just as Kithairon "seizes" the larger share of votes; and the Muses and Hermes all execute their tasks with speed. There is nothing particularly arresting in any part of the description. The local audience probably responded not so much to any special beauty of language as to the story itself and to the details chosen by the poet to characterize the two prominent features of the Boeotian landscape. If the opening lines do give us the conclusion of Kithairon's part in the competition, for example, the choice of the story of Zeus' birth as the subject matter of his song is highly appropriate for a site on which (as Pausanias reports) an important cult of Zeus was located.[21] There may perhaps be some touch of humor in the fact that his opponent, Helicon, despite close association with the civilizing forces of the Muses, loses not only the contest but also his temper.

The same papyrus also contains a slightly longer fragment from a similar narrative poem, of which only the middle portion survives. The intact section is narrated by the prophet Akraiphen, who is answering the questions of the river god Asopos as to what became of his nine maiden daughters. Here it is again important to realize the role of Boeotian geography in Korinna's poetry, for Asopos was the name of a major river on whose banks Tanagra was located, and according to local mythology, the daughters of the river god included not only Tanagra herself but other nearby cities and islands as well. The prophet explains the fate of Asopos' daughters as follows:

654.iii.12–51 PMG

Of [your] daughters
Zeus the father, king of all, has [three];
Poseidon, who rules the sea married
three, while Phoibos [Apollo] rules the beds
of two,

"And the fine boy Hermes, son of Maia,
[has] one. For this Eros
and Cypris persuaded [the gods]
to go into your house
and seize the nine maidens.

"One day they will bring forth a race
of demigod heroes,
and they will be exceedingly fruitful
and never-aging; [such are
the things I learned] from the oracle's tripod.

"This honor, I alone, Akraiphen,
the prophet, superior
among my fifty brothers,
obtained—the truth
from the holy inner sanctum.

"For first Leto's son
granted to Euonymos
to utter oracles from his tripod;
but Hyrieus, having cast him out of the land,
was the next to hold the honor—

"Poseidon's son. Then Orion,
my father [held the office],
having regained his own land;
he now frequents the heavens,
and this office fell to my lot.

". . . I utter
the truth as spoken through my oracles;
But you now, yield to the immortals
and [set your] heart [free from sorrow],
since you are father-in-law to the gods."

Thus spoke the bent, old prophet.
Asopos, gladly touching him by the right hand
and shedding a tear from his eyes,
answered aloud as follows. . . .

Asopos' reply is missing, but the description of his emotional
display of feeling in response to the prophet's account suggests that
Akraiphen was successful in persuading him to accept what has
befallen his daughters. It is likely that Korinna is here following a
local myth according to which the abduction of the nine girls by
the four gods is sanctioned as an act of fate that will bring future
glory to their family through their offspring—a pattern not uncommon in the chiefly patriarchal outlook of Greek mythology. In
any case, the prevailing tone of the fragment is one of submission.
Even the gods must submit to the will of Eros and Cypris; the
daughters of Asopos must submit to their husbands; and Asopos
is advised to yield to fate and submit to the will of the gods.

Besides giving us a further example of Korinna's use of the received tradition, the "Daughters of Asopos" fragment suggests that
despite the simplicity of her narrative, Korinna may have dealt with
the complexity of time in an interesting manner. Here the prophet
contrasts the past event (the rape of the girls) with future glory
(the heroes they will bear), at the same time pointing out that for
the daughters of Asopos themselves there will be, in effect, neither

past nor future, for they will be never-aging creatures in a world in which time does not exist. The prophet's own account of his predecessors, who include his father, the great Orion, and his grandfather, Hyrieus, is not merely (as one critic would have it) an otherwise pointless exercise in genealogy.[22] Rather, in addition to certifying the credibility of Akraiphen's prophecy, it changes the focus from times to come to times past, thus drawing together into the same continuum the heroes of old and the heroes of the future.

Another papyrus contains the only other fragment from Korinna's works that is of any length, a badly mutilated section of some twenty lines that may be the beginning of a poem from a series grouped together under the title "Geroia," perhaps meaning "Tales of Old." Although hardly of a personal nature, the fragment does seem to address the poet's role in preserving the traditions of the community through celebration in dance and song of its heroes of the past. Speaking in the first person, Korinna proclaims that Terpsichore herself, the Muse of dance, called upon her to sing:

655.i.1–16 PMG

Terpsichore [summoned me] to sing
beautiful tales of old [geroia]
to the Tanagraean girls in their white robes.
And the city rejoiced greatly
in my clear, plaintive voice.
For great things . . .

. . . the broad-plained earth . . .
I, having done honor to the oracles
in the time of our fathers . . .
. . . to the maidens . . .
I myself often honored with words
the leader Kephissos [the river god]
but often also great Orion
and the fifty mighty youths
whom [he begat] by mating with nymphs. . . .

Although we cannot be certain, the white-robed Tanagraean girls mentioned in line 3 are probably the members of the chorus to whom Korinna is to teach her songs for public performance.[23] We have fragments of apparently similar parthenia (maidens' songs) written by Pindar for performances by choruses of girls in Thebes, and fragments of Alkman's parthenia performed at Sparta (albeit quite different from Korinna's songs) survive as well. The mention of Terpsichore at the opening of the fragment suggests the element of dance involved in such choral performances, amply documented by scenes on vase paintings from various parts of Greece.

The word Korinna may have used here to describe the subject matter of her songs, *geroia* (evidently also used as the title of the book of poems of which this was a part), seems to be related to the word *geron* ("old man," as in *geriatrics*) and might mean something like "Tales of Old." In translations and commentaries of several decades ago, *Geroia* was uniformly rendered as "old wives' tales" (or in German, "Altweibergeschichten"), which was assumed to make sense in the context in which Korinna herself uses the word. The term "old wives' tales," however, generally implies ignorance, narrowness, and triviality—something thought to be of interest only to old women, who, it is presumed, have nothing better with which to occupy themselves. Since there is no good evidence that the Greek word *geroia* had any such coloring, a translation such as "tales of old" is much to be preferred, especially in the light of what is known of Korinna's subject matter. A recent German translation interprets the term along these same lines (but even more specifically) as "glorious songs of heroes" ("hohe Lieder von Helden").[24] Such an interpretation seems consistent with Korinna's statement of her subject matter elsewhere, in 664(b), where she says she sings of "the excellent deeds of male and female heroes."

Shorter Fragments of Korinna's Poetry

Of the fragments from Korinna's poetry preserved through brief quotations in grammarians who were interested in the peculiarities of her dialect, the most intelligible are the following:

657 PMG

Indeed do you sleep perpetually?
Hitherto you were not asleep, Korinna. . . .

658 *PMG*
[from "Boeotos"; Boeotos is a son of Poseidon]

You, O blessed son of Kronos,
you, O lord Boeotos . . . to Poseidon . . .

660 *PMG*
[from "Euonymia"; Euonymia is the granddaughter of Earth
and a Boeotian river, Kephissos]

Wanting to seize her child
in her dear arms . . .

662 *PMG*
[from "Kataplous" or "Return"]

Orion great in strength was victor
and named the whole land
after himself. . . .

674 *PMG*

[regarding one of the daughters of Asopos, the personified city
of Thespia]

Thespia, beautifully formed,
loving of strangers, dear to the Muses . . .

664(a) *PMG*

I myself blame even clear-voiced Myrtis,
because, though born a woman,
she entered into rivalry with Pindar.

Most of these excerpts reflect the same concern with Boeotian legend that we saw in the papyrus fragments. The first one, 657, however, is remarkable for its self-address, suggesting that perhaps not all of Korinna's poetry was so removed from the realm of personal experience. The last fragment, 664(a), has been much discussed in the scholarly literature, largely because it seems to be unreconcilable with the later reports of Korinna's own victory over Pindar; the discrepancy is particularly acute if one translates the last line as "entered a competition against Pindar." How can Korinna have entered such a poetry contest herself, it is argued, if she does not approve of Myrtis' doing the same?[25] It is worth noting, however, that the basic meaning of the crucial word in the last line, "eris," is simply "strife," "quarrel"; it need not bear the specialized meaning of "musical competition." If Korinna intended the word to be understood in its basic sense, she may simply be expressing disapproval of some literary or personal quarrel or perhaps criticizing Myrtis for attempting to rival Pindar in approach or subject matter that Korinna considered inappropriate for a woman writer. The latter interpretation would certainly fit with the essentially conservative impression given by the existing fragments of Korinna's poems, which indicate that she was interested only in transmitting received tradition, not in challenging it or in retelling it to focus on particular moral issues in the manner of a Pindar or a Bacchylides.

The paucity of fragments and the question of Korinna's dates prevent her from being assigned her appropriate niche in the history of Greek literature. To judge from the fragments themselves, she excelled at swiftly paced narrative that relied on simple, direct language and repetition of verbal ideas. With perhaps an intentional humorous twist, she draws parallels between the mythological world and everyday human behavior, as in the Muses' use of the democratic voting procedure or Mount Helicon's temper tantrum. Her verse may lack the brilliant imagery or philosophical profundity of other Greek lyric poets, but to label her style as "naive" or even "childish," as some critics have, does injustice to her refreshing simplicity in treating the relationship among the mythological, natural, and human worlds.

Despite the parochial nature of her dialect and even her subject matter, Korinna was a well-known poet outside her homeland, at least by the first century B.C. As we have already seen, Antipater of Thessaloniki pays tribute to her as one of the nine mortal Muses. During the same century, the Roman poet Propertius indirectly sings her praises by claiming that his lover surpasses Ariadne (a Cretan princess) in dance and Aganippe (a spring on Mount Helicon) in lyre playing and that when she compares her own verses to those of "ancient Korinna," they are of equal merit.[26] (His mention of "antiquae . . . Corinnae," incidentally, provides another indication of her early date, since it seems unlikely that he would have referred to someone of only a hundred or a hundred and fifty years before his own time as "ancient.") Korinna's poetry seems not only to have been read by educated Roman women such as Propertius' lover, but also to have been the subject of academic studies. The Roman poet Statius, writing in the first century A.D. to his schoolmaster father, praises his skill at "opening up the secrets of refined Korinna" ("tenuisque arcana Corinnae").[27] The descriptive epithet here, "tenuis," means, literally, "thin," "fine," but in a literary context generally carries the sense of "refined" or "delicate." What was doubtless intended by Statius as a compliment on Korinna's nicety of style is turned by one modern translator into "meagre" Korinna![28] The famous poet of Tanagra did not have the emotional power or the brilliance of Sappho, but "meagre" she was not, nor did she spend her days writing "old wives' tales."

Praxilla of Sikyon

Praxilla, the first poet mentioned in Antipater of Thessaloniki's list of the nine mortal Muses, lived in the mid-fifth century in the city of Sikyon on the Corinthian Gulf several miles to the west of Corinth. In the preceding century her city had enjoyed prosperous times during the benevolent rule of Kleisthenes, who fostered a well-known group of artists. The artistic fame of Sikyon continued into the fourth century, for at that time it was the home of a great sculptor named Lysippos. According to Tatian, the same Christian father to whom I have referred in connection with Sappho and Korinna, this Lysippos made a bronze statue of Praxilla "even though she said nothing useful in her poetry."[29] "Useful" or not, Praxilla's poetry was widely popular both in her own day and in later centuries as well. A late writer reports (see below) that her songs were a favorite part of the repertory of drinking-party music in fifth-century Athens, and the fourth-century statue of her by Lysippos also suggests a prominent reputation.

To judge from the scanty remnants of Praxilla's poetry—eight fragments in all, although some are only brief paraphrases of her actual words—she was a versatile author who wrote poetry of several different genres, including not only popular songs of the sort for which she was known in Athens, but also hymns about various gods and goddesses as well as dithyrambs, choral songs associated with the worship of Dionysos and generally performed at festivals held in his honor.

It is Athenaeus, a second-century A.D. compiler of literary excerpts and anecdotes, who reports that Praxilla of Sikyon was admired for her composition of *skolia* (drinking songs).[30] He goes on to claim that the name *skolia* (crooked) comes from the irregular criss-cross pattern formed by the participants at aristocratic drinking parties when, rather than everyone performing in some sort of regular order, only those with truly excellent voices would sing for the rest of the company. Athenaeus includes a group of twenty-five of these short Attic *skolia*, of which two can be connected with Praxilla through other sources. (He himself does not give the authorship of any of the songs, and some of them probably were in fact anonymous.) In general the songs consist of some aristocratic maxim illustrated through reference to nature, to Greek myth, or in some cases to events in Athenian history.[31] In one of the songs identified (by an ancient commentator on Aristophanes' *Wasps*) as from Praxilla's *Paroinia* ("Amidst the Wine" songs),[32] she alludes to the legend of Admetus, who, when offered the chance to extend his life by arranging for someone else to go to Hades for him, found that only his courageous wife, Alcestis, was willing to die in his stead:

749 *PMG*

> O my friend, since you know the story of Admetus,
>   love the brave.
> Keep away from cowards, knowing that from cowards
>   the return is small.

According to the version of the story as told in the play *Alcestis* by the Athenian dramatist Euripides, Admetus was exceptionally lucky, for Herakles took pity on his household and wrestled with Death himself in order to win Alcestis back. Although the *skolion* does not mention Alcestis by name, she is clearly the example of bravery par excellence whom Praxilla has in mind.

The other song identified with Praxilla (again by a commentator on Aristophanes)[33] is likewise cast in the form of advice:

750 *PMG*

O friend, watch out for a scorpion under every stone.

According to the anonymous version (of slightly different wording) given in Athenaeus, the second line of the song went, "Beware lest it sting you; trickery of every kind lurks in what you cannot see."[34]

The songs are typical of the others in the group of *skolia* preserved by Athenaeus in that, lacking reference either to wine or to drunkenness, they resemble proverbs more than what we might think of as drinking songs. Although the authorship of the two examples discussed is not absolutely certain (the ancient commentators use phrases like "attributed to Praxilla"), it is likely that Praxilla at least wrote poems similar to these, or her name would probably not have become connected in Athenaeus' remarks with *skolia*. Her association with such songs has led to one quite unreasonable conclusion, drawn not surprisingly by Wilamowitz (whose distortions of Sappho's poems were discussed in chapter 1). He concluded, in essence, that only a woman who was not a lady could have written drinking songs and that therefore Praxilla must have been a *hetaira*, roughly the ancient equivalent of a Geisha girl.[35] There is no evidence for such an assumption.

Another two-line song probably by Praxilla is preserved in an ancient treatise on meter in which the author quotes the verses as an illustration of the Praxilleion, a type of dactylic meter named after the poet:

754 *PMG*

O you who look prettily through the windows,
a virgin from the neck up, but below, an experienced
woman.

The preserver of the lines does not actually say that they are by Praxilla, but it seems likely that he chose some of her own verses to illustrate the meter named in her honor. Various interpretations of the song have been proposed. Presumably the person addressed is a young woman of innocent demeanor who is in fact not so innocent as she looks, but whether she is supposed to be a bride-to-be or a *hetaira* cannot be determined.[36] In any case, the lines capture the youthful charm of innocence only recently lost combined with knowledge only recently gained. At least one critic, however, finding such a carnal interpretation unbefitting a woman poet, proposed that the lines were in fact a kind of riddle and that the answer to the riddle is the moon; the moon, looking in through the windows, is inaccessible ("virgin") when she is high up in the sky, but when she sets "below" the horizon she becomes Endymion's consort.[37] This is a clever but unnecessarily complicated interpretation, given the simplicity and directness of the other songs associated with Praxilla. And even if the moon were the intended (veiled) subject, on the most obvious level the lines still seem to describe the transitional point in a young woman's life at which she is neither child nor adult.

The remaining fragments from Praxilla's work all have to do with mythological themes. The longest of them, from a hymn to Adonis, is preserved by the second-century A.D. Zenobius in a work on proverbs in which he is attempting to elucidate the expression "More foolish than the Adonis of Praxilla." (Adonis, a sort of vegetation deity, was the consort of Aphrodite who was killed by a boar at a youthful age and over whom Greek women held a ritual lament each spring.) Zenobius explains as follows: "An expression used of fools. Praxilla of Sikyon was a lyric poet. . . . She makes Adonis, when asked by those below what the most beautiful thing he had left behind was, answer as follows:

747 *PMG*

The most beautiful thing I leave is the light
   of the sun,
and after that the glimmering stars and the face
   of the moon,
and ripe cucumbers, apples, pears.

For only the simple-minded would equate cucumbers and the like with the sun and the moon."[38]

Whatever the origin of the expression which Zenobius is attempting to explain, it is unlikely that his reasoning here is correct. The lines themselves seem to portray Adonis not so much as a fool as an exuberant youth who cannot really decide what he misses most—the light of day, the night sky, or the fruit of the earth. He misses all these earthly pleasures, whether they appeal to his sense of sight or of taste.[39]

Another fragment is preserved in an ancient handbook on meter in which the author quotes a line from one of Praxilla's dithyrambs entitled "Achilles":

748 *PMG*

But they did not ever persuade the heart within
    your breast . . .

Presumably the reference is to Achilles' unceasing wrath against Agamemnon with which Homer in the *Iliad* begins his narration of the Greeks' war against Troy. The genre of this fragment, although most typically associated with the worship of Dionysos at Athens, is not surprising in view of the information, related by the fifth-century Herodotus, that in the preceding century the ruler Kleisthenes had for political reasons encouraged the worship of Dionysos at Sikyon through "tragic choruses," probably dithyrambs.[40]

The other fragments from Praxilla's work (751, 752, 753) are actually only allusions to her versions of various myths. Contrary to the usual account of Dionysos' parentage, for instance, she evidently said his mother was Aphrodite rather than Semele. She also told of the son of Pelops named Chrysippos (Golden Horse), with whom in the usual versions Laios (the father of Oedipus) fell in love and abducted; according to Praxilla, it was Zeus himself who was the abductor. In addition, Praxilla reported that the festival of the Karneia (celebrated in Sparta and other Doric cities in honor of Apollo) was named after an obscure deity, Karneios, who in her account was a son of Zeus and Europa but was raised by Apollo and his mother, Leto.

A general evaluation of Praxilla of Sikyon is difficult, but had more of her poetry survived, we would probably find that her work covered a broad range of subjects and was characterized by metrical originality and a certain charm in description (as in the "window" fragment) which no doubt contributed to the popularity of her poetry in the symposia of Athenian aristocratic circles.

Telesilla of Argos

Some thirty miles from Sikyon, further south in the Peloponnesos, lies the fertile Argive Plain, famous in the Bronze Age as the region ruled by Agamemnon, the powerful king of Mycenae. The chief city of the area in classical times was (as it is today) Argos, the home of the poet Telesilla "of wide fame" (as Antipater of Thessaloniki calls her), who was remembered in late antiquity more for her military courage in an incident in about 494 B.C. than for her poetry.

Not much can be seen of Argos as Telesilla would have known it in the early fifth century B.C., for some parts of the classical city still lie unexcavated beneath the modern town, and other parts were probably destroyed by subsequent construction during the Hellenistic and Roman periods.[41] Although we know comparatively little about the physical remains of the city, it is clear that Argos had a lively artistic tradition in the classical era. Herodotus informs us that in the late sixth century, the Argives were reputed to be "the best among the Greeks in the art of music."[42] At about the same time an important school of sculpture was founded, which in the next century produced one of the leading sculptors in all of Greece, Polykleitos. But the only writer who is associated with Argos besides Telesilla herself was a minor local historian by the name of Sokrates, who seems to have written during the Hellenistic period.

Of Telesilla's poetry, we have left only one short fragment, three one-word quotations, and several brief references to her poems in authors of late antiquity like Pausanias. Pausanias' apparent familiarity with her work suggests, however, that in the second century A.D. her poems were still in circulation some seven hundred years after her death. The one surviving fragment concerns the story of Alpheus, the river god who fell in love with and pursued the nymph Arethusa, who prayed to the virgin goddess Artemis to be transformed into a spring and thus escape his unwanted advances. The

fragment is quoted as an illustration of a meter named the Tele-
silleion:

717 PMG

> But Artemis, O maidens,
> fleeing from Alpheus . . .

Too little survives to allow any reconstruction of Telesilla's treatment of the myth. The address to "maidens" suggests that like some
of Korinna's songs, Telesilla's poem may have been written for a
choral performance by a group of local girls at one of the city's
festivals. Four of the other fragments (718, 719, 720, 721), actually
only single words or paraphrases, are connected in one way or
another with Artemis or with her brother Apollo, the city's most
important god and the one to whom the finest temple in Argos
was dedicated.[43] Whether Telesilla's range extended beyond such
religious poetry we cannot tell. In one poem she apparently spoke
of a threshing floor (723); in another (724) she used the epithet
"oulokikinnos" ("curly-haired"). Hardly any more informative is
an ancient commentator's remark that seems to indicate that Telesilla must have personified the qualities of excellence (*arete*) and
nobility (*kalokagathia*) in at least one of her poems; in elucidating
Homer's description of Athena as "beautiful and large," the commentator states that "Homer wants us to imagine her appearance
of beauty and awe, just as Xenophon and Telesilla of Argos portray
the image of Excellence and Nobility" (725).

Although virtually nothing of Telesilla's writing has survived,
thanks to the biographical accounts in Pausanias and Plutarch (probably derived from the Argive historian Sokrates, mentioned above),
she stands out as a vivid figure in the fifth-century history of her
city. Pausanias tells the story in connection with a statue of Telesilla
which he saw during his visit to Argos:

> Beyond the theatre is the temple of Aphrodite; in front of the seated
> statue of the goddess, Telesilla the composer of songs is represented on a
> stele. Her songs are shown hurled down at her feet, while she herself looks
> at a helmet she holds in her hand as she is about to put it on her head.
> Telesilla was famous especially among women, and was respected all the
> more on account of her poetry.

It happened that the Argives had been miserably defeated by Kleomenes son of Anaxandrides and the Spartans . . . [Kleomenes] led his Spartan forces against Argos after the town had been emptied of its troops. But Telesilla made all the slaves go up on the walls—as many as had been unable to bear arms on account of youth or old age. She herself collected all the weapons left behind in houses and temples and armed those among the women who were in the prime of youth. After arming them she lined them up at a point where she knew the enemy would approach. When the Spartans came, the women were not frightened by the shouting, but, expecting the attack, fought vigorously, until the Spartans, thinking that for them to defeat women would be seen as an invidious victory and that defeat by women would be shameful, yielded their arms. The Pythian priestess [of Delphi] had already predicted the outcome of the battle; her oracle is preserved by Herodotus, whether he understood it or not:

> But whenever the female shall conquer
> And drive out the male, winning glory
>   among the Argives,
> Then she will cause many an Argive woman
> To rend both cheeks.[44]

This prophecy, typical of other Delphic oracles in its conditional phrasing and in the ambiguity of its wording (in that it seems to predict both victory and defeat at the same time), is included in Herodotus' fifth-century account of the battle without any indication of how he interpreted it. In fact his report, which appears to be based largely on Spartan sources, makes no mention at all of either Telesilla or the role of the Argive women, so we have no confirmation of the story from any contemporary source. Plutarch, however, writing in the second century A.D., makes the same point as Pausanias regarding the respect women felt for Telesilla as the result of her poetic skill and gives essentially the same account of her heroism but in less detail, adding that the women who were killed in battle were buried along the Argive Way and that the survivors were honored by the setting up of a shrine to Enyalios, the war god. According to his report, even in his own time the Argives still celebrated a festival each year on the day of Telesilla's victory, in which the men and women of the city wore the clothing of the opposite sex.[45]

Modern scholars have reacted to the story of Telesilla's heroism with varying degrees of skepticism. Lisi, for example, notes that according to the second-century A.D. Maximus of Tyre, Telesilla's poetry "roused" her people just as Alcaeus roused the Lesbians and Tyrtaeus the Spartans (the latter being the author of explicit call-to-arms songs), and concludes that the whole episode is probably derived from Telesilla's martial poetry.[46] This is certainly a possible explanation, but what little we know of Telesilla's work suggests that her chief sphere was religious poetry rather than war songs. In any case, Maximus of Tyre does not explicitly label her as a composer of martial poetry. Other scholars are less skeptical, though still cautious in assessing Pausanias' account: "The role of Telesilla may have been exaggerated."[47]

Whether or not the story of Telesilla's heroism as a soldier is fabrication, exaggeration, or historical truth (indeed, there is at least nothing inherently improbable in Pausanias' account), there is no doubt that she was a poet of considerable reputation even in late antiquity and one whose work was known to Greek chroniclers and grammarians alike, if apparently not to any Roman readers. The almost total loss of her poetry represents a serious gap in our understanding of fifth-century Argos. Telesilla's city, about whose culture her poems might have told us so much, remains in the shadow of the Argos of the Bronze Age.[48]

Conclusion

The classical period of Greek literature, then, which we usually think of as being centered in Athens and as being represented exclusively by male authors, did have at least a few women writers, all of whom lived and worked in Boeotia or the Peloponnesos. Of Myrtis of Anthedon in Boeotia, we know virtually nothing, except for possibly unreliable biographical information about her role as a teacher of other poets. But Korinna of nearby Tanagra, despite the dispute over her dates, is represented by fragments sufficient in number for us to form some limited judgment of the qualities of her work. In contrast to the most famous Boeotian poet, Pindar, Korinna wrote in the local dialect on local myths, legends, and folk motifs such as the singing contest between the two Boeotian mountains (654.i). Unlike Sappho's, her poetry is not particularly woman-centered, even though she seems to have written some of her songs for performance by a female chorus. As Skinner has noted, "While Sappho's work is intensely female-oriented, Corinna's is not. Instead, her treatment of legendary material pays marked deference to the canonical, male-dominated literary tradition and presents its narrative from a frankly patriarchal perspective."[49] Among the extant fragments of Korinna's work, the clearest example of this perspective is seen in 654.iii about the abduction of the nine daughters of the river god Asopos. Her poetry was admired long after her own time (whether the fifth century, as we have argued, or the third century), most notably by the Roman poets Propertius and Statius.

Finally, we have only the barest scraps from the work of two fifth-century poets of the Peloponnesos, Praxilla of Sikyon and Telesilla of Argos. Praxilla seems to have written hymns, dithyrambs, and what we would call proverbs, the last of which became popular as drinking songs among male aristocratic circles in Athens. Telesilla, whose work was still known in the days of the second-century A.D. travel writer Pausanias, seems to have written on typical mythological themes. It is possible that she was also the author of martial poetry, which may have enhanced the biographical tradition of her military heroism in defending the city of Argos against the Spartans.

3 _Women Poets of Hellenistic Greece_
Anyte, Nossis, Moero, and Erinna

This chapter brings us to the Hellenistic period of Greek history and to the rest of the "earthly Muses" named by Antipater in the epigraph of this book: Anyte, Nossis, Moero, and Erinna. All of these poets lived in the early part of the Hellenistic era, which is commonly defined as beginning with the death of Alexander the Great in 323 B.C. and ending with the death of Cleopatra VII, queen of Egypt, in 30 B.C., at which time her kingdom was incorporated into Rome's spreading empire. The famous Cleopatra was one in a long line of Hellenistic queens, including Berenice, Arsinoe II, and Cleopatra III, who acquired tremendous political power in an era in which women writers were unable to achieve comparable influence within literary circles.

The political unity of the enormous empire which Alexander had conquered fell apart after his death, and decades of warfare among his successors resulted eventually in the establishment of three separate kingdoms: Macedonia, Egypt, and the Seleucid Empire of Asia Minor. In the face of these three powerful kingdoms, the small communities of mainland Greece soon banded together into two political and military leagues, the Aetolian League in the north and the Achaean League in the south. Athens and Sparta remained independent of either league, but always in the shadow of the powerful Macedonian kingdom to the north. Despite her political decline, Athens remained an important intellectual center in the Mediterranean, fostering as she did the development of the influential philosophical schools of the Stoics and the Epicureans (see chapter 4). Yet it was Alexandria in Egypt that quickly became not only the largest city in the Greek world but also the leading cultural center of the time.

Significantly, the three men who are remembered today as the major poets of the Hellenistic period (besides the comic poet Menander of Athens) were all connected in one way or another with Alexandria. Callimachus, author of learned hymns and polished epigrams, was closely connected with the court circle of King Ptolemy II Philadelphus and enjoyed the privileges of association with the famous Library of Alexandria. Apollonius Rhodius, who composed an epic account of Jason and the Argonauts, likewise benefited from court patronage, even holding the post of head of the Library. Theocritus, generally regarded as the father of the pastoral poetry which later inspired such diverse writers as Vergil, Shakespeare, Milton, and Shelley, left his homeland in Sicily and travelled abroad, staying at least a short time in Alexandria; in one of his poems, *Idyll* 18, he sings the praises of Ptolemy. Alexandria's Library, which eventually boasted some half a million volumes, along with the Museum (that is, the "Muses' Sanctuary" or what would today be called a center for advanced research), lent institutional support to the work of these and other poets, scholars, and compilers. A similar center under court patronage existed at Pergamum on the coast of Asia Minor, and other centers of intellectual activity could be found on the islands of Rhodes and Cos.[1] But of all the cultural centers of the Hellenistic era, only the Epicurean School in Athens has left record of active participation by women. In contrast to Callimachus, Apollonius, and Theocritus, all of whom lived in the middle of the third century B.C., none of the four women poets discussed in this chapter can be connected with any of these major centers. Whatever local support they may have found in their own communities, none seems to have enjoyed the financial or intellectual patronage of a major institution.

It is impossible to characterize the cultural complexities of the Hellenistic period in a few words, but perhaps some comparisons between literature and the visual arts will help establish a context in which to consider the poems translated and discussed below. If the art of classical Greece can be described as idealistic, the art produced for the new markets after Alexander's conquests must be called realistic. The repertory of subjects expanded to include not just gods, heroes, and upper-class citizens, but the ordinary people as well—old women, fishermen, babies, children, and non-Greeks. The new naturalism is especially noticeable in the artists' technical proficiency in the rendering of children and animals.[2] In Hellenistic literature, a comparable emphasis upon the ordinary can be found in the expanded subjects covered in the increasingly popular poetic form called the epigram. The epigram was a short poem in elegiac couplets, that is, pairs of lines of which the first was a hexameter line and the second a shorter line derived from the hexameter. Originally the epigram had served the limited purpose of epitaph, as its name implies (the Greek *epigramma* means "inscription"), but in the Hellenistic period, epigrams had come to be used to treat any number of subjects—laments, dedications, love affairs, family pets, and so on—and need not always have been intended to be used as actual inscriptions. Such poems may be distinguished from those intended as actual inscriptions by the term *epideictic* (display), which denotes a poem meant to show off the poet's art.

With the exception of a long fragmentary hexameter poem by Erinna, "The Distaff," and a short hexameter piece by Moero, all of the poems discussed in this chapter belong to the genre of the epigram, and nearly all of them have been preserved for us among the large collection of similar poems called *The Greek Anthology*. This collection is based on several anthologies made during the Hellenistic, Roman, and Byzantine periods, the earliest of which was compiled by Meleager of Gadara about 100 B.C. Among the poems preserved from his collection (which he called the *Stephanos* or "Garland") is his own introduction, in which he speaks of the Muses' garland of sweet words which he has woven together, including many "lilies" of Anyte and Moero; only a few flowers of Sappho—"but," he says, "they are roses"; and the sweet "crocus" of Erinna, "just like the complexion of a young girl."[3] While the "lilies" and "crocuses" of the Hellenistic women poets may seem pale by comparison with the fiery intensity of Sappho's "roses," we should remember to judge them by the same standards that are applied to "occasional verse" of any era, keeping in mind as well the general tendency of Hellenistic literature towards what might be called elegant ordinariness.

Anyte

Of the words of all the women poets discussed in this book, more remain of Anyte than of anyone else besides Sappho. *The Greek Anthology* has preserved for us twenty-four poems attributed to her, of which at least twenty-one or twenty-two are taken by modern scholars to be certainly by Anyte.[4]

According to a compiler of the second century A.D., Anyte was a native of Tegea in the mountainous district of the Peloponnesos called Arcadia.[5] Although another source assigns her to Lesbos (probably on the assumption that all women poets should conform to the model of Sappho), her Doric dialect and references in her poetry to Tegea and the Arcadian god Pan suggest that she may indeed have come from the region of Greece that later came to epitomize the ideal of the shepherd's pastoral landscape—the remote and idyllic land of Arcadia as it was portrayed by Vergil in his *Eclogues*. In any case, Anyte, writing perhaps about 300 B.C., or slightly earlier than Theocritus, seems to have been among the first Hellenistic poets to describe pastoral settings within the context of the epigram.[6] To translate the remarks of a modern critic, "Anyte's significance for the history of the Greek epigram should not be underestimated. She appears to have created the type of bucolic landscape-epigram and animal epitaph which remained in use for a very long period."[7]

The one surviving biographical anecdote about Anyte can tell us little about historical realities, but it is interesting both as an example of a miracle tale and as an indication that Anyte's reputation survived in some form into the second century A.D., when Pausanias recorded the story in his travelogue of Greek sites—an invaluable resource for today's archaeologists.[8] Pausanias reports that the Sanctuary of Asclepius in Naupactos (on the northern side of the entrance to the Gulf of Corinth) was in ruins when he visited the site but that it had originally been built by a man named Phalysius. Phalysius was going blind, so the story goes, and his prayers to Asclepius at

Epidauros were heeded when the god delivered a sealed wax tablet
to the poet Anyte and inspired her to sail to Naupactos. There she
met Phalysius and urged him to remove the seal and read the
message. To his amazement, he was able to read the tablet, which
instructed him to make a present to Anyte of 2,000 gold staters—
a sum the equivalent of many thousands of dollars. It is impossible
to tell just how the tale of this profitable trip originated, but as is
often the case with ancient pseudobiographical material, it may
have been derived from one of Anyte's poems, perhaps a dedicatory
epigram like the ones translated below.[9]

Seven of Anyte's surviving poems reflect the original use of the
epigram as an inscription for a tombstone. Of these, four concern
the death of young women and girls:

1 (*Anth. Pal.* 7.646)

Throwing her arms around her dear father,
 Erato, melting away in moist tears, spoke these last words.
"Father, I am no more; dark black Death
 covers my eyes as already I perish."

2 (*Anth. Pal.* 7.486)

Often in lamentation upon this girl's tomb, her mother Kleina
 bewails her beloved child, who died before her time.
She calls forth the soul of Philanis, who—before her
 marriage—
  crossed the pale stream of the River Acheron.

3 (*Anth. Pal.* 7.649)

No bed-chamber and sacred rites of marriage for you.
 Instead, your mother put upon this marble tomb
A likeness which has your girlish shape and beauty,
 Thersis; you can be addressed even though you are dead.

4 (*Anth. Pal.* 7.490)

I mourn for the maiden Antibia, to whose
 father's house many suitors came, drawn by
Report of her beauty and wisdom. But deadly Fate
 whirled away the hopes of all of them.[10]

Although we cannot be positive, these poems have the ring of
actual epitaphs composed for the grave monuments of the people
named in them, particularly 2 and 3, in which the tomb provides

the focus for the poem. An English translation fails to convey the elegance of the language in these verses, in which Anyte makes skillful use of the flexibility of Greek word order so as to emphasize the pathos inherent in an untimely death. For example, each of the poems stresses the grief of a surviving parent, whether it is the father addressed in the imaginary dramatic scene of 1, the grieving mothers of 2 and 3, or the father indirectly alluded to in 4; in nearly every instance, the parent is mentioned in the most prominent positions within the verse—the beginnings and endings of the line. Sometimes the framework of the whole couplet is used to good effect, as in 1, in which the second couplet begins in the Greek with the address to the father—representative of the world of the living—and ends with the word *thanatos* (death). Although such refinements cannot be reproduced in a positional language like English, these examples should suffice to suggest Anyte's careful attention to the niceties of word order that are possible in an inflected language like Greek.

These four epitaphs for girls also suggest a considerable versatility in the treatment of a given theme. Poem 1 makes use of a dramatic vignette to capture the moment of death; 2 focuses on the actions of the living in mourning the dead; 3 is in the form of an ironic address to the deceased and her statue, which must be the focus of future addresses now that Thersis herself is dead; and 4, expressed in the first person, emphasizes the pathos of unfulfilled promise (the girl's beauty and intelligence) and the frustration of unfulfilled hopes (the many suitors who were attracted by the girl's qualities.) These epitaphs—whether real or epideictic—indicate that Anyte's handling of a "stock" theme is marked by freshness and originality, qualities that can be seen also in her pastoral epigrams.

Three other epitaphs that are probably all by Anyte also survive.[11] Two commemorate the heroism of men who have died for their country:

5 (*Anth. Pal.* 7.724)

Death took you in your prime [text uncertain];
    dying, you brought dark grief to your mother Pheidia.
But the poem on this stone above you sings
    of how you died doing battle for your beloved fatherland.

6 (*Anth. Pal.* 7.232)

The Lydian dust holds this Amyntor, son of Philip,
    who touched iron-hard battle with his hands many times.
Nor did grievous sickness send him to the House of Night,
    but he perished holding his round shield over his
        comrade-in-arms.

A third is of a more general sort expressing the philosophical sentiment that death brings equality to all people, regardless of their status in life—whether they be a Phrygian slave (commonly named "Manes") or the king of Persia:

7 (*Anth. Pal.* 7.538)

This man, while he was alive, was Manes; now that he has
    died,
    his power is equal to that of the great Darius.

If these poems are in fact by Anyte, they suggest she had a wider range of contact within the Greek world than we might otherwise guess; poem 6 refers apparently to the death of a Macedonian in Asia Minor, and 7 also suggests connections with Asia Minor.

In addition to epitaphs for women and men, Anyte also composed several epigrams that either served as or at least posed as memorial poems for animals. Since the subjects of this group of epigrams range from a soldier's war-horse to a child's pet grasshopper, it seems likely that some of the poems were meant as epideictic pieces, not as actual inscriptions to be put on a tombstone. If such is the case, Anyte was probably among the earliest Hellenistic poets to experiment with the traditional genre of the epigram by playing on the expectation that the theme be one of great solemnity; certainly the kind of mock seriousness created in a poem posing as the ultimate tribute to a deceased grasshopper prepared the way for later use of the epigram as a vehicle for wit and satire. At least two of Anyte's animal epitaphs sound, however, like they might have been intended as actual inscriptions,[12] for horses and dogs were commonly commemorated in Hellenistic epitaphs:

8 (*Anth. Pal.* 7.208)

Damis erected this memorial for his steadfast horse
    when Ares struck its tawny flanks;

Black blood boiled up through the thick hide,
and amidst the slaughter it smeared the earth with gore.

9 (Poll. 5.48)

You, too, perished once beside a well-rooted shrub,
Locrian hound, swiftest of noise-loving dogs;
Into your nimble limbs a viper of intricate-colored neck
put such cruel poison.

Compared to other poems of its kind, the epitaph for the war-horse (8) is remarkable for the vivid description of the animal's death. Instead of glossing over the moment of death, the poet chooses to emphasize the horse's bloody end in the thick of battle. Poem 9 also focuses on the manner of the animal's death, in this case by snakebite. In the Greek, this poem in memory of a type of animal that the poet labels "noise-loving," is appropriately filled with alliterative *p*'s and *k*'s, sharp sounds imitative of the dog's barking.

Three other animal epitaphs preserved from among Anyte's poems seem likely to be epideictic pieces, including memorials for a bird, a dolphin, and a girl's pet grasshopper and cicada:

10 (*Anth. Pal.* 7.202)

No longer will you rouse me from my bed as before, waking
early in the morning and flapping your fast-beating wings;
For a plunderer, coming upon you stealthily as you slept,
swiftly put his claws upon your neck and killed you.

11 (*Anth. Pal.* 7.215)

No longer will I take delight in floating seas,
and toss up my head, raising it from the depths,
Nor will I snort and leap about the ship's beautiful beak,
delighting in the figurehead, my likeness.
The purple swell of the sea cast me upon the shore,
and I lie along this narrow beach.

12 (*Anth. Pal.* 7.190)

For her grasshopper (nightingale of the fields)
and her cicada (dweller in the oak) Myro made a common
tomb;
The girl shed maidenly tears, for Hades, who is hard to
persuade,
twice came and took away her playthings.

The epitaph for the bird, presumably a cock, while retaining the focus on the manner of death, betrays its self-consciousness in playing with the reader's expectations by referring so mysteriously to the agent of death (a "plunderer," presumably a fox) and by hinting at the irony involved in the death during sleep of an animal so closely associated with wakefulness.

The dolphin poem, longer than a typical epitaph, centers more on the animal's delight in life rather than the moment of death, and also departs from the usual form in that the point of view is the dolphin's. The allusion to the dolphin figurehead on the ship seems to play against a common theme in actual epitaphs, namely a reference to a likeness of the deceased. The poem simply uses the genre of the epitaph as a framework within which to conjure up the sight, seen with some frequency in the Mediterranean, of dolphins gracefully cavorting in the water alongside a ship.

But the most charming example of Anyte's ability to play with the conventions of the epitaph is in the piece on Myro's loss of her pet grasshopper and cicada to the inexorable forces of Hades. Here the poet delights us with the epic-sounding epithets that she attaches to the two tiny insects buried in the same grave—the one "nightingale of the fields" and the other "dweller in the oak." Yet despite the tone of mock solemnity, there is an underlying sense of pathos in the girl's mourning over the loss of her pets, even if they were only insects kept in a box or tied on a string. The poem evidently captured the imagination of a later imitator, one Marcus Argentarius, who pictures Myro sprinkling dust over the common tomb of the grasshopper and the cicada, one of whom (the "songster") had been snatched away by Hades, the other by Persephone.[13] His version lacks the edge of pathos that colors Anyte's poem, as does a similar epigram by another later imitator, Aristodicus of Rhodes, on the death of a locust which has flown off to be among the flowers of Persephone (*Anth. Pal.* 7.189).

Another group of Anyte's surviving epigrams are the dedication poems—pieces written in connection with the dedication of a gift by someone to a god or goddess in return for some favor. Although these poems could be epideictic, they have the ring of an actual inscription:

13 (*Anth. Pal.* 6.123)

Stop here, O spear which slays mortals; no longer drip
    the mournful blood of enemies from your brazen claw.
But sitting in the craggy marble home of Athena,
    proclaim the manhood of Echecratidas of Crete.

14 (*Anth. Pal.* 6.153)

This bowl could hold an ox; the son of Eriaspidas dedicates
    it—
        Kleobotos, whose fatherland is broad-plained Tegea.
To Athena this bowl is given, made by Aristoteles
    of Kleitor, who has the same name as his father.

The dedication in 13 is expressed in the form of a command to the
object dedicated, namely Echecratidas' spear, which now rests in a
marble sanctuary of Athena, perhaps the temple of Athena Alea in
Tegea that Pausanias describes as superior to all others in the Pelo-
ponnese.[14] It is as though the spear would continue to do its work,
were it not for the poem's imperative that it must remain fixed in
the temple of the armed goddess of war.

Poem 14 also involves a dedication to Athena—but whether in
her militaristic role or in some other aspect, the poem does not
clarify. The piece depends for its effect on exaggeration, since no
doubt the bowl was in fact hardly large enough to hold an ox, and
on its economy of expression, through which we learn the name
of the dedicator, his father's name, and the name of his country,
along with the same information for the maker of the bowl—all
within the space of two couplets. Nothing is known about the artist
Aristoteles, but the fact that he is mentioned with as much detail
as the dedicator himself suggests that he may have been well known
at least within the area of Arcadia (Kleitor is a town in the northern
part of the district).

Another dedicatory poem concerns a shrine to Pan and the
nymphs:

15 (*Anth. Plan.* 291)

Lonely Theodotus set up this gift to shaggy Pan
    and to the rustic nymphs at the foot of the hill,
Since they checked his great suffering caused by the burning
    heat,
        stretching forth to his hands honey-sweet water.

This poem has all the elements that appear in Anyte's pastoral epigrams. If indeed it was intended as an actual inscription, it seems to refer to some sort of shrine at a spring, the "gift" possibly being a vessel into which the water flowed. The epithet that describes Theodotus ("oionomos"), here translated as "lonely," seems to mean literally "feeding alone," but it may derive from a root that would give it the meaning "pasturing sheep"; in any case, it is an adjective applied to shepherds, whose solitary life in the countryside forms the basis for the Greek pastoral tradition. The rustic, goatlike Pan and the nymphs who inhabit springs and woods are of course pastoral deities par excellence, and the poem's reference to the blazing heat and to thirst quenched by honey-sweet water completes the vignette of an idyllic place of rest and respite.

With this poem we come to the group of Anyte's epigrams for which she is most important in terms of the development of later Greek literature—her pastoral poems. Many of these maintain the tradition of the epigram in that they could have been intended as inscriptions on statues or shrines. But perhaps of more significance than their possible practical origins is Anyte's creation of a poetic pastoral landscape—a peaceful world of hot, blazing sun and cool, refreshing fountains; a world inhabited by goatherds, travelers, children, and pasturing flocks, graced by the presence of Pan, Hermes, and other rustic deities. It is a place of delightful refreshment and of escape from the mundane realities of work, war, or death:

16 (*Anth. Plan.* 228)

Stranger, rest your weary limbs under this rock;
    a sweet breeze murmurs among the green leaves.
Drink cold spring water from the fountain, for in the
    burning heat this is welcome respite for wayfarers.

17 (*Anth. Pal.* 9.313)

Sit, everyone, under the blossoming leaves of laurel
    and draw a sweet draught from the timely spring
So that you may rest your limbs, weary from the harvest's
toils,
    smitten by the breath of Zephyrus.

18 (*Anth. Pal.* 9.314)

I, Hermes, stand beside an airy row of trees
    in the crossroads near the surf-lined beach,
Offering rest for men weary from their journey;
    my fountain drips with fresh cold water.

19 (*Anth. Pal.* 9.144)

This is the precinct of the Cyprian, since she likes to come
  here
    always to watch the sunlit sea from the mainland
So that she may accomplish a lovely voyage for sailors.
    The waves tremble as they behold her gleaming wooden
    image.

20 (*Anth. Pal.* 6.312)

Placing crimson reins on you, billy goat,
    and a noseband around your shaggy mouth,
The children train you in equine contests near the god's
  temple,
    so that he may see them in their childish delights.

21 (*Anth. Pal.* 9.745)

Behold the horned goat of Dionysus, how spiritedly
    it holds its gaze, looking down over its shaggy jaws,
Exulting because often in the mountains a Naiad
    put a lock of hair from his cheek into her rosy hand.

22 (*Anth. Plan.* 231)

—"Why, rustic Pan, do you sit and pipe on this sweet-
  sounding reed
    that echoes throughout the lonesome shady grove?"
—"So that the young heifers plucking the leafy grasses
    might pasture in these dew-covered mountains."

Like her other epigrams, Anyte's pastoral poems display considerable variety in form, ranging from direct address to the passerby to simple description and from statement in the first person to an exchange written in dialogue form. The tone of the poems also ranges from the serious, as in the description of Aphrodite's precinct overlooking the sea (19), to the playful, as in the account of the children's attempt to convert their billygoat into an Olympic steed (20), much to the tolerant amusement of the god who observes their game. But despite differences in form and tone, all of these poems describe an attractive world of peace and prosperity under the protection of the gods. Like the heifers of 22, we are drawn to Anyte's shady groves by the sweet sound of the Pan pipes.

Although too little of Anyte's poetry remains for us to make absolute judgments about lines of influence on other writers of her own period and of later periods, we must certainly grant her a position of importance in the development of the pastoral tradition. Contemporary scholars disagree as to the extent of her importance, but few would go so far as to ignore her altogether, as Tarn did in claiming with regard to Theocritus that "the pastoral idyll of literature is his and his only—so entirely his that from him derives the modern sense of 'idyllic.'"[15] As T. B. L. Webster has observed, Anyte's dedication poem for the spear of Echecratidas appears to be the model for similar epigrams by Callimachus and by Theocritus' close friend Nikias; if this is so, her work—including her pastoral epigrams—must have been known in Alexandria and other parts of the Greek world and could thus easily have been available to Theocritus as he was developing his own approach to poetry.[16]

Whatever Anyte's place in the history of ancient literature may be, it is not surprising that in the twentieth century she, like Sappho, attracted the attention of the imagists, who were no doubt drawn to her work by her vignettes of nature. Richard Aldington, a British novelist and poet who married the American poet H.D. in 1913 and lived with her until their separation six years later, published a book of translations from Greek and Latin poetry that begins with the poems of Anyte, whom he hails (after Antipater's epigram on the nine earthly Muses) as the "woman-Homer." Aldington speaks of the beauty of the Greek and Latin poems on which his book is based as being like Parian marble or bronze plaques, of which his translations are copies done as *Medallions in Clay*. His accurate and close translations of Anyte reveal his understanding and appreciation of her work, however romantic may have been his concept of the person: "In the imagination I saw you, Anyte, chaste, frail and fierce, a huntress on the hills of Tegea, crowned with cold violets, a lover of lonely forests. . . ."[17]

Another view of Anyte almost contemporary with Aldington's may be found in Frederick Wright's remarks published in the *Fort-*

nightly Review: "Curiously enough the qualities of [Anyte's] verse are all of the kind that it is usual to call masculine. Simple, vigorous, restrained, she has none of that somewhat florid exuberance which marks the inferior feminine in art: she is a Jane Austen rather than a George Eliot, an Ethel Smyth rather than a Chaminade."[18]

No doubt it is as profitless to view Anyte as a "masculine" writer as it is to envision her as a virgin huntress. If we look at the poems themselves—epitaphs, dedications, and pastorals—we see a master of the epigram and a creative artist whose work helped shape the idyllic dreamworld of Arcadia.

Nossis

Another Hellenistic woman poet whose epigrams are represented in *The Greek Anthology* is Nossis of Locri. There is little doubt about her place of birth, for she announces it in one of her twelve surviving epigrams. Locri, a Greek colony located in southern Italy along the east coast of the "toe" of the peninsula, was founded in the seventh century B.C. A second-century B.C. historian described it as having an aristocracy based on matrilineal descent[19]—an unusual system in any Greek city. As to whether women in Locri enjoyed any unusual social or legal status as well, we have no information either from historical tradition or from the archaeological research conducted in the area. It is perhaps only a curious coincidence that the epigrams of Nossis, written about 300 B.C., seem to reflect a distinctly female world centered around the worship of Hera and Aphrodite; of the twelve extant epigrams, only two focus on males.[20]

Unlike Anyte, who chooses to remain absent as a first-person character in her verse, Nossis presents herself by name in three of her epigrams, creating a vivid persona of a woman who celebrates the delights of Eros and who proclaims herself a follower of the poetic tradition of Sappho:

I (*Anth. Pal.* 5.170)

Nothing is sweeter than Eros. All other delights
  hold second place—I spit out from my mouth even
  honey.
Nossis declares this: whoever Cypris has not loved
  does not know what sort of blossoms her roses are.

2 (*Anth. Pal.* 7.718)

Stranger, if you sail towards Mytilene of the beautiful dances
    to be inspired by the flower of Sappho's charms,
Say that the land of Locri gave birth to one dear to the Muses,
    and when you have learned that my name is Nossis,
        go your way.

3 (*Anth. Pal.* 6.265)

Honored Hera, you who often come down from heaven
    and look with favor on your Lacinian temple fragrant
    with incense,
Receive this linen cloak which Theophilis, daughter of
    Kleocha,
        wove for you, together with her noble daughter Nossis.

The first epigram suggests that if we possessed more of Nossis'
work, it would surely include love poetry, a speculation confirmed
by Meleager's reference, in describing the sweet-scented iris of
Nossis that he has woven into his "garland," to the fact that Eros
himself helped Nossis prepare the wax tablets on which to write
her verse.[21] As it is, all we have is Nossis' declaration proclaiming
the superiority of Eros over all other earthly delights. The first
couplet of the poem is direct and vivid in declaring that Eros is
sweeter even than honey, the rejection of which is emphasized in
the original Greek by the spitting sounds of repeated *p*'s and *t*'s.
The second couplet is more subtle, depending for its effect on
the associations of the word for "roses" ("rhoda"), the final word
of the poem in the original text. Given the erotic context of the
couplet, it is surprising that not until recently has anyone commented on the use of "rhoda" here, as elsewhere in Greek poetry,
to refer to the "flower" of a woman's genitals.[22] Thus the second
couplet, though more subtly expressed than the first, is equally
vivid. Any woman to whom Aphrodite ("Cypris") has not yet
taught the arts of love remains ignorant of the delights that her
sexuality holds in store for her. Yet various ambiguities in the
original Greek also allow the lines to bear a more generalized
meaning. The gender of "whoever" in the phrase "whoever Cypris
has not loved," for instance, can be either masculine or feminine.

In addition, the grammar allows "her roses" to be interpreted as "the roses of Aphrodite," presumably symbolizing sensual pleasure, so that the couplet as a whole can be paraphrased on a more general level as follows: "Whoever has not been loved by Aphrodite does not know the pleasures of sex." In either case, it is Aphrodite who is in control, for it is only those whom she has chosen to love who are knowledgeable in the arts of Eros.

Nossis in effect makes another proclamation about Eros in 2 by declaring herself within the poetic tradition of Sappho of Lesbos (Mytilene). This epigram poses as an address (after the manner of actual inscriptions on tombstones) to the passerby who is envisioned as a traveller to Sappho's homeland. The message is clear enough: "Locri has produced a second Sappho, and I am she." This again suggests that a fuller representation of Nossis' work would probably reveal the same sort of emphasis on Aphrodite which we find among the fragments of Sappho. In any case, the two couplets may well have served as an epilogue for a collection of Nossis' verse.[23]

Poem 3 also places Nossis within a tradition, but this time it is her family tradition of which she speaks. The fact that she identifies her aristocratic ancestry only by "matronymics," that is, the name of her mother and her mother's mother, is in accord with the matrilineal system that may have been practiced in Locri.[24] The setting of the poem is the temple of Hera on the Lacinian promontory near Croton, some distance to the north of Locri. The Roman historian Livy describes the temple—of which only one column now remains standing—as sacred to all the people of the area.[25] The poem is in the form of a dedication of a cloak woven by Nossis and her mother for the goddess and presumably carried by them on a pilgrimage to the famous temple. In the original text, the names of all three generations of women are reserved for the final line, which begins with the name of Nossis and ends with the name of her grandmother Kleocha.

All but one of the other dedication poems by Nossis which survive focus on women, and all of them seem likely to have been composed for the purpose of an actual inscription. Three concern dedications to Aphrodite:

4 (*Anth. Pal.* 9.332)

Coming to the temple, let us look at the image of Aphrodite,
    how it is wrought with golden trim.
Polyarchis set it up, after reaping the benefits of great wealth
    gained from her own splendid body.

5 (*Anth. Pal.* 9.605)

Kallo has set up a picture of herself in the house of
    fair-haired Aphrodite;
      she had a portrait made, a close likeness.
How sweetly it stands; behold how much grace blooms upon
    it.
      May she fare well, for her life is blameless.

6 (*Anth. Pal.* 6.275)

It is fitting for Aphrodite, rejoicing indeed, to receive
    this gift, a headband from the hair of Samytha.
For it is of many colors, and smells sweetly of nectar;
    with this she, too, anoints beautiful Adonis.

Poem 4 dedicates a statue of Aphrodite, perhaps of marble or bronze
with gilt decoration, on behalf of a courtesan (*hetaira*) named Polyarchis, whose name means "ruler of many" or "ruler of much."
The Greek text puns on her name by saying that "much-ruler" has
earned much money ("Polyarchis . . . pollan ktesin"), with which
she was able, presumably, to dedicate a relatively expensive sort of
statue. The gilt statue of the first couplet, then, becomes not only
a fitting offering to the goddess of love, but also an appropriate
reflection of the splendor of Polyarchis' body as described in the
second couplet.

    Since prostitution was a standard institution in most Greek cities,
it is not surprising to find many dedications by *hetairai* of various
kinds of presents for their patron goddess. One ancient source even
reports that an entire temple to Aphrodite on the island of Samos
was financed by a group of Athenian *hetairai* from their earnings.[26]
Possibly Nossis' other poems in this group (5, 6) were also written
for *hetairai*, but we cannot be sure that the dedicators had what
might be called a professional relationship with Aphrodite. For
example, the word "blameless" in 5, thought by some commentators
to imply that Kallo could not have been a prostitute, would, from

the Greek point of view, carry no such information. The point of the poem is that Kallo has dedicated a portrait of herself to Aphrodite, who will be honored by the beauty of the picture and its close resemblance to the giver. The grace of the portrait is seen as a reflection of Kallo's own qualities, and forms the basis for the prayer in the poem's final line. Poem 6 adds a new twist by treating the subject of dedication from the viewpoint of the recipient, who is sure to accept the wonderful headband offered by Samytha because of its attractive colors and perfume.

Three other epigrams by Nossis are also connected with portraits of women:

7 (*Anth. Pal.* 6.354)

This likeness, even from a distance, can be seen to be
   Sebaithis',
      because of its beauty and its dignity.
Behold: I think I see before my eyes the prudent lady
and her kindness.
      May you fare well in every way, blessed woman.

8 (*Anth. Pal.* 6.353)

The essence of Melinna has been captured; look how gentle
her face is.
      She seems to look back at us graciously.
How truly the daughter resembles her mother in all respects;
      indeed, it's good when children look like their parents.

9 (*Anth. Pal.* 9.604)

This picture captures the beauty of Thaumareta;
      it likens well the lively youthfulness of her gentle face.
Looking upon you, the little puppy-watchdog wags its tail
      and thinks it sees the mistress of the house.

In these three portrait poems, the emphasis is on the accuracy of the likeness and its success in capturing the personal qualities of the women portrayed, particularly the traditional "female" virtues such as beauty, gentleness, and graciousness. In addition, 7 emphasizes the dignified character of the woman represented. The formula is varied in 8 with the approving reference to the close resemblance of Melinna to her mother. Poem 9 adds a touch of humor in the claim that the family puppy, supposedly acting as watchdog of the house, is fooled by the accuracy of the resemblance.

The only three other surviving epigrams by Nossis treat a range of subject matter, including an epitaph for a Sicilian writer of *phlyax* plays (farces making fun of classical tragedies), a dedication of captured armor, and a prayer to Artemis in her role as goddess of childbirth:

10 (*Anth. Pal.* 7.414)

Pass by laughing loudly, and say a friendly word
    to me: I am Rhinthon of Syracuse,
A small nightingale of the Muses; yet we have culled
    our own ivy wreath from tragic phlyax-plays.

11 (*Anth. Pal.* 6.132)

The Bruttian men cast these shields off their doomed
    shoulders,
        struck by the hands of swift-fighting Locrians.
They celebrate their courage, resting in the temples of the
    gods,
        nor do they miss the arms of the cowards whom they left.

12 (*Anth. Pal.* 6.273)

Artemis—you who hold Delos and lovely Ortygia,
    give over your holy arrows to the bosom of the Graces.
After you have washed clean your skin in the streams of
    Inopus,
        go inside the house to release Alketis from harsh pangs of
        childbirth.

Poem 10 suggests possible contact with a fellow writer, in this case the Syracusan Rhinthon, who probably lived and wrote in southern Italy toward the close of the third century B.C.[27] Nossis seems to indicate that he was a superior artist in the genre of *phlyax* plays, which, as we know from surviving fragments and titles, as well as from portrayals of such dramas on south Italian vase painting of the fourth century B.C., featured grotesquely costumed players who engaged in ribald burlesque of the old tragedies about Oedipus, Helen of Troy, Antigone, Herakles, and so on.[28] But whether she wrote her praise of Rhinthon's comic artistry as an actual inscription for his grave or as a tribute to his memory many years after his death, we cannot be sure. Poem 11 also sounds like an actual dedication poem, written for Nossis' fellow Locrians after they had won a victory over a neighboring native people called the Bruttians.

Poem 12, the last of the surviving poems of Nossis, returns to the characteristically female world of her other epigrams. This poem is in the form of a prayer addressed to Artemis, who is asked to put aside her bow and arrow and turn from her activities as virgin huntress to her role as goddess of childbirth. The reference to the islands of Delos and Ortygia in the opening line stresses this aspect of the goddess, for according to ancient tradition, Leto, mother of the twin deities Artemis and Apollo, had given birth to Artemis on Ortygia, after which Artemis assisted with the birth of her brother Apollo on Delos.[29] Although the epigram could be epideictic, it has the ring of an actual prayer inscribed and delivered to a temple of Artemis as a means of assisting Alketis during her difficult labor.

Despite the meagre remains of her verse, Nossis has been the source of inspiration for at least one poem by a well-known writer in the twentieth century—not surprisingly, the imagist H.D. She wrote a poem of some eighty lines entitled simply "Nossis," in which the narrator converses with a Meleager figure, a poet who is making a garden "wrought of flame and spirit" from poets of the past. The narrator, looking along a path lined with iris, seems to see the ghost of Nossis, whose verses (adapted from the first epigram quoted above) are recalled:

> *"I Nossis stand by this:*
> *I state that love is sweet:*
> *if you think otherwise*
> *assert what beauty*
> *or what charm*
> *after the charm of love,*
> *retains its grace?*
>
> *"Honey," you say:*
> *honey? I say "I spit*
> *honey out of my mouth:*
> *nothing is second-best*
> *after the sweet of Eros."*

"*I Nossis stand and state*
that he whom Love neglects
has nought, no flower, no grace,
who lacks that rose, her kiss."

I thought to hear him speak
the girl might rise
and make the garden silver
as the white moon breaks,
"Nossis," he cried, "a flame."[30]

Moero

Besides the "iris" of Nossis and the "roses" of Sappho, the an-
thologizer Meleager speaks of weaving into his garland of poetry
many "lilies" of Moero to go along with those of Anyte.[31] Unfortunately, only two epigrams of Moero have survived in *The Greek
Anthology* in its present form. The only other example of her work
consists of ten lines from a hexameter poem quoted by an author
of the second century A.D. Beyond these, no other traces of her
work survive. If we can believe the entry in the tenth-century A.D.
lexicon called the *Suda* (under Myro, an alternate spelling of her
name), she was the author not only of epigrams and hexameter
poems, but also of lyric verse as well. The *Suda* and other sources
report that she was from Byzantium. According to Tatian, Cephi-
sodotus the son of Praxiteles made statues of both Anyte and Moero.
If such information as well as conclusions based on stylistic evidence
do not mislead us, we may thus date Moero to about 300 B.C., or
in other words, to the early part of the Hellenistic period.[32]

Like many of Anyte's poems, the two surviving epigrams by
Moero involve dedications:

1 (*Anth. Pal.* 6.119)

You lie in the golden chamber of Aphrodite,
    O cluster of grapes, full of Dionysus' liquid.
Nor any longer does your mother, throwing forth around you
    a lovely branch,
give birth to the nectarous leaf above your head.

2 (*Anth. Pal.* 6.189)

O water nymphs, daughters of the river,
　　you who as divinities always tread these depths with your
　　　　rosy feet,
Hail, and preserve Kleonymus, who set up statues
　　to you, O goddesses, under the pine trees.

The first epigram strikes one as affected, particularly in comparison
with the directness of the dedications of Anyte and Nossis. In
language that is high-flown and exaggerated, Moero addresses the
dedicated grapes in metaphorical terms calling them repositories of
"Dionysus' liquid" (as though the grape juice were already wine)
and referring to the vine as the grapes' mother. Such metaphors
become even more artificial if the piece was meant to accompany
not a real bunch of grapes but a painted or sculpted representation
of grapes.

Poem 2 is less precious, addressing some sort of nymphs (the
Greek text of line 1 is questionable) who apparently inhabit a spring
located near a grove of pine trees. It is hard to tell whether the
epigram was intended to accompany Kleonymus' dedication of the
statues of the water nymphs or whether it is simply a prayer for
Kleonymus' continued good health. In either case, the poem evokes
none of the pastoral mood so evident in the rustic settings described
in Anyte's epigrams.

The ten hexameter lines by Moero are preserved in a series of
quotations in Athenaeus (second century A.D.) that have to do with
the constellation of the Pleiades. These stars, because of the similarity between their name and the Greek word for doves (*peleiades*),
were often thought of as doves being pursued by the hunter Orion.
According to Moero's version, the doves were transferred to the
heavens by Zeus out of gratitude for their services to him while he
was still a helpless infant:

Great Zeus was raised in Crete, nor did any
Of the blessed gods know of him; but he grew strong in all
　　his limbs.
Doves nourished him in his sacred cave,
Bringing ambrosia from the streams of Ocean.
A great eagle, always drawing nectar from a rock,

Would bear the drink in its beak to all-wise Zeus.
To him far-seeing Zeus, after he had overcome his father
    Kronos,
Gave immortality and a place to dwell in heaven.
So also he granted honor to attend on the trembling doves,
Who are the harbingers of summer and winter.[33]

The final line refers to the fact that the Pleiades rise in the spring and set in the fall. The subject of the passage—the infancy of Zeus—is reminiscent of the song sung by one of the competing mountains in Korinna's musical contest (chapter 2), in which the secrecy of Zeus' upbringing in a cave is emphasized. There is no way to guess what the topic or length of Moero's whole hexameter poem may have been, but the Homeric diction of the Greek and the generally unremarkable narrative suggest a work of no great originality. Although Meleager seems to have thought highly of Moero and to have regarded her as comparable to Anyte, the three extant bits of her work do not entirely justify his high opinion, for none of them exhibits the freshness or power of the poems of Anyte and Nossis.

Erinna

Of all the women writers discussed in this book, none—including Sappho—is more enigmatic than Erinna. She and her poetry form the subject of no fewer than five poems by various writers preserved in *The Greek Anthology*, all of whom praise her work highly, and a sixth poem mentions her in the same breath with Callimachus. For us, however, there is very little left by which to judge, for all that survive are three epigrams that are probably by Erinna, a two-line hexameter fragment attributed to her, and the partial remains of approximately fifty-four lines from a long hexameter poem usually referred to as "The Distaff." The fragments of this hexameter poem came to light only recently, in 1928, when they were discovered by Italian scholars. Published the following year, they have since been the subject of considerable scholarly controversy. Unfortunately, there are many gaps in the papyrus of the fragment. Approaches to the text range from conservative statements based only on the few words that can be deciphered with certainty, to imaginative interpretations based on conjectural reconstruction of the missing parts of the lines.

As is the case with so many classical literary figures, the ancient biographical tradition about Erinna must be regarded with skepticism. The Byzantine lexicon known as the *Suda* includes a lengthy entry on Erinna as follows:

Erinna, of Tenos or Lesbos, or, as some say, of Telos. (Telos is a little island near Knidos.) Some think she was from Rhodes. She was a writer of hexameters and composed "The Distaff." This poem is in Aeolic-Doric dialect, and consists of 300 hexameters. She also wrote epigrams. She died a virgin at the age of 19. Her verses have been judged equal to Homer's. She was a companion of Sappho's and her contemporary.

A thorough review of the biographical tradition has recently demonstrated that nearly all of the above statements seem to be derived from the epigrams by or about Erinna in *The Greek Anthology* and that consequently the report has little value as an independent source of information about the life of this mysterious figure.[34] The epigrams about Erinna may, in turn, have been based largely on Erinna's literary work rather than on any independent information about her life. Three of them appear to have been introductions to a collection of her verse:

(*Anth. Pal.* 9.190)

This is the Lesbian honeycomb of Erinna.
    Even though it is small, it is all flavored with
    the Muses' honey.
Her three-hundred lines are equal to Homer,
    though she was only a girl of nineteen.
Applying herself to her distaff out of fear of her mother,
    and working at her loom, she stood as servant of
    the Muses.
Sappho is better than Erinna at lyric verse
    by as much as Erinna is better than Sappho in hexameters.

Anonymous

(Anth. Pal. 7.11)

"This is the sweet work of Erinna—not much, to be sure,
  for it is the work of a girl of nineteen—
But more powerful than many other books. If Hades
  had not come early to me, who would have had such a
    name?"   *Asclepiades*

(Anth. Pal. 7.713)

Erinna is a writer of few verses, nor is she wordy in
her songs,
  but she received this brief epic from the Muse.
So she does not fail to be remembered, nor is she confined
  under the shadowy wing of black night.
But we, O stranger, we wither away in heaps—the numberless
  myriads of later singers.
Better the small murmuring of the swan than the
  cawing of jackdaws sounding all through the spring clouds.
                                                             Antipater of Sidon

All three epigrams suggest that Erinna—whatever the biographical facts may have been—enjoyed a wide reputation as a writer of hexameter verse. The anonymous epigram compares her favorably with Sappho (possibly the origin of the biographers' asssumption that she was born on the island of Lesbos and was Sappho's contemporary). The poem by Asclepiades, who was born perhaps about 320 B.C., poses as an address to the reader by the deceased Erinna herself. Asclepiades' probable date suggests that Erinna's poetry must have been in circulation sometime before 300 B.C., perhaps as early as 350 B.C.[35] The third epigram, by Antipater of Sidon, shows that her reputation continued at least into the first century A.D., for Antipater was writing in the period of 20 B.C.–20 A.D.[36] All three poems emphasize the high quality of her verse despite its small quantity, which is attributed to her premature death.

Two other epigrams in *The Greek Anthology* also focus on Erinna, stressing as do the three prefatory poems her inspired work cut short by cruel Hades:

(Anth. Pal. 7.13)

While Erinna, the maiden honey-bee, new singer among
  the minstrels, was gathering the flower of the Muses,

Hades snatched her away to be his bride. A true word,
  indeed, the girl spoke while she lived: "Hades,
  you are envious."   *Leonidas or Meleager*

(*Anth. Pal.* 7.12)

Just as you were giving birth to the springtime of honeyed
  hymns,
    just as you were singing with the voice of a swan,
Fate, mistress of the distaff that spins out the thread,
    carried you to Acheron across the broad waves of the
    dead.
But the beautiful work of your verses proclaims that you
    have not perished, but mingle in the dances of the
    Pierian Muses.   *Anonymous*

Besides the focus on Erinna's untimely death, this group of epigrams about her shares certain recurring motifs: the honey or honeybee image in all but 7.713, the swan of 7.713 and 7.12, and the reference to the distaff in 9.190 (Erinna's) and 7.12 (Fate's). Possibly some or all of these images are derived from Erinna's own poetry. The mention of the distaff in two of the epigrams is particularly intriguing, since the biographical notice in the *Suda* claims that Erinna wrote a hexameter poem called "The Distaff" ("Elakate"). In fact it was the appearance of the word *elakate* among the intelligible portions of the papyrus fragment found in 1928, together with the names of Erinna herself and her friend Baukis (mentioned in two of Erinna's own epigrams), that led scholars to assume that the discovery was of Erinna's "Distaff." It has since been noted that this is an odd name for a poem that seems to be primarily a lament (see discussion below), and that the *Suda*'s report of such a title may be erroneously derived from the epigrams quoted above.

One further epigram in *The Greek Anthology* mentions Erinna, this time in the context of a satirical piece railing against grammarians who pride themselves on their knowledge of Erinna and Callimachus and who enjoy tearing apart the creative efforts of any poets who do not measure up to them:

(*Anth. Pal.* 11.322)

Busybody pack of grammarians, you're always digging up
    somebody else's Muse, you miserable bookworms who
    walk on thorns.

You're a disgrace to the great, priding yourselves on
your Erinna,
   you bitter and dry hounds of Callimachus.
You're a bane to poets, oblivion to rank beginners.
   Go to Hell, you bugs who nip in secret at the eloquent.

         Antiphanes

Although the piece is not particularly complimentary to Erinna or
Callimachus, it does suggest that Erinna's work, like that of the
famous Alexandrian poet, was considered worthy of praise by the
grammarians. Whatever Erinna's literary output may have been, it
is clear from the amount of attention she receives in *The Greek
Anthology* that she must have held the rank of a major figure among
the poets of the Hellenistic era.

As for Erinna's own epigrams, *The Greek Anthology* preserves
three under her name. All three concern women. The first is about
a portrait of a woman named Agatharchis, much in the manner of
similar poems by Nossis, while the remaining two concern the death
of the young woman Baukis:

1 (*Anth. Pal.* 6.352)

This painting is from tender hands: My fine Prometheus,
   there are people who are equal to you in wisdom.
Indeed, if whoever painted this maiden so true to life
   had added a voice, it would have been the real
   Agatharchis.

2 (*Anth. Pal.* 7.712)

I am the tomb of the bride Baukis; passing by
   this much lamented stele, say this to Hades beneath the
     earth:
"Hades, you are envious." But to you who see them,
   these beautiful monuments will announce the cruel fate
   of Baukis:
How with the pine-torches with which Hymenaios was
   hymned
   her father-in-law set the girl ablaze upon this pyre,
And you yourself, Hymenaios, changed the tuneful song of
   marriage
   into the mournful sound of lamentation.

3 (*Anth. Pal.* 7.710)

O stele and Sirens and mournful urn of mine,
    you who hold this small heap of ashes that belong to
        Hades,
Give greetings to those who pass by this my grave,
    whether they are citizens, or visitors from other towns.
Say that this tomb holds me, who was a bride; say also this,
    that my father called me Baukis, and that my family
Was of Tenos, so they may know, and that my companion
    Erinna inscribed these words upon my tomb.

The first epigram, whether intended as an actual inscription or, more likely, as an epideictic piece, emphasizes the painter's skill by calling attention to the sensitive hands that have created such a lifelike portrait and by comparing the artist to the god Prometheus, who in Greek mythology had created human beings out of clay. The painter has been almost as successful as the god in fashioning a real woman—all but her voice. The similarity of this poem to the portrait epigrams of Nossis raises the question as to whether Erinna (assuming she predates Nossis) might not have influenced the Locrian poet in her treatment of such themes.

The other two surviving epigrams attributed to Erinna both concern the death of Baukis. Poem 2 poses as the address of Baukis' tomb to the passerby, who learns that Baukis died as a bride and that the torches to have been used to honor Hymenaios, the god of marriage, were instead used to light her funeral pyre.[37] This is the poem to which the author of *Anth. Pal.* 7.13 alludes when he quotes the statement, "Hades, you are envious," in the context of his own epitaph for Erinna herself. Poem 3 provides more presumably biographical detail about Baukis, namely that she was from Tenos, one of the Cyclades islands in the middle of the Aegean, and that she was a "close companion" ("synetairis") of Erinna. Poem 3 is in the form of an address to the passerby by the deceased herself, and like 2, displays many of the conventional features of an ancient epitaph or epideictic piece in the form of an epitaph. The existence of two such poems about Baukis suggests that they were not in fact written for purposes of inscription; rather, Erinna seems to be exploiting the genre of epigram as a means by which to express grief over the death of Baukis.

Although we may assume that Erinna wrote many other epigrams that have not survived, she seems to have attracted the most attention as a writer of hexameter verse, the meter which had since the time of Homer's *Iliad* and *Odyssey* been used to treat serious themes of broad (if not always strictly epic) scope. A writer of the second century A.D. quotes two lines of hexameters that he says are from a poem by Erinna "or one attributed to her." The immediate context in Athenaeus involves a discussion of various kinds of fish, particularly the pompilo addressed in the quotation:

> Pompilo, fish that brings sailors a fair voyage,
> May you follow along behind the stern of my sweet
>   companion's ship.[38]

There is no clue in Athenaeus as to what sort of poem these lines are excerpted from, nor do we know who the speaker or the companion (*hetaira*) are. The fragment seems unlikely to be part of "The Distaff," which, although it is in hexameters, appears to focus on the narrator's childhood affection for Baukis and grief over her death. It is possible that the lines belong to the genre of the "send-off" poem, a type of verse commonly written for a friend or relative who was about to undertake a journey, as exemplified by Sappho's *propempticon* for her brother in fragment 5 (see chapter 1).[39]

The hexameter fragments that are assumed to belong to Erinna's "Distaff" raise by far the most interesting and yet most difficult questions concerning her work. One scholar has commented that "the newly discovered remains . . . are both Sapphic in their intensity and Hellenistic in their preoccupation with the minutiae of everyday life."[40] Yet the degree of intensity and the details of the minutiae are matters of great controversy, partly because the gaps in the text allow considerable latitude in the interpretation of the lines. Since many of the problems involve the technicalities of papyrology, this survey can only give a sketch of the current opinion about the fragment. To show how difficult the text is, I provide below a translation based only on those words which can either be easily deciphered on the papyrus or restored with the addition of no more than two or three missing letters:

1–14	of a girl . . . maidens [or dolls?] . . . tortoise . . . tortoise . . . wave
15	from white horses
16	I shouted loudly . . . tortoise . . .
17	the yard of the great court . . .
18	wretched Baukis, I cry out this lament. . . .
19	these games lie in my heart
20	still warm. But [those are] already ashes.
21	of dolls . . . in the bed-chambers . . .
22	maidens [or dolls] . . . once at dawn
23	Mother . . . to the wool-workers
24	. . . sprinkled with salt
25	little . . . Mormo brought fear.
26	. . . she roamed on her four feet
27	and changed her visage from [one thing to another].
28	But when into the bed . . . , you forgot everything
29	which still in your innocence . . . having heard your mother,
30	dear Baukis. Forgetfulness . . . Aphrodite.
31	Therefore you, weeping . . . but other things I leave;
32	for my feet [are] not permitted . . . from the house,
33	nor [am I able] to look upon a corpse, nor to lament
34	with uncovered hair . . . shame
35	tears me around my cheeks . . .
36–54	nineteen . . . Erinna . . . distaff . . . shame . . . maiden-songs . . . looking . . . hair . . . dear Baukis. . . flame . . . Hymenaios . . . Hymenaios . . . alas, wretched Baukis. . . .[41]

Such are the bare bones of Erinna's "Distaff." The fragment has been interpreted in widely differing ways, ranging from "a genuine cry of grief" on the part of the young Erinna, to a "brilliant" forgery by a male writer from Cos or Rhodes who catered to the public taste for the details of everyday life spiced with romance and drama.[42] The attempt to reconstruct the sense of the fragment is not quite as hopeless as it might seem if compared to an analogous scrap of English prose. For example, lines 15–35 of the papyrus are missing only a portion of the middle of each line; a papyrologist can determine in this instance the precise number of letters missing and, with the aid of the metrical requirements of the line along with the sense conveyed by the existing words, has some reasonable chance of guessing what possible combinations of words might have once been written in the gaps. The papyrologist is further aided by the inflectional endings of the Greek language, by which one can tell, for instance, whether a noun is the subject or object of a sentence even if the sentence is missing its verb or other important elements.

There is general agreement that the chief topic of the fragment was a lament for Baukis, who, it is assumed on the basis of Erinna's two epigrams about her, died as a nineteen-year-old bride. It has even been suggested that "Distaff" was perhaps a nickname given to the poem by Alexandrian scholars because of the poem's reference to wool working and possibly to the metaphor of the thread of Fate and that the poem's original title would probably have been something more along the lines of "Lament for Baukis."[43] In any case, the words "wretched Baukis" in lines 18 and 54 indicate a refrain of lamentation bewailing the loss of Baukis.

Recent studies of the fragment generally agree with Bowra's suggestion that the opening section up through line 27 deals with childhood games recalled by the narrator, including a game referred to by a second-century A.D. author, Pollux, as *Chelichelone*, or "Torty-tortoise." This was essentially a game of tag, in which girls gathered into a circle with one child in the center playing the role of the tortoise. According to Pollux's description, the following exchange took place:

Children: "Tortoise, what are you doing in the middle?"
Tortoise: "Weaving my wool and the Milesian woof."
Children: "Your child, what was he doing when he died?"
Tortoise: "From white horses he leaped into the sea."[44]

Whereupon, we can assume, the tortoise leaped up and tagged another of the children, who then became the next tortoise. In a convincing psychoanalytic interpretation of the "Distaff" fragment, in which the word for tortoise occurs three times in the opening sixteen lines, Arthur has shown that the symbolism of this girls' game provides a framework around which to understand the extant portions of the poem.[45] The tortoise traditionally symbolizes the home and the interior space of the female; the white horses mentioned by Pollux and referred to in line 15 of the fragment represent the opposing, exterior sphere, and the leap into the sea symbolizes death and rebirth. On the basis of such symbolism, we can view the poem as a "statement of self-discovery" in the context of remembering the everyday life of the past (childhood games, dolls, bogeys like Mormo, weaving) and of confronting the reality of death, in this case the death of the narrator's childhood friend Baukis.

Following the lines of reminiscences about the terrible beast Mormo, a female bugaboo used in ancient as well as modern Greece to keep children in line ("Be good or Mormo will eat you!"), the poem seems to shift to a new section. Line 28, in view of the references shortly afterward to Aphrodite and towards the end of the intelligible section to Hymenaios, has been supplemented by some scholars so that it reads "But when *you went* into the bed *of a man*, you forgot everything," the "everything" being taken to mean all such childhood games as have just been described. This is certainly a possible interpretation, but it must be stressed that the reference to the bed might equally well have been in connection with hiding from Mormo, or even—in view of the poem's "Sapphic intensity"—to sharing the bed, erotically or otherwise, with the narrator.[46]

The "forgetfulness" section is apparently followed in lines 31–33 by a reference to some sort of prohibition against the narrator's viewing of a corpse, presumably that of Baukis. Various theories have been proposed to explain the prohibition, such as the possibility that Erinna was perhaps a priestess for whom viewing a corpse would have been taboo; alternatively, it has been suggested that it was taboo for a woman of childbearing age to be subjected to the taint of death by taking part in a funeral or that since Erinna was not a relative of Baukis', she was prohibited by law or by custom from attending the funeral.[47]

Lines 34–42 introduce the subject of "shame" ("aidos") twice, which has generally been interpreted as the narrator's shame over not being able, for whatever reason, to express her grief at Baukis' death. Unfortunately, from line 35 to the end of the fragment only the beginnings of the lines survive, so that restoration of the text becomes much more problematic. The reference to "nineteen" is usually taken to refer to Erinna's age at the time of composition (on the basis of the epigrams about her), particularly in view of the mention of the name Erinna in the very next line. Also clear are references to a distaff, maiden songs, Baukis again (twice), and Hymenaios, the god of marriage. But it is impossible to restore the sense of this last section with any confidence.

Three recent studies of "The Distaff" fragment have called attention to the problems in West's 1977 argument that this sophisticated poem could not have been written by a nineteen-year-old girl kept at her loom all day and living on an obscure island somewhere in the Aegean and that it must therefore have been the work of an expert (male) forgerer from an intellectual center like Cos or Rhodes. Pomeroy, for example, has shown that education and wool working for women in the fourth century were hardly incompatible and that there is no reason to assume that Erinna could not have both written poetry and worked at her weaving.[48] Arthur has pointed out the unreliability of the biographical tradition on which much of West's argument is based, and Skinner notes that the ancients themselves never doubted the authenticity of "The Distaff."[49] There is little reason to doubt that these lines were the work of a woman called Erinna. The ancients thought of her as a writer in the tradition of Sappho, no doubt partly because of the presence of some Aeolic forms in her language (the dialect of Greek used by Sappho) but also because of her description of intense emotional involvement with another woman.[50] Perhaps, like Sappho in fragment 94 (see chapter 1), the speaker of this lament is calling upon the memory of pleasant times past to help assuage the grief of the present moment. Whether or not "The Distaff" was in any sense autobiographical, we can safely assume that it is a genuine record of female experience transmuted and transmitted through the medium of poetry.

Although there is certainly room for further speculation about the fragments of "The Distaff" and about Erinna's proper place in the history of Hellenistic Greek literature, significant advances in our knowledge are not likely to occur in the absence of new discoveries. But a new papyrus find—another text of "The Distaff," for instance—may someday help scholars begin to fill in some of the gaps in our very sketchy appreciation of this enigmatic poet who was once greatly admired in the ancient world.

Conclusion

Other women poets of the Hellenistic age are little more than names. Meleager, in the same poem in which he announces that his "garland" of verses will include the "roses" of Sappho, the "lilies" of Anyte and Moero, the "iris" of Nossis, and the "crocus" of Erinna, also mentions that he is weaving in a few blossoms of someone called Parthenis.[51] However, none of her poetry survives, nor is her name known from any other source. From an inscription, we learn that one Aristodama of Smyrna was granted honorary citizenship by the people of Lamia in Thessaly, who were grateful to her for praising their ancestors in one of her poems.[52] Again, nothing of her work survives. The second-century A.D. writer Athenaeus mentions a poet named Moschine and her daughter Hedyle, both of Athens and probably from the second half of the fourth century. He records that Hedyle wrote a mythological poem called *Scylla*, from which he quotes a few lines concerning the minor sea god Glaukos.[53]

Such information gives us little to draw from beyond names and a few scattered lines of verse. But judging from the range of examples surviving from the works of the Hellenistic poets Anyte, Nossis, Moero, and Erinna, women writers of postclassical Greece treated not only some of the standard themes characteristic of contemporary male writers as well—epitaphs for a fallen soldier, praise of the dead, dedications to gods and goddesses, references to poets of the past, descriptions of pastoral scenes, and so on—but also themes which can be identified particularly with the female experience in the ancient world. Especially in Greece, male and female spheres were sharply defined, a distinction reflected, for example, in the design of a typical Greek house, in which the women's quarters (*gynaikeion*) were clearly demarcated from the rest of the rooms.[54] Hence it is not surprising that we find certain themes among the verses of these women writers that are not common in the work of their male counterparts. One such theme involves descriptions of children's play, such as the tortoise game and dolls evidently alluded to by Erinna in "The Distaff," or the play involving pet grasshoppers and billy goats mentioned by Anyte. Another theme that recurs in the work of these women writers centers around the special relationship between women and the goddess Aphrodite, as in Nossis' poems about Eros and Cypris and her various portrait-dedication poems. Weaving is another subject of slight interest to male writers, who on the whole refer to the process only in metaphorical contexts.[55] But in the women writers we find references to actual weaving as a normal part of the female world, as for example Nossis' dedication of the cloak woven by herself and her mother for Hera, or Erinna's allusions to wool workers and to the distaff. Finally, the women poets represented in *The Greek Anthology*, especially Erinna in her expression of affection for Baukis, treat the subject of emotional attachment and commitment between women in a way that is almost wholly absent from the works of their male contemporaries.[56]

4   *Women Philosophers of the Hellenistic and Roman Worlds*

So far all of the works discussed in this book have been in poetic form—whether solo lyrics such as those of Sappho, choral songs of the sort Korinna wrote, or the elegiac couplets favored by poets of the Hellenistic era. Prose was a relatively late development in the history of Greek literature, not appearing on the scene until the sixth and fifth centuries B.C., when it began to be used by Greek philosophers and chroniclers of Asia Minor to record their findings. Anaximander of Miletus (c. 610–540 B.C.), for example, was said to have written the first prose treatise on philosophy. Heraclitus of Ephesus (c. 500 B.C.) was another of the first Greeks to write philosophy in prose rather than verse, and his contemporary Hecataeus of Miletus appears to have led the way in prose accounts of what today would be called geography and ethnography. Since their work, and that of others like them, exists only in short fragments, it is difficult to trace the origins of prose writing, but it is clear that the new form, freed from the established conventions of the poetic genres (not to mention the restrictions of the metrical patterns in quantitative verse), opened up the path for the later full-blown development of history (Herodotus and Thucydides), rhetoric (Lysias, Demosthenes, etc.), and philosophy (Plato and Aristotle).

Although history is represented by no women writers of the ancient world and rhetoric by only one of whom we know (see chapter 5), philosophy attracted many female exponents. Unfortunately, little, if anything (depending on the authenticity of certain philosophical letters), survives from the works of these women. It is, after all, much easier to collect and preserve short poems than long treatises. Moreover, during the Middle Ages and the Renaissance, philosophical inquiry became almost exclusively a male province; no doubt monks and scholars had little interest in copying or studying the works of obscure female philosophers, whose minds (according to the prevailing Aristotelian doctrine) would by nature have been inferior to those of their male counterparts anyway. Given the lack of models available to women thinkers in the twentieth century, it is perhaps not surprising that while a typical contemporary anthology of Western poetry will contain at least a few poems by women, a parallel anthology of philosophical essays will often contain no work at all by a woman. This chapter, then, attempts to recover what little is known about ancient women philosophers from such sources as the titles of their works, allusions to them by male authors, and letters or fragments of letters addressed to them.

Fortunately for the intellectual history of women writers, the abundance of notable women thinkers in the ancient world attracted the attention of a classical scholar of seventeenth-century France, a man named Gilles Ménage. Ménage wrote on many topics, but primary among his interests was the third-century A.D. work of Diogenes Laertius on the lives of ancient philosophers. Having published a commentary on Diogenes Laertius, Ménage then produced his own supplement to the ancient biographies in which he presented brief lives of women philosophers, expanding on what he found in Diogenes Laertius and collecting information from a wide variety of classical and patristic sources. The book, called *Historia Mulierum Philosopharum* (*History of Women Philosophers*), was published in Latin in 1690 and again in 1692, with English and French translations following in the next century.[1]

Ménage dedicated his work to his friend Anne Lefebvre Dacier, daughter and wife of classical scholars and a published scholar in her own right as well. In his preface, Ménage explains that he has found no fewer than sixty-five women philosophers of the past, whose history he proposes to write as an appropriate token of his respect for Madame Dacier. He then proceeds to organize his findings according to the various philosophical schools with which the women were associated—Stoics, Epicureans, Platonists, and so on, including one catchall category for those women philosophers whom he cannot identify with any particular sect.

Ménage's definition of philosopher seems to be the one suggested by the Greek roots of the word, that is, "lover of wisdom." In his enthusiasm to collect material, he is inclined to label any woman a philosopher if she was associated with the traditional male philosophers through family ties or through marriage. He also includes literary figures such as Socrates' advisor in Plato's *Symposium*, the seer Diotima, whom Plato depicts as Socrates' teacher on the subject of the nature of love. Here we shall narrow the definition to include only those thinkers who are known to have written treatises of a philosophical or scientific nature—a definition that, to be sure, would exclude even Socrates himself, since his (entirely oral) teachings are known only through the works of Plato. Moreover, rather than attempt a kind of encyclopedic list similar to Ménage's, we shall deal only with those women writers about whom we have more than a passing reference by a late author of dubious reliability. Such an approach narrows the list down from Ménage's sixty-five to some half-dozen women philosophers. Each of these contributed in some degree to the intellectual growth of her times, although the exact nature of these contributions cannot be determined in the total or near-total absence of surviving fragments.

The Epicurean School

Epicureanism, one of two ancient philosophical systems which advocated the emancipation of women, had its formal beginnings in 306 B.C. At that time its founder, Epicurus, moved to Athens and bought a house, together with a large garden, which served as living and working quarters for both himself and his followers. The school itself became known as the *Kepos* or "Garden." The members of the Garden included not only full Athenian citizens like Epicurus himself but also several women and slaves, who, within the context of Athenian society at large, enjoyed few legal rights or privileges.

Within the enclosure of the Garden, however, all members of the group—male and female, free and slave—were entitled to the benefits and responsibilities of the Epicurean school.

Before we consider further what is known about the women members of the Garden, we should first review the doctrine on which the Epicurean system was based. Drawing on work of earlier Greek philosopher-scientists, Epicurus taught that all matter is composed of atomic particles, which combine and recombine to form the universe and everything in it. Death is not to be feared, for at death the atoms of the human soul simply disperse to rejoin the universal supply of particles, just as the atoms do that make up the body. The gods exist in a state of perfect tranquillity and for that reason should be emulated by human beings, but they pay no attention to us or our pleas for help and should be worshipped only insofar as it is proper to show admiration for their peaceful existence, not because one expects any quid pro quo from them.

Epicurus anticipated not only Isaac Newton and other founders of modern atomic theory but also Darwin and his theory of natural selection. Epicurus argued that the various life forms, including humans, evolved naturally out of Mother Earth, without any intervention or plan on the part of the gods. He was opposed to teleology, the notion that things are created for specific purposes, stressing instead the natural processes through which everything evolves. It is perhaps this antiteleological viewpoint that underlies the equal treatment given to women and men within the Epicurean system, for if human beings were not created for some purpose, it follows that neither men nor women have any special role to play within society (beyond the obvious reproductive roles). Man was not created to serve anyone, nor woman to serve man.

Another factor contributing to women's equal status in the Garden derived from the doctrine that a person's happiness depends not on any external conditions but strictly on an internal sense of peace of mind, or what the Epicureans called *ataraxia* (tranquillity). Thus an individual's marital status, family connections, political influence, or amount of wealth were all considered of little or no value to—or in some cases actually detrimental to—one's true happiness. This focus on individuals, rather than families or political groups, meant that both sexes were left free to develop their intellectual understanding of the universe through the study of atomic theory, instead of following gender-defined roles designed for economy in attaining material success.[2]

The names of seven of the women members of the Garden are known, and all of them appear to have been classed by the sources who mention them (usually several centuries later) as *hetairai*. In the rigid social structures in Athens, *hetairai* (literally "companions") were distinguished from "respectable" Athenian women by their (generally) non-Athenian birth, their often high levels of education and musical training, and their availabiltiy (at a price) as sexual partners for Athenian men. Now it is difficult to tell whether all of the women members of Epicurus' school really were *hetairai* or whether they were merely reputed to be so because of the unconventional mixing of the sexes within the Garden, not to mention the school's unorthodox views of marriage. In any case, many of them do seem to have been of foreign origin, and it is important not to envision the Garden as a refuge for an ordinary Athenian-born woman who wished to escape the confines of her rigidly controlled existence within the Athenian family.

Of the women members associated with Epicurus' school, the most famous was undoubtedly Leontion.[3] Although not even a fragment of her writing has survived, we know that she wrote a treatise criticizing one of Aristotle's followers, for Cicero, the famous first-century B.C. Roman orator and politician, alludes to her work in one of his philosophical dialogues: "Was it on such dreams that Epicurus and Metrodorus and Hermarchus relied in speaking out against Pythagoras, Plato, and Empedocles? Or the little prostitute Leontion in daring to write a treatise against Theophrastus? Of course, she writes in fine Attic style, but really! Such license the Garden of Epicurus allowed!"[4]

Cicero, himself one of the finest stylists in the ancient world and without question a major influence on the prose styles of the Renaissance, Victorian, and even modern periods, grudgingly acknowledges the superiority of Leontion's Greek prose. At the same time, he steers attention away from the actual subject matter of her writing by focusing on her status as a nonrespectable woman. In

Latin, the term *meretrix*, used by Cicero here in its dimunitive form, carries the same associations as the English "prostitute," as opposed to the idea of "courtesan" or "Geisha" suggested by the Greek term *hetaira*. Cicero further detracts from any appreciation of Leontion's work as a philosopher by emphasizing her presumed audacity in daring to direct her treatise against the ideas of Aristotle's most famous pupil, Theophrastus.

Indeed, the fact that a woman explicitly challenged a male philosopher seems to have struck the Romans as so appalling that Leontion's attack on Theophrastus is again alluded to in the century after Cicero. Pliny the Elder (who died in the great eruption of Vesuvius in 79 A.D.), toward the end of the preface to his monumental *Natural History*, defends himself from criticism by saying that he realizes that more could be written on the topics at hand and that doubtless various of his critics, who have so far "miscarried," will eventually "give birth" to responses to his work. One must be prepared for anything from critics, he concludes, for after all, even the "divine" Theophrastus was attacked—and by a woman![5]

Leontion's social status as a *hetaira* seems also to have been the center of attention for the major biographer of ancient philosophers, Diogenes Laertius. Leontion is mentioned on five occasions in Laertius' life of Epicurus, all but one of them in the context of sources that Laertius identifies as hostile to Epicurus and most of them referring to Leontion as a *hetaira*.[6] As we noted at the outset of chapter 2 vis-à-vis Megalostrata's presumed connection with the famous Spartan poet Alkman, women writers in ancient times (as well as in modern) were viewed in relation to male writers rather than as independent figures, so it is perhaps not surprising that Laertius devotes so little attention to the philosophical activities of Leontion. He does at least mention Epicurus' philosophical correspondence with Leontion (as well as with other *hetairai*) and even quotes the beginning of one of Epicurus' responses to a letter from Leontion: "By Apollo, my dear little Leontion, with what uproarious applause you filled us as we read your letter."[7]

As with Leontion's treatise against Theophrastus, however, we have nothing left at all from her side. Epicurus' use of the dimunitive form of her name would seem to suggest affection. His reference to applause certainly implies that he thought highly of her opinions. In another, badly mutilated fragment of one of Epicurus' letters, we learn that Epicurus was criticized by a disillusioned former member of the Garden for evidently allowing Leontion to hold the office of "directorship" (*prostasia*), the duties of which were passed around among the various members of the community regardless of their personal social status.[8]

Besides Leontion, the names of six other women members of Epicurus' school are known. In most cases, their position as *hetairai* seems to be confirmed by the typically suggestive meanings of their names: Hedeia ("Sweety"), Mammarion ("Tits"), Boidion ("Ox-eyes," or something to that effect), Demetria ("Ceres"), and Erotion ("Lovey").[9] But neither these women nor Themista (wife of Leonteus), to whom Epicurus is supposed by Cicero to have dedicated many of his works, seems to have engaged in philosophical writing.[10]

The Cynics

Cynicism was the other ancient school of philosophy (besides Epicureanism) which seems to have taken a position favoring the equality of women. The Cynics, or *Kunikoi*, were so named because their founder, the fourth-century Diogenes of Sinope (on the coast of the Black Sea), was perceived by more conventionally minded Greeks as advocating living one's life after the manner of a dog (*kuon*). Although Diogenes organized no formal school, his unusual teachings attracted many followers, particularly in the third century B.C. He taught that one should reject both current conventions and material possessions, live as a beggar, and practice "shamelessness" (*anaideia*)—hence his identification with dogs and their uninhibited approach to bodily functions and to sexual intercourse.[11]

It was perhaps Diogenes' doctrine of *autarkeia*, or self-sufficiency of the individual, that contributed most to an enlightened view of women. Since material needs of an individual were reduced to a mere subsistence level, there was no requirement for an organizational structure within which to increase efficiency through division of labor or assignment of certain tasks to males and other tasks to females. Instead, the emphasis was on the reduction of material wants on the part of everyone. Individuals were to rely on their own inner resources to satisfy these minimum wants, and privileges of birth, rank, and sex were to be abolished. Men and women were to dress in like manner and to exercise nude in public gymnasia. Marriage was not particularly advocated, except in cases where both the man and the woman desired such a union (we must remember that in the typical Greek marriage, the girl had no choice of husband, who was selected for her by her family). Evidently no restrictions of any kind were placed on sexual relations between adults, and the children of heterosexual unions were to be the common responsibility of everyone.

Whether or not the Cynics attracted a large female following is unclear, but certainly one woman who became a Cynic was regarded as an object of amazement among several ancient writers. This was the famous Hipparchia, who in the late fourth century B.C. married the Cynic Krates of Thebes, practiced the Cynic way of life, and may have written Cynic philosophy. The most extensive ancient source about Hipparchia is from the *Lives* of Diogenes Laertius. Rather than mentioning Hipparchia incidentally in connection with a male philosopher, as he did in the case of Leontion and Epicurus, the ancient biographer devotes a separate section to her in her own right. Despite its anecdotal nature, his account is worth quoting as evidence for the widespread fame of this strong-minded Cynic philosopher:

Hipparchia fell in love with Krates—both his words and his life—and ignored all her other suitors despite their wealth, noble birth, or good looks. Krates was everything to her. Indeed, she even threatened to commit suicide unless her parents gave her in marriage to Krates. Krates was then called upon by her parents to dissuade their daughter, and he did everything he could. Finally, he stood up, took all his clothes off in front of her, and said, "Here is the groom; here are his possessions. Plan accordingly, for you cannot be my mate unless you take part in the same pursuits."[12] The girl made her choice, and adopting the same sort of clothes as her husband, lived with him outdoors and went around to dinner-parties with him. She attended a drinking-party at the house of Lysimachus, where she refuted Theodorus ("The Atheist," so he was called) with the following sophism: "That which would not be considered wrong if done by Theodorus would also not be considered wrong if done by Hipparchia. Now if Theodorus strikes himself, he does no wrong. Therefore if Hipparchia strikes Theodorus, *she* does no wrong." Theodorus had no reply to this argument, but started to pull up Hipparchia's clothing. But she was neither alarmed nor distraught, the way a woman usually would be. When he said to her [quoting Euripides' *Bacchae*, line 1236], "Is this she who has abandoned her loom and shuttles?," she replied, "It is I, Theodorus. But do I seem to you to have made such a bad plan, if I gave over the time I would have spent at the loom to learning instead?" These and countless other stories were told of the Female Philosopher.[13]

Diogenes Laertius' colorful account of Hipparchia's strong will and quick wit makes no mention of actual writings by the philosopher herself, and most of the other ancient sources that refer to Hipparchia seem more intrigued by the unorthodox, vagabond mode of existence practiced by the Cynics than by their philosophical writings. But one Byzantine source, the (probably tenth-century A.D.) compilation known as the *Suda*, does state that Hipparchia wrote "hypotheses" ("hypotheseis") and "preliminary proofs" ("epicheiremata"), as well as "propositions" ("protaseis") directed against Theodorus the Atheist, the last presumably being similar to the sophism quoted above from Laertius' account of the confrontation between Hipparchia and Theodorus.[14] Unfortunately, we have no way of knowing whether or not such a late source is based on reliable information, but the possibility exists that part of Hipparchia's fame rested on her writing, not just on her choice of unusual lifestyle and her complete rejection of the sine qua non of Greek womanhood and literal center of female life—the loom.

Yet it was chiefly for their unorthodoxy that Hipparchia and her husband, Krates, were remembered. The only near-contemporary reference, a fragment from one of the comedies of the third-century B.C. Menander, alludes to the Cynics' gypsy lifestyle and unusual attitude toward marriage: "You'll go around with me wearing an old cloak, just like the woman [Hipparchia] did with Krates the Cynic, the one who gave his daughter in marriage, as he himself remarked, on a thirty-day trial basis."[15] Hipparchia herself was memorialized in an epigram (purporting to be an inscription for her tomb) by the influential poet of the second century B.C., Antipater of Sidon:

I, Hipparchia, did not choose the tasks of women, with their ample garments, but rather the hardy life of the Cynics. No pleasure for me in fine robes fastened with brooches, nor thick-soled slippers, nor anointed headbands. Instead, I like a leather pouch and its companion, the staff, and the heavy cloak which goes with them. I shall be much more famous than Arcadia's Atalanta, by so much as wisdom far surpasses running in the mountains.[16]

It is no small comment on the intellectual history of women in western society that Antipater's prediction in this epigram proved, alas, to be false. Whereas Hipparchia has gone largely unnoticed, the Roman poet Ovid and many other writers have been captivated by the story of Atalanta's defeat. Ovid tells the ancient myth of the virgin huntress who refused to marry any suitor who could not beat her in a footrace, the penalty for defeated suitors being death.[17] Finally, after many competitors had been executed, Hippomenes, with the help of Aphrodite, defeated Atalanta by distracting her with the beautiful golden apples of the Hesperides, which he dropped alongside the course, thus winning both the race and the woman. Like many stories in Greek mythology, the tale endorses both male competitiveness and male triumph over the competitive female.

The Pythagoreans

The Pythagorean philosophical school of sixth-century B.C. Italy and its Neopythagorean imitators in Hellenistic Greece also offer some evidence for the active participation of women followers. The most important indication of such activity consists of a collection of Hellenistic letters addressing various ethical and practical topics of traditional concern to women (the care of infants, the virtues of moderation, the need for tolerance, etc.) that were attributed to female authors such as Theano, Periktione, Myia, Phintys, and Melissa. Much contemporary controversy surrounds the authorship of these letters, a debate to which we must return, but for the moment, suffice it to say that even if the letters were in fact written by men under female pseudonyms, it must at least have been thought credible by the Neopythagorean audience to whom they were directed that such letters were written by women.

Before we examine some samples of these letters, however, we must look briefly at the somewhat shadowy figure who inspired what later became one of the most influential sects in ancient Greece and Rome, even in late antiquity after Christianity had gained a foothold. Pythagoras is known to us through a variety of relatively late sources (some as late as the third century A.D.), many of them clearly unreliable, and through scattered allusions to his theories and doctrines in earlier authors such as Empedocles, Heraclitus, Herodotus, Plato, and Aristotle.[18] He seems to have been born on the island of Samos, one of the large islands just off the coast of Asia Minor, some distance to the south of Sappho's homeland of Lesbos. In 531 B.C., he is said to have moved to the Greek colony of Croton in the "toe" of Italy, where he established a religious society open to both men and women. Although separation of early and later Pythagorean doctrine is problematic, it appears that the core of Pythagoras' teachings included purification of the spirit through study and proper diet (vegetarianism) and an emphasis on self-control and self-examination through silent meditation. Pythagoras seems also to have engaged in various forms of arithmetic speculation and to have experimented with numerical ratios in connection with musical intervals (he evidently discovered that the octave represents a ratio of 2:1, the fifth 3:2, the fourth 4:3, and a whole tone 9:8). In fact, his interest in music in general seems to have led to a tradition whereby he was regarded with as much awe as the legendary musician Orpheus, whose singing to the lyre could charm not only beasts but also the dread Hades. Pythagoras himself is described in the tradition as a kind of mystical bard whose music was thought to have cured ailing psyches.[19]

According to several of his ancient biographers, Pythagoras had various female pupils, and Diogenes Laertius reports that one Theano was either Pythagoras' wife or his pupil.[20] Iamblichus' *Life of Pythagoras* (third century A.D.) lists the names of sixteen women associated with the society, and elsewhere various of his daughters are named.[21] As Demand points out, "The survival within the tradition of the names of these women, despite some confusion about their actual identity, perhaps in itself implies something about the significance of women in the early days of the society."[22]

Whatever the actual representation of women in Pythagoras' circle was, it is clear enough that by the fourth century B.C., female participation in Neopythagoreanism was strong enough to elicit "targeted-audience" literature, namely a series of pamphlets directed at a female readership. The extant pamphlets are attributed to women named Theano (the same name that is assigned in the biographical tradition to Pythagoras' wife), Myia, Periktione, Melissa, and Phintys. Although some scholars regard these names as mere pseudonyms for male writers who wished to encourage women in preserving traditional values, others are more cautious in passing judgment on the gender of the authors, asserting, for example, that they "are at least as likely to have been male, but this cannot be conclusively proven."[23] Here we shall not attempt to determine the matter of gender, but only to show a sample of what issues these pamphlets dealt with.

The pamphlets are generally cast in the form of a letter addressed to a particular woman. For present purposes, three examples will illustrate the approach and general range of concerns addressed.[24] The first is a letter attributed to Theano, who, according to the tenth-century A.D. lexicon known as the *Suda* (under "Theano"), was a Pythagorean woman from Metapontum, a coastal town along the "instep" of the heel of Italy not far from the Pythagorean community at Croton. She is said by the *Suda* to have written several treatises, including *Peri Pythagorou* (*Concerning Pythagoras*), *Peri aretes Hippodamoi Thourioi* (*For Hippodamos of Thurii, Concerning Excellence*), *Paraineseis gynaikeias* (*Advice for Women*), and *Apophthegmata Pythagoreion* (*Sayings of the Pythagoreans*). Other titles are attributed to her as well, but the only extant works (besides a short excerpt said to be from a treatise called *Peri eusebeias, Concerning Piety*), are eight letters of various lengths addressed to various women.[25] Here is one example, a short letter on the topic of a husband's infidelities:

Theano to the admirable Eurydike:

What pain weighs down your spirit? You have lost heart for no other reason than the fact that your husband has gone off to a *hetaira* and indulges in bodily pleasures with her. But you ought not to be dispirited—you who are the finest of women [gap in text]. For don't you see that the ears, too, when they have taken their fill of pleasure, become satiated with the sound of an instrument [such as the lyre] and with an elegant melody, and that after they reach this point of satiety they lust after the *aulos* and want to listen to the Pan-pipes?[26] Yet what does an *aulos* have in common with the elegant strings [of a lyre] and with the admirable sound of an instrument of honey-sweet quality? This is the way in which you should also think about yourself and the *hetaira* with whom your husband sleeps. Your husband will care for you out of habit, nature, and rational thought, but whenever he reaches a point of satiety, he will sleep with a *hetaira* on the side. For those in whom destructive fluid has accumulated have a lust for nourishment that is not wholesome.[27]

The musical references in this letter attributed to Theano are consonant with Pythagorean interests in musical intervals, not to mention their concept of self-attunement and inner harmony. The recommendation that a wife should tolerate her husband's sexual diversions is also typical of the other letters attributed to Neopythagorean women, which generally advocate strict self-control for women in matters of sex, diet, and dress, coupled with patient endurance of any faults on the part of a husband.

We turn now to another example of one of these Neopythagorean treatises, this one a slightly more lengthy pamphlet that might be said to be a precursor of a guide to child rearing. The presumed author, Myia, was said to be the wife of Milo of Croton (the center of the original Pythagorean community):

Myia sends greetings to Phyllis:

Since you have become a mother of children, I want to give you the following advice. Choose someone for a nurse who is suitable and well-groomed, yet modest, and who is not prone to sleep or drunkenness. Such a nurse would make the best judgments as to how to rear children in a manner worthy of a free person, especially if she has nourishing milk and does not easily succumb to intercourse with a man. For a great part—indeed, the first and foremost part—of one's entire life depends upon the nurse's knowledge of good nursing so that she does the right things at the right time. She should offer the nipple and breast and nourishment not according to whim, but with some forethought; in this way she will guide the infant toward good health. Let her not succumb whenever she wants to sleep, but whenever the infant has a desire for rest, for in this way she will bring much relief to the child. Let the nurse not be inclined to anger, nor too talkative, nor negligent in the taking of food, but rather orderly and prudent; if possible, she should be a Greek woman rather than a foreigner.

It is best if the infant is pleasantly filled with milk and thus falls asleep. Such a feeding is a sweet relaxation for newborns and best for their digestion. If you give any other sort of food, it must be of the simplest sort. In general, you should refrain from using the strong force of wine, or only occasionally put in a small amount (together with milk) in mixing the afternoon meal.

Baths should not be given too frequently—it is better to give occasional, lukewarm ones. Furthermore, the air should be suitable and should have an equal mix of warmth and coolness, and the house should be neither too breezy nor too enclosed. Also, the water should be neither too hard nor too soft, and the bedding should not be too rough, but should embrace the skin accommodatingly. In all of these matters, nature yearns after what is fitting, not what is expensive.

It is perhaps useful to add at present that these expectations resulting from proper nourishment are based on certain guiding principles. With God's help, we will provide you with additional appropriate suggestions about child-rearing.[28]

The advice contained in this miniature handbook to child rearing is typical of the other letters in stressing the need for simplicity and moderation and for steering a middle course. It also reflects the earlier Pythagoreans' advocacy of a natural diet. The assumption that a wet nurse will be employed is consistent with aristocratic practices throughout the classical, Hellenistic, and Roman periods.

One last example of the Neopythagorean letters attributed to women writers differs from most of the others in that it reads more like an actual letter than a pamphlet in the guise of a letter. In this instance, Theano shares her frustrations—evidently over her (presumably platonic) admiration for a man named Kleon—with a fellow woman philosopher:

Theano to Rhodope the philosopher:

Have you lost heart? I, too, have lost heart. Are you distressed that I haven't yet sent you Plato's book, the one which is entitled "Forms, or Parmenides"? I myself am at loose ends, because no one has yet met with me to discuss Kleon. I don't want to send off the book until someone comes to offer an explanation about this man. I feel an excessive longing for his soul, for he is both a philosopher and one who is eager to do good deeds, and he also fears the gods of the Underworld. Do not suppose that the story is otherwise than what I am telling you: I'm half dead and can hardly bear to look on the light of day.[29]

In this instance, there seems little reason to suppose that the author of the letter was a man writing under a female pseudonym. Unlike most of the other letters, this one offers no advice about appropriate behavior for women. Instead, we seem to have an example of personal correspondence between two women whose studies included a common interest in the dialogues of Plato, an influential figure in fourth-century Neopythagoreanism. Besides the reference to book lending, the cryptic quality of the personal allusions in the letter also suggests actual correspondence rather than pamphleteering.

In sum, the body of letters attributed to Theano and other women associated with the Pythagoreans of the fourth century and later constitutes one of the more curious collections of ancient philosophical writings. The collection is certainly worthy of a more detailed study than space allows here. In general, it seems unwise to assume that the entire collection was authored by men masquerading as women, and one must certainly allow the possibility that all of the letters were indeed written by latter-day Pythagorean women whose names reflect the names of famous women connected with the early Pythagorean association at Croton. As Pomeroy observes, the essentially misogynistic attitudes in some of the letters "need not persuade us that the Neopythagorean treatises were written by men. It would be unreasonable to expect the Neopythagorean women to write like modern feminists."[30]

Hypatia, Neoplatonist

Of all the women discussed in this book, none—with the possible exception of Sappho—has enjoyed more enduring fame than Hypatia, the philosopher-mathematician who was murdered in Alexandria, Egypt, by a mob of antipagan Christians in 415 A.D. In the nineteenth century the figure of Hypatia was romanticized in Charles Kingsley's lengthy novel, *Hypatia, or New Foes with an Old Face*. Kingsley offers what no doubt tells us more about his own peculiar views of a woman scholar than about the real Hypatia. Here is the Kingsley Hypatia—literally quivering with emotion after delivering a lecture to her students on Book 6 of Homer's *Iliad:*

> And the speaker stopped suddenly, her eyes glistening with tears, her whole figure trembling and dilating with rapture. She remained for a moment motionless, gazing earnestly at her audience, as if in hopes of exciting in them some kindred glow; and then recovering herself, added in a more tender tone, not quite unmixed with sadness—
> "Go now, my pupils, Hypatia has no more for you today. Go now, and spare her at least—woman as she is after all—the shame of finding that she has given you too much, and lifted the veil of Isis before eyes which are not enough purified to behold the glory of the goddess. —Farewell."[31]

Far from being represented as a figure of authority imparting information to her students, this Hypatia is a curious mixture of helplessness, pretentiousness, and titillation.

Hypatia seems to have fared somewhat better in the present century. She has been mentioned in recent popularizing accounts of the history of science such as Carl Sagan's television series, "Cosmos," and she (along with Sappho) has a place setting among the women honored in the artist Judy Chicago's "Dinner Party." She has also been written about in journals of the history of mathematics, and her name appears routinely in recent biographical dictionaries of women in science. As Alic notes, she is often the only woman cited in contemporary histories of astronomy and mathematics.[32] Moreover, an American journal founded in 1983 as a forum for research in feminist philosophy was appropriately titled *Hypatia.*

Although not a word of anything that can be definitely attributed to Hypatia remains to us today, a rough idea of the circumstances of her life and death and a reasonably complete sketch of her interests in mathematics, astronomy, Platonic philosophy, and what might be termed engineering can be reconstructed through the accounts of the fifth-century A.D. ecclesiastical historian, Sokrates, and especially through several letters of her student Synesios of Cyrene. The correspondence of Synesios (who was elected Bishop of Ptolemais in Libya) with and about Hypatia represents the closest we can come to Hypatia's own thinking. Further details of more dubious accuracy can be supplied from late sources such as the *Suda* or the ninth-century scholar Photius, whose hostile comment nevertheless shows Hypatia's continuing reputation in the Byzantine period: "Isidore (of Seville) was much different from Hypatia, not only as a man differs from a woman, but also as a real philosopher differs from a woman who knows geometry."[33]

Before we examine what can be deduced about Hypatia's written contributions to scholarship, let us first review briefly the main facts of her life and death insofar as they can be gleaned from the ancient sources. The task of presenting a coherent sketch of her biography is complicated by inconsistencies among these sources and even within the same source; the unusually long encyclopedia entry on Hypatia in the *Suda*, for example, is quite obviously a patchwork of at least two variant sources, for it begins with a very brief description of her family, works, and death, claiming that she was the wife of Isidore, and then begins over again with the phrase "Concerning Hypatia the philosopher"; in the second (much lengthier) account, she is described not as anyone's wife but as a beautiful virgin.[34]

The ancient sources do agree that Hypatia was the daughter of the Alexandrian geometrician and philosopher Theon, who may have been connected with the research institute known as the Museum in Alexandria, where Hypatia was raised and educated. She herself is described as a geometrician, mathematician, astronomer, and exponent of Platonic and Aristotelian philosophy—interests that are borne out by the known titles of her works (see below). The sources also generally agree on the period of her activity; she was born in 370 A.D. and was murdered at the age of forty-five in 415.

As has been recently noted, the "spectacularly brutal murder . . . as well as its subtle political and religious overtones encouraged both friends and enemies to remember her. Not surprisingly, all of the reports place more emphasis on the social impact of her life than on her contributions to science and mathematics.[35] The first section in the *Suda* provides only the barest outline: "She was torn to pieces by the Alexandrians, and her body was shamefully treated and parts of it scattered all over the city. She suffered such treatment on account of envy and because of her superior wisdom, especially in the area of astronomy; some say the envy was on the part of Cyril [Bishop of Alexandria], while others claim that these events took place on account of the innate rashness and proclivity towards sedition among the Alexandrians."[36] For a more detailed report, we must turn to the contemporary account provided by the ecclesiastical historian, Sokrates:

> There was in Alexandria a certain woman named Hypatia, daughter of Theon the philosopher. She had achieved such heights of erudition that she surpassed all the philosophers of her time, succeeded to the Platonic school derived from Plotinus, and delivered all the philosophy lectures to those who wished to listen. Accordingly, everyone who wanted to study philosophy flocked to her from all directions. On account of the majestic outspokenness at her command as the result of her education, she came face to face even with the magistrates without losing her composure, and felt no shame at being in the presence of men. Everyone revered her for her outstanding composure, and at the same time found her a source of amazement. It was at that time that envy arose against this woman. She happened to spend a great deal of time with Orestes [Prefect of Egypt], and that stirred up slander against her among the people of the Church, as if she were the one who prevented Orestes from entering into friendship with the Bishop [Cyril]. Indeed, a number of men who heatedly reached the same conclusion, whom a certain Peter (who was employed as a reader) led, kept watch for the woman as she was returning home from somewhere. They threw her out of her carriage and dragged her to the church called Caesareum. They stripped off her clothes and then killed her with seashells. When they had torn her body apart limb from limb, they took it to a place called Cinaron and burned it. This deed brought no small blame to Cyril and to the Alexandrian Church. For murder and fighting and other such things are completely alien to those who profess Christianity. These deeds were done in the fourth year of Cyril's bishopric, in the tenth consulship of Honorius and the sixth of Theodosius, in the month of March during Lent.[37]

Ironically, Hypatia's unfortunate end seems to have led Sokrates, as a Christian historian, to regard her as a kind of pagan martyr whose Christian murderers should be condemned for their violent act. It is worth remarking that both in the *Suda* and in Sokrates' contemporary account, although the exact reasons behind the plot to assassinate Hypatia are not clear, the exceptional character of her position as an outstanding woman scholar is noted as a source of hostility toward her. As Lefkowitz remarks, "We may well ask whether her death was to some extent caused by her being a woman."[38] Whether or not we agree with Gibbon, who argued that Cyril "prompted, or accepted, the sacrifice of a virgin," it is clear that Hypatia's fame as a learned woman made her a vulnerable target for the antipagan factions in Alexandria.[39] In the ancient biographies, at least, she takes on the mythical proportions of an Antigone figure—a female whose extraordinary nature and deeds are the source of her downfall at the hands of male authority.

Turning from Hypatia's life and death to the question of her writing, we must again note that our only sources of information about her scientific and philosophical interests are the titles of her works (insofar as they have been preserved), and a collection of eleven letters of her pupil, Synesios, in which she is either the addressee or the subject of a passing reference. According to the *Suda*, Hypatia wrote three major works: a commentary on Diophantos (an Alexandrian author of a treatise on algebra), a treatise entitled *Astronomical Canon* (presumably on the movements of the planets), and a commentary entitled *On the Conics of Apollonius*, in which she treated the subject of conic sections previously expounded upon in the third century B.C. by Apollonius, yet another scholar from Alexandria.[40] But for one book, Apollonius' treatise survives to this day (either in the Greek original or in Arabic translation), but not a word of Hypatia's study is extant. (Ironically, several works by her less famous father, Theon, do survive.) These three titles suggest a focus on mathematics and astronomy, but the ancient biographical notices and the letters of Synesios imply that Hypatia's intellectual interests ranged from Plato and Aristotle to Homer to technological inventions as well.

Since we do not have even fragments of Hypatia's work, the nearest we can come to some sense of her as a thinker and a writer—rather than as a martyr—are the letters of her student, Synesios, who, despite his interest in Neoplatonism, was a Christian who held office as Bishop of Ptolemais. Three of these letters are translated here as representative samples of this one-sided correspondence between master and pupil. The first is interesting for its allusion to Synesios' hope for regular correspondence from his former teacher, whom he depicts as flourishing in a group of like-minded individuals:

To the philosopher Hypatia:

Blessed lady, I send greetings both to you yourself and, through you, to your most fortunate companions. For a long time I would have been eager to accuse myself of not being worthy of your letters; but now that I know that I have merely been overlooked by all of you—in this case, while I have done no wrong, I have encountered a good deal of ill luck, as much ill luck as a man could encounter. But if indeed I were able to receive letters from you, and to learn how you are spending your time (certainly you are in good company and are experiencing good fortune), I would fare only half so badly, and in all of you I would find my own good fortune. But as it is, this is only one of the difficulties that have overtaken me. I am deprived both of my children and of my friends, and of goodwill from everyone; and most of all, of your divine spirit, which alone I had hoped would remain with me as a force stronger than this heaven-sent ill fortune and the fluctuations of fate.[41]

Another letter similarly alludes to Synesios' own bad fortune, while at the same time appealing to Hypatia to exert her influence on behalf of two young men who seem to be in some kind of unspecified (financial?) difficulty:

To the Philosopher:

Even if fate is unable to take everything away from me, it seems to want to take away as much as it can:

". . . which has made me bereft of many noble sons."

[*Priam to Hektor, Iliad* 22.44]

But it will not take away from me the ability to bring forth the best and to render it to those who have suffered injustice. May it not overpower my judgment! I detest injustice. To be sure, it exists; yet I would wish to prevent it. But this ability, too, is one of those things that have been snatched away from me, and this, too, is gone as far as my children are concerned.

"It was long ago that the Milesians were brave."

[*Aristophanes, Plutus* 1002, 1075]

There was a time when I was a help to my friends; you called me "a good thing for other people" as I lavished on others the reverence directed at me by those who had great power; they were like my own hands. But now

I am left bereft of everything, unless you can do something. Indeed, I count you and your excellence an inviolate good. You always have power, and you can bring about good by using that power. Let it be a concern to all who respect you, both private citizens and magistrates alike, as to how Nikaios and Philolaos—fine young gentlemen and kinsmen—may return to being masters of their own affairs.[42]

The exhortation towards the end of the latter letter to both private citizens and magistrates implies that whatever Hypatia's official standing may have been vis-à-vis the Museum, she was in a position to influence the members of the city government. Indeed, Synesios sharply contrasts his own present helplessness with Hypatia's continuing position of power. Another point of interest in the letter is Synesios' use of literary allusion, through which he reinforces his message by referring to a famous passage in the *Iliad* and to a scene from one of Aristophanes' comedies. The allusions show that Hypatia's wide-ranging interests included, besides strictly philosophical or scientific subjects, the standard classics of the Greek literary tradition.

A final example from Synesios' letters to Hypatia will serve to illustrate her interest in technology and applied mechanics. This letter is sometimes cited in modern surveys of the history of science as evidence of Hypatia's invention of a device called the hydroscope, but a close reading of Synesios' actual words indicates only that he expected her to be able to follow and interpret his own rather sketchy directions for the construction of the instrument.[43] In modern terms, the device described would be called a hydrometer, an instrument used to measure the density of liquids (most commonly now, perhaps, in connection with automobile batteries). Synesios opens the letter with another reference to his own unfortunate circumstances, this time evidently an illness during which for some reason he wanted to test the weight of water (for his diet? for purposes of hydrotherapy?):

To the Philosopher:

I am faring so badly that I need a hydroscope. Please arrange for this to be constructed and paid for. The tube is cylindrical and is the shape and size of an *aulos* [oboelike pipes]. This is marked with notches along its length, by which we determine the weight of the water. For an [upside-down] cone sitting evenly placed covers the tube up at the bottom end, so that there is a common base for both the cone and the tube; this device is what is called the *baryllion* [little weight]. So, whenever you put the tube into water, it will stand up straight and allow you to note the number of notches [floating above the surface of the water]; these notches indicate the weight of the water.[44]

After Hypatia's death in 415 A.D., the philosophical school of thought that she represented—the blend of Platonic, Aristotelian, Pythagorean, and Stoic elements conveniently known as Neoplatonism—continued as a dominant intellectual force through the end of the ancient world and even on into the medieval and Renaissance periods. Other Neoplatonist philosophers (such as Hierocles and Hermeias) succeeded to the leadership of Neoplatonic teaching in Alexandria, but none seems to have captured the imagination of later writers in the way that Hypatia did.[45] One of the Greek epigrammatists, Palladas (fifth or sixth century A.D.), honors her place as philosopher, astronomer, and teacher in the following poem:

> Whenever I look upon you and your words, I pay reverence,
> As I look upon the heavenly home of the virgin.
> For your concerns are directed at the heavens,
> Revered Hypatia, you who are yourself the beauty of
>   reasoning,
> The immaculate star of wise learning.[46]

Some scholars have argued that the second line of the poem refers to the constellation Virgo, but it may be that the "virgin" ("parthenon") is Hypatia herself and that her home is "heavenly" because of its occupant's astronomical concerns (as explained in the next line).[47] The metaphor is extended through the last line of the poem, in which the addressee herself, in her role as teacher, becomes a star.

Conclusion

While Gilles Ménage may have been overly optimistic in claiming to have discovered definite evidence of sixty-five women philosophers in the ancient world, many of the major philosophical schools of antiquity were represented by women writers. Yet most of their works, along with those by women whose very names have been lost along with their writings, have been buried under a mountain of devaluation (Hypatia was a mere geometer) or outright hostility (Leontion was a "little prostitute" who dared to challenge Theophrastus). Of the four schools of philosophical inquiry examined here, Epicureanism and Cynicism were clearly the most favorable towards the intellectual development of women. Both sects tended to de-emphasize the traditional division of labor between men and women. The Pythagorean and Neopythagoreans, although they seemed to have fostered the participation of women, held to a more traditional view of the family and of women's place within the family. Neoplatonism, on the other hand, which concerned itself largely with theology and mysticism, apparently did not attract many female followers, Hypatia's fame notwithstanding.

In contrast to the stories about the women poets discussed earlier, the anecdotal evidence about women philosophers often implies a sense of female intrusion into male territory. A pattern emerges whereby women are praised for their "modesty" or their composure in male company. Hipparchia the Cynic, we recall, was not flustered when Theodorus attempted to pull up her clothing in the middle of a philosophical exchange; the Neopythagorean Theano is reported to have responded to a male admirer who told her that her arm was beautiful, "Yes, but it is not public";[48] and Hypatia, Sokrates reports, felt no shame at being in the presence of men. In all of these remarks, the implication is that women thinkers really do not belong in the company of men. Given the long-standing hostility towards women as thinkers—whether philosophers, theologians, or scientists—it is indeed remarkable that the classical world affords us even half a dozen models of women writers who were "lovers of wisdom."

5 Women Writers in Rome and Their Successors

We turn now from women authors of antiquity who wrote in Greek to those who wrote in Latin, both Romans and non-Romans. Paradoxically, although Roman women generally enjoyed more legal protection and economic freedom than their Greek counterparts (especially Athenian women), this improved social status does not seem to have fostered the same degree of literary creativity that we find among women writing in Greek. The history of Latin literature is rich and varied, even though most of its genres derive from Greek precedents, but the evidence for women writing in Latin is comparatively sparse, particularly in the earlier period (second century B.C. through first century A.D.). It is interesting to speculate on the possible reasons for the apparently less hospitable climate for women as writers within the Roman context. Perhaps, as Eve Cantarella notes, "their responsibilities of wife and mother impeded Roman women from leaving the confines of an inflexible role."[1] Whatever the reasons, there is no evidence on the Roman side of the coin for the kind of Greek female subculture that seems to have provided a creative milieu for a Sappho on Lesbos or a Nossis in Locri.

However, some women did write in Latin—particularly in the genres of elegiac poetry and in various forms that could be generalized under the category of memoirs. In modern histories of Roman literature, one is likely to find no mention of any writers who were women, but here I would like to correct that picture by examining the general evidence for women as authors (including those from whose works nothing survives) and by turning to an analysis of the surviving works of Sulpicia, Proba, and Egeria. Egeria, who probably lived in the fifth century A.D., the period that is generally regarded as the end of the classical world, provides a convenient (if somewhat arbitrary) stopping point for a study of women writers in antiquity. She might just as easily—as she in fact does—form the basis for a study of the beginning stages of the female literary traditions of the medieval period.[2]

Quintilian, the Roman rhetorician and educator of the first century A.D., cites three examples of Roman women of letters in his discussion of the importance of maternal influence in the education of (male) children. Often discussed in modern studies of the history of education, Quintilian provides us with a typically Roman view of the role of women as writers and public speakers—not so much in their own right as in relation to their capacity to educate the next generation. In the following excerpt from his treatise on rhetoric and education, Quintilian refers to three women writers, all of whom are known to us in varying degrees through other sources:

I would hope that there is as much learning as possible in parents. Nor do I speak only about fathers; for we have heard that the mother of the Gracchi, Cornelia, whose learned way of speaking has been passed down to posterity in her letters, contributed a great deal to her sons' eloquence. And Laelia, daughter of Gaius [Laelius] is said to have reflected her father's eloquence in her speaking ability, and the oration of Hortensia, daughter of Quintus [Hortensius], delivered to the triumvirs [in 42 B.C.] is read not just for the honor shown towards the female sex. But let not those parents who happen not to have received a good education themselves have any less concern for the education of their children—but rather let them for this very reason be all the more diligent regarding other matters [in which they can be of help].[3]

Of Laelia, little else is known except for a similar reference in Cicero to her oratorical eloquence, but Cornelia is, of course, a famous figure in Roman history.[4] Herself the daughter of the famous consul and conqueror of Hannibal, Publius Scipio Africanus, Cornelia was the mother of twelve children, of whom Tiberius and Gaius Gracchus were among the few to survive to adulthood. During the second century B.C., the Gracchi brothers, in their capacity as tribunes of the people, attempted to bring about various reforms aimed at a more equitable distribution of land, and both were killed in acts of political unrest. Their relationship with Cornelia is encapsulated in the traditional story according to which Cornelia, upon being asked to display her jewels to another Roman lady who was visiting her house, presented Tiberius and Gaius and announced, "These are my jewels."[5]

Cicero, like Quintilian, alludes to the eloquence of Cornelia's letters. In his dialogue on the history of Roman oratory, Cicero has one of the interlocutors remark about the role of parents in general and Cornelia's influence in particular upon her two sons: "It makes a great deal of difference whom one hears at home on a daily basis, with whom one speaks from childhood on, and also in what manner one's father, teachers, and mother speak. We have read the letters of Cornelia, mother of the Gracchi. It is clear that her sons were nursed not so much by their mother's breast as by her speech."[6] These letters to which both Quintilian and Cicero allude are no longer extant, with the possible exception of two fragments from a letter addressed to Cornelia's son Gaius Gracchus and preserved along with the *Lives* of Cornelius Nepos. Although the authenticity of these fragments is debated, there seems to be nothing particularly anachronistic in their style or content that would clearly prove them to be forgeries. Indeed, the author comes across as a demanding and lively matriarch of the sort we would be led by the Roman historians to expect in the case of Cornelia:

(a)

You will say that it is a beautiful thing to avenge one's enemies. No one thinks this more important or more beautiful than I do, but only if one can pursue such an undertaking and keep the safety of the republic intact. But insofar as this cannot happen, during much of the time and in many places our enemies will not perish; they will continue to exist just as they are now—better than that the republic should go to wrack and ruin.

(b)

If I could think of an oath, I would swear that—except for those who killed Tiberius Gracchus—no enemy has given me more trouble and vexation over these matters than you. It was appropriate that you—of all the children I had before—should sustain their duties and take care that I should have as little disturbance as possible in my old age, and that whatever things you do, you should especially want your actions to be pleasing to me, and that you should regard it wrong to do anything against my judgment on important matters, especially since only a small part of my life remains. Can't even this brief space of time aid in preventing you from opposing me and from ruining the republic? When will there be a respite? When will our family cease its madness? When will there be able to be moderation in this affair? When will we stop both having vexations and offering to desist from them? When will we be thoroughly ashamed that the republic is shaken up and thrown into turmoil?

But if this cannot happen at all, then seek the tribuneship—when I am dead. For my sake, do whatever you please when I am no longer alive to feel the effects. When I am dead, you will make the appropriate offerings to me and call upon me as your ancestral deity. Will it not at that time shame you to seek fulfillment of prayers by those deities whom, while they were alive and present, you treated as abandoned and deserted? Let not Jupiter allow you to persevere in these matters, nor such madness enter your mind. But if you do persevere, I fear that throughout your life you will take on so much work—through your own fault—that at no time will you be able to enjoy yourself.[7]

If we accept these two fragments as authentic, Cornelia appears to have written this letter to dissuade her son Gaius from canvasing for the tribuneship in 124 B.C. after his brother Tiberius had been killed while seeking reelection to that office. Appealing to the Roman sense of duty to the state, she advocates ceasing conflict and preserving the republic through moderation. At the same time, she appeals to the particularly Roman value placed upon respect for one's ancestors; if Gaius is going to engage in traditional ancestor worship after his mother reaches the end of her life at some point in the not-too-distant future, why does he not respect her wishes now while she is still alive? The effective use of irony conjures for the modern reader an image of a matriarch whose will is not to be crossed by her offspring. Despite the vividness of the image, the Latin of the original is relatively simple and uncomplicated by the standard rhetorical devices characteristic of Cicero's speeches.

The third figure whom Quintilian mentions as an object of literary admiration, Hortensia, was herself the daughter of Cicero's principal rival, a famous orator of the first century B.C. Quintilian's comments indicate that at least one of Hortensia's speeches was still preserved and studied during the following century, namely

the oration she delivered in the Roman Forum in 42 B.C. on behalf
of herself and other women of the Roman aristocracy who were
protesting a war tax about to be levied on them during a prolonged
period of civil war. Unfortunately, no fragments of the original
speech survive, but we do have a Greek version of her remarks
preserved by Appian in an historical work of the late first or early
second century A.D. We can assume that Appian offers a reasonably
close paraphrase of her speech, which is addressed in particular to
the triumvirs Octavian (later Augustus Caesar), Mark Antony, and
Lepidus, following an edict from them that fourteen hundred of
the richest women in Rome had to submit valuations of their
personal property and to be prepared to turn over as war tax whatever the triumvirs demanded:

As was appropriate for women such as ourselves in need of something
from you, we dispatched ourselves to your womenfolk. But we were rudely
treated by Fulvia [wife of Mark Antony] and have thus been forced to
come to the Forum. You have already taken away from us our fathers,
sons, husbands, and brothers, whom you accused of having done wrong
to you; if you should also take away our possessions, you will reduce us
to straits unworthy of our birth, manners, and female nature. If you claim
that you have been wronged at our hands, as you say you have by our
husbands, then proscribe us as you do them. But if we women have neither
voted any of you an enemy, nor torn down your houses, nor destroyed
your army, nor led one of you against another, nor prevented you from
obtaining public office or honor—then why should we have a share in the
penalty even though we had no share in the guilt?

Why should we pay taxes when we have no share at all in public office,
in honors, in military commands, or in government—all of which you
fight over to our detriment? "Because," do you say, "this is war"? And
when have there not been wars? When have women ever been taxed—
whose very nature exempts them among all peoples?

Still, our mothers once did go beyond what is natural and did pay taxes,
when you were in danger of losing the entire empire and the City itself
during the Carthaginian troubles. But they contributed the tax of their
own free will—and not from their land or estates or dowry or houses,
without which life is unlivable for freeborn women; rather, they contributed
only from their jewelry, and these items were not appraised by informers
and accusers through force or violence. The women themselves gave whatever amount they wished.

What, then, is your fear now on behalf of the empire or our fatherland?
Let there be war with the Celts or the Parthians, and we will come to the

rescue no less readily than our mothers did. But may we never contribute towards civil war nor lend aid for you to fight with each other. We did not help Caesar or Pompey, nor did Marius or Cinna or even Sulla—that tyrant of the fatherland—impose taxes on us. And you—you claim to be re-establishing legal government![8]

Although the Greek paraphrase of Hortensia's speech can only give us an approximate idea of her Latin style, we may note some general qualities such as the effective use of rhetorical questions and the appeal to historical precedent. Hortensia, speaking as a member of the privileged class of wealthy women, also emphasizes the injustice of levying a war tax on nonparticipants. As she points out, the women have never engaged in any hostilities against the triumvirs or their associates; further, she continues, as women they have no share in public office, so why should they pay taxes to a system that excludes them? We note that she does not argue that women should be included; rather, she simply accepts women's nonparticipatory status as a universal phenomenon and argues that therefore any resources provided by women to a war effort should be voluntary and directed only toward foreign wars, certainly not civil wars.

Since no other speech of Hortensia is preserved or even alluded to, we have no way of knowing whether her oration of 42 B.C. was an isolated phenomenon or whether she might have delivered public speeches on other occasions as well. Judging both from Quintilian's praise of the speech and from Appian's version of it, we may at least conclude that the piece reflects a professional touch due either to her father's training or to experience or to both. As Valerius Maximus (a Roman historian of the first century A.D.) puts it in his comment about Hortensia's speech of 42 B.C., "Quintus Hortensius at that time lived again through the female line, breathing through the words of his daughter."[9]

Elsewhere among the works of Roman historians and poets we find occasional references to women as authors, but none of their writing has survived. The famous historian of the first century A.D., Tacitus, for example, mentions that for some particular details he consulted a work by Agrippina the Younger, the daughter of Germanicus and mother of the emperor Nero: "This . . . I found in the commentaries of Agrippina the Younger, who, as the mother of the *princeps* Nero, recounted for posterity both her own life and the misfortunes of her family."[10] No doubt this would have been a fascinating document to compare with the account of the times given by Tacitus, who chronicles Agrippina's marriage to her uncle, the emperor Claudius (as his fourth wife), her poisoning of him, her son Nero's attempt to murder his mother through the device of a sailing vessel rigged with a collapsible ceiling, and her subsequent assassination at the hands of Nero's henchmen.

Women poets are also mentioned with some frequency in Latin literature. The historian Sallust discusses Sempronia, mother of Mark Antony's wife, Fulvia, as a woman who—despite what he labels as her loose morals—deserves praise for her considerable skill in lyre playing and in writing poetry.[11] The elegiac poet Propertius says that his beloved "Cynthia" (presumably a "code" name, according to the usual custom among Roman elegiac poets) composes poetry and that her songs are the equal of the poetry written by "Korinna of olden days," referring to the Boeotian poet (see chapter 2).[12] Ovid speaks of a woman whom he calls Perilla and claims that she is surpassed only by Sappho in the quality of the verse she writes.[13] The epigrammatist Martial, writing in the second half of the first century A.D., refers to a contemporary of his named Sulpicia as a poet who sings not of mythological themes like the banquet of Thyestes, but rather of "pure and honest love, amusements, delights, and jokes."[14]

Sulpicia of Messalla's Circle

Although Roman women writers of lyric and epigrammatic poetry are alluded to in the works of Propertius and Ovid and others, only one such poet is actually known to us through extant pieces— the six surviving elegies of an earlier Sulpicia, who lived during the reign of Augustus (31 B.C.–14 A.D.). The six extant elegies of this Sulpicia are preserved along with the poems of Tibullus. Hardly enough to be called a corpus, these six poems (totalling only forty lines of Latin) nevertheless provide some basis for an appreciation of her work and afford a glimpse at how her efforts may have differed from those of the male writers connected with the same literary circle. The patron of the circle was Marcus Valerius Messalla Corvinus (64 B.C.–13 A.D.), himself a well-known historian and orator of the day. His circle included Ovid, Tibullus (who, after Propertius, was the most famous exponent of Roman elegiac poetry), a poet known as Lygdamus, and Sulpicia herself. References in her own poetry and elsewhere led nineteenth-century scholars to the conclusion, probably accurate, that Sulpicia was the niece of her patron.[15]

As Santirocco has noted in a recent article on Sulpicia, her six poems have attracted little serious attention in modern times on the part of classical scholars, who tend to regard her work as amateurish and emotional.[16] As he further points out, however, her few extant lines did capture the admiration of a twentieth-century poet—Ezra Pound, who commented that "it would be worth ten years of a man's life to translate Catullus; or Ovid or perhaps Sulpicia."[17] While one may find some exaggeration in Pound's statement, in that no man (or woman) would be likely to spend ten years translating forty lines, one may nevertheless take stock of the fact that Pound speaks of Sulpicia in the same breath as Catullus and Ovid. Certainly it is worth an effort to see what qualities of Sulpicia's verse may have appealed to such a distinguished, if controversial, poet as Pound.

Sulpicia's six elegies have been preserved—along with five poems about her or her lover "Cerinthus" (no doubt a pseudonym, according to the usual practice of the Roman elegists) and some other anonymous poems of the Messalla circle—as part of the works of Tibullus. Although some scholars have tried to rearrange the "about Sulpicia" and the "by Sulpicia" poems into some sort of chronological sequence to reflect the course of the presumed affair between Sulpicia and Cerinthus, here we shall avoid such a biographical approach and simply examine the poems in the order in which they are preserved in the manuscripts.[18] Since the first poem is obviously introductory, the preserved order possibly reflects the intention of the author, or at least of an early compiler, in presenting a particular sequence of short pieces.

Sulpicia's opening poem announces the speaker's delight in her lover and in proclaiming her relationship to the world:

I

> Finally a love has come which would cause me more shame
>   were Rumor to conceal it rather than lay it bare for all.
> Won over by my Muses, the Cytherean goddess [Venus]
>   brought me
>   him, and placed him in my bosom.
> Venus has discharged her promise; if anyone is said
>   to have had no joys of his own, let him tell of mine.
> I would not wish to entrust anything to sealed tablets,
>   lest anyone read my words before my lover does.
> But I delight in my wayward ways and loathe to dissemble
>   for fear of Rumor. Let me be told of:
> I am a worthy woman who has been together
>   with a worthy man.[19]

This bold declaration asserts the speaker's absolute joy in the fulfillment of her prayer to Venus, who has given her the unnamed lover (the "him" of line 4). Significantly, the speaker attributes this success to the power of poetry, for it was her Muses who "won over" Venus. Such an attitude is not likely to be the mark of an amateur who writes poetry solely as a means of venting emotion, as Sulpicia has sometimes been viewed.[20] On the contrary, the poem itself reflects a polished style that indicates a high level of conscious artistry.

In the Latin, the poem is organized around its central couplet, the statement that Venus has fulfilled her promise and has provided the speaker with joy enough for others to have a share in by recounting, should they have no joys of their own of which to tell. The theme of "Rumor" ("fama"), introduced in the opening couplet, is reiterated in the poem's final couplet: the speaker actively wishes Rumor to carry abroad the news of the announced relationship so that others will know of her "gaudia" ("joys"). Yet two ironies pervade this programmatic statement of the speaker's intention to publicize her love affair. First, although she vehemently proclaims her desire to lay bare all, the (pseudonymous) name of the lover is never mentioned in the introductory poem itself, but appears only in the second and fifth of the six preserved elegies. Second, although the narrator announces here that she does not want to write anything down in tablets for fear that someone else might see her words before the unnamed lover does, she is of course writing down this poem of announcement of the joyous gifts she has received from Venus.

A more detailed analysis of the poem's Latinity would reveal various refinements typical of the Roman elegists of the Augustan period: alliteration, assonance, the use of a diminutive form as the last word of a line (line 7, "tabellis," "little tablets"), and skillful treatment of the couplet as a unit of meaning, to name a few examples. Such an analysis would doubtless produce a more realistic appraisal of Sulpicia's style than the florid evaluation arrived at by Kirby Flower Smith in the early part of this century. After describing her poetry as "difficult," he asserts that

her way of thinking is distinctively feminine, and though we may be familiar with it in the modern sphere of our own personal experience, it is less easy to follow in Latin, because Latin as we know it in the surviving literature is distinctively and exclusively masculine. She is feminine in what she says and in the way she says it. On the other hand, and this is the real difficulty, she is quite as feminine in what she does not say.[21]

According to this peculiar analysis, Sulpicia could hardly be expected to have any success as a writer, for she attempts to express "feminine" thoughts through the vehicle of a "masculine" language.

The next two poems in the preserved collection constitute another feature characteristic of Roman elegy: the device of paired poems. In this case, both poems have to do with the narrator's impending birthday. The first of the two poems, consisting of a complaint and a plea, is answered by the second of the pair, which presents us with a complete reversal of the earlier situation:

2

> My hateful birthday is at hand, which I must celebrate
> without Cerinthus in the irksome countryside.
> What can be sweeter than the City? Or is a country villa
> fit for a girl, or the chilly river in the fields at Arezzo?

Take a rest, Messalla, don't pay so much attention to me;
  journeys, my dear relative, are often untimely.
When I'm taken away, I leave my mind and feelings here,
  since force keeps me from acting as my own master.[22]

3

Do you know of the dreary journey just lifted off your
  girl's mind?
    Now she gets to be in Rome on her birthday![23]
Let's all celebrate that day of birth,
    which has come to you by chance when you least expected
    it.[24]

In the first poem of the pair, the narrator establishes the tone of
the whole poem with the opening word in the Latin, "invisus"
("hateful"). She is a city girl (the Latin *puella*, "girl," is actually a
diminutive form of the word for "boy," *puer*). She prefers Rome
to the drudgery of the countryside, to which Messalla is about to
take her just at the moment when she should be enjoying the
celebration of her birthday together with Cerinthus. Yet in the final
couplet, the speaker asserts her control, albeit limited, over the
situation: she may be in the country, but she will leave her "mind"
("animum") and feelings in Rome. Suddenly, in the second poem
of the pair, the speaker's "mind" ("animo") is completely at ease.
This time she addresses not her uncle, but her lover. Only half the
length of the previous poem, this piece gaily announces the reversal
of the situation: the birthday will be in Rome after all. The "sad"
("triste," a favorite elegiac word) journey has vanished, and the
celebration will take place in the preferred surroundings of the city
and, of course, in the company of the unnamed Cerinthus ("tibi,"
line 4). Taken as a unit, the two pieces provide a charming vignette
of the vagaries of fortune in the arena of love. At the same time,
as Santirocco notes, there is an implied cause and effect relationship
between the two poems; the attempt to persuade Messalla in the
first of the pair may be what led to the happy occasion proclaimed
in the second.[25]

The next piece in the collection suggests a broader range of tone
in Sulpicia's work than one might suspect on the basis of her other
poems. Here the author, who, like Sappho in some of her songs,

becomes the stated persona of the poem, adopts a biting, sarcastic mode as she lambastes her lover for his infidelity:

4

> It is pleasing—the fact that in your carefree way you allow
>   yourself so much on my behalf, lest I suddenly take a bad
>   fall.
> So you care more for a skirt—a wench loaded down with
>   her wool-basket—than for Sulpicia, daughter of Servius.
> There are people concerned about me, and they especially
>   worry
>   that I might give way to that lowly mistress of yours.[26]

The poem begins and ends ambiguously, but the central couplet of mordant accusation is stated as boldly as possible: the addressee chases after a low-class "skirt" (a "toga," as opposed to the more respectable *stola* [robe] of the Roman matron) instead of remaining faithful to Sulpicia. The author has written the opening couplet in such a way that its meaning only becomes fully clear after the accusation is levelled. The liberties taken on the speaker's behalf turn out to consist of sexual license, and the "fall" from which the speaker is saved seems to be falling in love with the unfaithful addressee. In the final couplet, after the accusation, the speaker returns to the ambiguous mode: unspecified persons have Sulpicia's interests at heart and think that she might "yield" or "give way" to the lowly wool worker—meaning, perhaps, that Sulpicia might choose to end her affair with the addressee and leave him to his philandering pursuits. There is the further implication that the people concerned on Sulpicia's behalf might be potential replacements for the unfaithful lover.

As in Sulpicia's other poems, particularly the opening piece, the style of this sarcastic attack is marked by a variety of refinements that enhance its effect. The preponderance of *s* sounds in the Latin creates a hissing effect, and there is a pun involved in the "falling" of line 2 ("cadam") and the "giving way" in line 6 ("cedam"). The lowly status of the other woman is emphasized by her association with wool working through the image of her being weighed down by a little wool basket, "quasillo," again a diminutive form reserved for the end of a line. Such poetic devices are similar to those used by Sulpicia's fellow elegists such as Tibullus and Ovid.

The next piece in the collection falls into the tradition within classical poetry of love-as-disease. In this case the speaker refers to a literal fever that wracks her body but in such a way that she also manages to suggest the fever of passion and the desire on her part for an equally fervent response from the addressee:

5

> Do you feel any sense of dutiful concern, Cerinthus, for your
> girl,
>> now that a fever wracks my tired limbs?
> I wouldn't want to triumph over sad diseases
>> unless I thought you also wished me to.
> For what good will it do me to triumph over disease,
>> if you can bear my troubles with an unfeeling heart?[27]

The word that Sulpicia uses here for "fever," "calor," bears a variety of meanings ranging from "heat of the sun" to "bodily temperature" to "vehemence," "ardor." Thus the speaker's literal fever almost becomes a metaphor for her passion for Cerinthus, who is urged to display evidence of his own passionate interest in the feverish victim. The particular quality that the speaker hopes for is a very Roman one—"dutiful concern" ("pia cura," line 1).

The final poem in the collection is unusual in that it consists of one breathless sentence spread out over three couplets. Cast in the form of an apology, the piece pursues the themes of concern (*cura* again) and the folly brought on by passion:

6

> Light of my life, let me not be so burning a concern to you
>> as I seemed to have been a few days ago,
> If in my whole youth I in my folly have ever done anything
>> which I admit to have been more sorry for
> Than last night, when I left you alone,
>> wanting to hide my passion.[28]

The emphasis in the final line of the apology on the deliberate attempt at concealment provides an ironic contrast to the theme of openness announced in the first poem, in which the narrator wants to lay bare her joyous affair. This time, however, the speaker, far from wanting to reveal her feelings, claims to have intentionally hidden them by temporarily abandoning her lover without explanation—a rash action for which she now apologizes. The passionate intensity of the opening line in the wish not to be a "burning concern" ("fervida cura") is reiterated in the poem's final line when the speaker refers to her own "passion" ("ardorem"). In between, the central couplet offers a charming exaggeration: this is the worst thing the narrator has ever done!

Given such a small surviving sample of Sulpicia's work, what are we to make of her place in the context of Roman elegy? A typical evaluation is represented in the comments of Luck: "Sulpicia is no Roman Sappho or Erinna, and her craftsmanship cannot be compared to that of Nossis or Anyte, whose epigrams always have a professional touch."[29] While we certainly may agree that Sulpicia is not a "Roman Sappho," it seems prudent to avoid the kind of patronizing assumptions behind statements implying that she was obviously an amateur who wrote spontaneously. As we have seen, her poems reflect many of the same stylistic devices used by her male counterparts, and the language and structure of the pieces suggest conscious artistry rather than amateurish outpourings. Luck also complains that Sulpicia "moves in a limited world of images. In her forty lines there is not a single mythological allusion."[30] Such a criticism, even if it were valid with reference to such a small selection of poems, is hardly to the point in evaluating the effectiveness of Sulpicia's elegies. If indeed these six pieces are typical of her work, it may be that she tended to avoid mythological allusion in favor of direct description of emotions and events.

As Santirocco concludes, Sulpicia's work has much in common with traditional Roman elegy, especially in the choice of themes (illness, separation of lovers, infidelity, etc.). Yet, as he further notes, her preference for brevity (the longest poem is ten lines of Latin) suggests that we should view her work not so much as part of the body of relatively lengthy elegies of the sort written by Ovid, Tibullus, and Propertius, but rather as part of the tradition of the short elegiac epigram represented by many of Catullus' poems.[31] In some ways, then, Sulpicia does continue the tradition of her

Greek predecessors Nossis and Anyte in writing artful elegiac pieces that are short, direct, and immediate—without an overlay of allusions to mythology or to contemporary political events.

Proba and Other Christian Authors

Within the tradition of ancient Christian Latin writing, Proba and Egeria, probably of the fourth and fifth centuries A.D., respectively, are among the most notable women writers.

Proba, whose full name seems to have been Faltonia Betitia Proba, was the Christian daughter of a Roman consul and wife of a pagan prefect of Rome. Her one extant hexameter poem reflects the blend of Christianity and paganism widely evident in the fourth century, for it is an account of the Old Testament version of the Creation and of the birth, life, death, and resurrection of Jesus, all told almost entirely in the words of Rome's greatest epic poet, Vergil; Proba simply borrows lines or half-lines from the *Aeneid*, the *Georgics*, and the *Eclogues* and cleverly weaves them together into the biblical narrative.[32] Such a verse form—a patchwork of existing lines—is referred to as a *cento*, the Latin word for a quilt made of old garments sewn together. Centos derived from Vergil's works were especially popular in the fourth century, for many readers of Vergil had begun to assume that the poet was himself a Christian; this (patently incorrect) assumption was based on the interpretation of his fourth eclogue, in which he speaks of the birth of a child who will bring hope to the world, as a prophecy of the birth of Christ.[33]

Proba's cento, 694 lines long, opens with a statement of purpose that forms the most original part of the work. Only this opening section is presented in translation here, for the rest of the work is chiefly of interest to the Latin specialist who wishes to see how the author has skillfully combined Vergilian half-lines to tell the biblical story. Cacioli has made such a study, in which she points out the various techniques that Proba uses to adapt Vergilian lines to suit her own purposes.[34] For example, when she wants to refer to the biblical Eve, for whom there is no counterpart in Vergil, she combines two half-lines from Vergil's *Aeneid* into the phrase "insignis facie / et pulchro pectore virgo," ("maiden distinguished in her features and her beautiful breast").[35] The context makes the reference of the periphrasis perfectly intelligible to the reader who is versed in the story of Adam and Eve in Genesis. Proba's work is also of interest to church historians who examine the document for what it can tell us of the author's presentation of Jesus as a kind of epic hero, the social virtues that the poem reflects through its selection and shaping of material, and the place it holds as an early example of Christian Latin poetry.[36]

In her prefatory remarks, Proba proclaims herself a "vatis," using a word that had a long history of referring not only to seers and prophets but also to bards, who were regarded as divinely inspired. She opens her poem with an apology for the subject matter of her previous work and announces her new direction in telling of the "sacred offices of Christ"[37] through the words of Vergil:

> For a long time now I have written of how our leaders have
>   profaned the sacred pacts of peace,
> leaders whom in their wretchedness dire greed for power
>   held fast.
> I have written, I confess, of many slaughters, cruel wars
>   of kings,
> battles among kin, famous shields polluted by the murder
>   of parents,
> and trophies taken from those who should not be enemies,
> of bloodstained triumphs that Rumor had reported,
> and of cities widowed over and over again of countless
>   citizens.
> It is enough to have recalled these evils.
> Now, O all-powerful God, accept, I pray, my sacred song,
> and unloose the voices of your sevenfold, eternal spirit.
> Unlock the innermost regions of my heart,
> so that I, Proba the seer, may tell of everything that is hidden.
> No longer is it my concern to seek ambrosial nectar,
> nor does it please me to draw down the Muses from
>   Mt. Helicon;
> let not vain error persuade me that rocks speak,
> or to pursue as my subject laurel-bearing tripods, useless vows
> and quarrelling gods of noblemen, and defeated household
>   deities.
> For my task is not to extend my fame through words

nor to cultivate meager praise through the pursuits of men.
Rather, wet from the Castalian spring, imitating the blessed,
I who in my thirst have drained the draughts of the holy day
from this point I shall begin to sing. Be present, O
    God, and direct my mind.
I shall tell how Vergil sang of the sacred offices of Christ.
I shall proceed from the beginning as I recall a matter
    obscure to no one,
if there be any faith within my heart, if a true mind,
    pouring through my limbs
stirs up my strength and the spirit mingles itself
    throughout my whole body,
and at the same time no poisonous bodies slow it down,
nor earthly limbs and mortal parts make it dull.
O Father, eternal power over humankind and all matter,
grant me an easy course, and come to enter my spirit.
And you, the Son, be present, and run alongside us
    as we undertake the task,
strength from our Father on high, heavenly source,
whom we are the first to worship and whose honors,
    well-deserved, we repeat anew,
now a new offspring, whom every age has come to believe.
For I recall, turning over in my mind the monuments of
    you ancient men,
that your Musaeus first sang throughout the world
of what things are, what things have been, and what
    things people said were soon to come.
All matter—and the tender orb of earth itself—
    condensed into firmness.
Happy is he who is able to understand the causes of things,
whence has come the race of men and beasts and the
    life of birds
and those creatures that the sea bears under its smooth surface,
and the nature of liquid fire and shifting moisture of
    the heavens.
By no means otherwise would I believe that the day dawned
at the first beginnings of the world, nor held any other course.
A greater design of things now begins,
if somehow its antiquity will produce faith in so great a task.
For—and I will confess this—I always used to sing
of the spectacles of trivial things—horses, the arms
    and battles of men,
and eagerly I wanted to pursue a vain task.

To one who was attempting everything, there seemed
  a better purpose
in opening up matters deep and buried under earth and
  darkness.
Every day for a long time now my mind has been eager to
lay hold of something great, and it is not content with
  peaceful quiet.
All of you—keep propitious silence and pay attention—
mothers and men, boys and unmarried girls.[38]

After this programmatic opening in which she renounces the
themes of pagan epic, Proba goes on for roughly the first half of
the poem to recount the Old Testament version of creation, always
by patching together phrases or modified phrases from Vergil's
Aeneid, Georgics, or *Eclogues*. Readers of Vergil suddenly find familiar
language in rather different contexts, as, for example, the words
spoken by Jupiter to Venus about the destiny of Aeneas and the
empire of Rome, "imperium sine fine dedi" ("I have given rule
without end"),[39] which in Proba's version are spoken by God to
the newly created Adam and Eve. After a second invocation, Proba
continues with an account of the birth and baptism of Jesus, whom
God addresses in the words of Anchises to his son Aeneas in the
Underworld, "tu regere imperio populos" ("your task is to rule
humankind with authority").[40] Her narrative goes on to describe
various episodes from the life of Christ, including the temptation
in the desert, Jesus' walking on the water, his entry into Jerusalem,
the Last Supper, the Crucifixion, the empty tomb, and Jesus' As-
cension into heaven. The poem concludes with a short epilogue in
which Proba appeals to her friends to celebrate the appropriate
sacred rites; in the final lines, she addresses her "sweet husband"
("O dulcis coniunx,"[41] the words of Creusa's ghost addressing her
husband Aeneas as he flees Troy) and asks him also to hold to the
way of worship that she had advocated, ending with the wish that
"if we are deserving through our piety, may our grandchildren keep
the faith."[42]

In the century after Proba wrote her cento, the Christian emperor
Theodosius II (401–50 A.D.) displayed what had become a fairly
typical combined interest in both pagan and Christian learning. We

know, for instance, that he had special copies made for himself not only of the biographies of pagan generals, poets, and so on, written by Cornelius Nepos (first century B.C.) but also of Proba's cento.[43] Her poem was praised in the seventh century A.D. by the encyclopedist Isidore of Seville, who points out that her ingenious verse was still read in his own day among the apocryphal writings, where it had been assigned by Pope Gelasius at the end of the fifth century.[44] The popularity of her work in the Middle Ages is also attested by its preservation in many different manuscripts, several of which contain a verse preface to the cento (presumably written by a copyist) inviting the "Romulidum ductor" ("leader of the sons of Romulus," i.e., the ruler of Rome) to read "Maronem mutatum in melius" ("Vergil changed for the better") and to ensure that the work of Proba should be preserved for posterity. While her poem cannot be said to have had any special significance in modern times other than as one example among several of the curious phenomenon of the cento, Proba's work was clearly read and appreciated for several centuries after its composition.

Another woman writer who demonstrates the combination of classical and Christian traditions is the empress Eudocia Augusta. Eudocia, wife of emperor Theodosius II, does not properly belong in this chapter, for she wrote in Greek rather than in Latin. Nevertheless, she can be closely associated with both Proba, in using classical forms to treat Christian themes, and with our final author, Egeria, with whom she shares in common a pilgrimage to Palestine that shaped her writing.

Eudocia, whose name was Athenais before she was baptized, was the daughter of a pagan philospher named Leontius; she was educated in the classical tradition in Athens before she moved to Constantinople and married Theodosius in 421 A.D. Her classical training is reflected in all of her surviving poetry, which is written in the epic meter of Homer and Vergil. Having made a pilgrimage to Palestine sometime about 438–439, Eudocia later separated from her husband and moved to Jerusalem, where she evidently lived in celibacy until her death in 460. The fragments of her poetry were collected and studied at the end of the nineteenth century, and recent excavations in Israel have uncovered an additional fragment of her work.[45] The new fragment, a seventeen-line inscription found in excavations of the baths at Hammat Gader in the Yarmuk Valley, is a hexameter poem identified in the first line as the work of Eudocia Augusta. The poem, which attempts to be Homeric in its language, is a praise of the baths and of the healing powers of the hot springs.[46] I have not translated any of the fragment here, for it is full of obscure names of what seem to be various rooms in the complex of the baths, and like most of the other fragments of Eudocia's work, it displays little purely literary merit. Nevertheless, her poems deserve a modern reexamination from a historical point of view for what they can tell us of how a woman writer combined pagan and Christian influences in her work.[47]

Egeria

It seems a fitting conclusion to this survey of women writers in the world of classical antiquity to end with the earliest known example of what was later to become a literary form of major importance for women as authors and as readers—the diary.[48] In this particular case, the diary takes the form of travel memoirs, or, as one scholar characterizes the work, a "pilgrimage narrative."[49]

The date and even the name of the author of the eleventh-century manuscript now generally referred to as the *Itinerarium Egeriae* (*The Travel Memoirs of Egeria*) have remained uncertain ever since the discovery of the work in 1884 by G. F. Gamurrini. The narrative as it exists today is a partial account (perhaps only about a third of the original)—probably dating to the fifth century A.D.—of a three-year religious pilgrimage undertaken by the author to Jerusalem and to several places in Egypt, Palestine, Syria, and Cilicia. A great deal of scholarly controversy has centered around the name of the author, which never appears in the existing portion of the manuscript; external evidence has yielded more than four different names, including Silvia Aquitana, Aetheria, Etheria, and Egeria. Of these, I shall adopt the last, more for the sake of convenience than because any certain proof of the author's identity has been discovered. In any case, until recently there has been general agreement that the author was a nun from Spain, for her narrative is punctuated by addresses to her "ladies, reverend sisters" ("dominae venerabiles sorores") or to "Your Charity" ("affectio vestra," presumably referring to a superior in her religious order), and her Latin has been analyzed as having much in common with that of authors from northwestern Spain.[50]

Beyond these two pieces of educated guesswork, both of which are open to question, little can be deduced about the author's personal life, background, or education. She seems not to know any Greek beyond an occasional brief phrase—a not uncommon phenomenon among Latin-speaking people during the probable time at which she lived. The grammatical "errors" in her Latin can also be attributed more to the changing nature of the language as it prefigured the development into the various Romance languages rather than to any particular lack in Egeria's education. Her biblical quotations and some of her descriptions have been traced to a pre-Vulgate version of the Bible and to a translation by Jerome of Eusebius' *Onomasticon*.[51] Her use of such literary sources would seem to indicate some degree of formal education.

Known to the modern world for only a little over a hundred years, Egeria's travel diary has captured perhaps a greater quantity of scholarly attention than the work of any other writer in this book except for Sappho and possibly Hypatia. As the medievalist K. P. Harrington put it, "The document is of surpassing interest to historians and linguists. That a woman should have undertaken such a journey in those times is in itself sufficiently remarkable."[52] In general, however, the focus of the scholarship has been less on the fact that the author was a woman writing for women and more on the details of the Latinity, the descriptions of places regarded as sacred in the Judeo-Christian tradition, and the various liturgical practices at Jerusalem as reported by the author in the second half of the extant text. Since the work, even in its partial state, is both relatively lengthy and available in several Latin editions and English translations, here I will examine only a few excerpts from the first half of the manuscript (the pilgrimage section) in order to observe some of Egeria's qualities as a writer.

In the following selections, Egeria's style is marked by a formulaic quality in that she generally follows the same pattern in relating a particular pilgrimage, including a general description of the site, an account of the reading aloud of an appropriate passage from the Bible connected with the site, praise of the local guides for their hospitality and holiness, and assurances to her audience of the beauty and significance of the place visited and/or of the truthfulness of the information imparted.

In the brief excerpts that follow, the diary first describes Egeria's visit to Mt. Sinai (chapter 3), the journey from there to Pharan, a region in the north central area of the Sinai peninsula, and on to the port of Clysma, near the present-day Suez (chapters 5, 6). The final excerpt (chapters 22, 23) describes her visit from Antioch in Syria further north to Tarsus in Cilicia and to a nearby shrine of Saint Thecla. In this context Egeria makes the only reference by name to a contemporary figure, a deaconess called Marthana, whom she had previously met in Jerusalem; no other guides or acquaintances are mentioned by name anywhere else in the extant portions of the manuscript.

Chapter 3

On Saturday evening we proceeded onto the mountain [Mt. Sinai], and, arriving at some monastic cells, we were received very hospitably by the monks dwelling there, and they offered us every courtesy. Since there is a church there with a priest, we stopped there for the night. Early on Sunday morning, accompanied by that priest and the monks who lived there, we began climbing the mountains one by one. These mountains are climbed with very great difficulty, since you do not ascend them slowly going round and round, in a spiral path as we say, but you go straight up all the way as if scaling a wall. Then you have to go straight down each of these mountains until you reach the very foot of the central mountain, which is properly Sinai. By the will of Christ our God, and with the help of the prayers of the holy men who were accompanying us, I made the ascent, though with great effort, because it had to be on foot, since it was absolutely impossible to make the climb in the saddle. Yet you did not feel the effort; and the reason it was not felt was because I saw the desire which I had being fulfilled through the will of God. And so at the fourth hour we reached the summit of the mountain of God, Holy Sinai, where the Law was given, at the place, that is, where the Glory of the Lord descended on the day when the mountain smoked.

In this place there is now a church, though not a very large one, because the place itself, the summit of the mountain, that is, is not very large. Yet this church has great charm all its own. When through God's will we had reached the mountain top and had arrived at the church door, there was the priest who was assigned to the church coming forth from his cell to meet us. He was an old man, beyond reproach, a monk from his youth, and, as they say here, an ascetic; in a word, he was a man worthy of being in this place.Then the other priests and all the monks who dwell there by the side of the mountain, that is to say, at least those who were not impeded either by age or by infirmity, came forth. Indeed, no one lives on the very top of that central mountain, for there is nothing there save the church alone and the cave where the holy man Moses was. All of the proper passage from the Book of Moses was read, the sacrifice was offered in the prescribed manner, and we received Communion. As we were about to leave the church, the priests gave us gifts native to this place, that is, some fruit which grows on this mountain. Now this holy Mount Sinai is itself all rock, without even a shrub. Down at the foot of these mountains, however, either around this one which is in the middle or around those which encircle it, there is a small piece of ground. There the holy monks carefully plant bushes and lay out little orchards and cultivated plots, next to which they build their cells, and the fruit which they have seemingly raised with their own hands they take from, as it were, the soil of the mountain itself.

After we had received Communion, then, and the holy men had given us gifts, and we had come out the church door, I asked them to show us each place. At once the holy men consented to point out each one. They showed us the cave where the holy man Moses was when he ascended the mountain of God a second time to receive anew the tables, after he had broken the first ones because the people had sinned. Moreover, they consented to show us whatever other places we desired and with which they were very well acquainted. Ladies, reverend sisters, I would like you to know that we were standing around the enclosure of the church on top of the central mountain, and from this place those mountains which we had first climbed with difficulty seemed, in comparison with the central mountain on which we now stood, as far beneath us as if they were hills. Yet they were so high that I do not think I have ever seen any higher, except for the central mountain which towers very much above them. And from there we saw beneath us Egypt and Palestine, the Red Sea, and the Parthenian Sea which leads to Alexandria, and finally the endless lands of the Saracens. Hard as this may be to believe, the holy men did point out each of these things to us.

Chapters 5–6

We took a route by which we would go down the length of the center of the valley, which, as I mentioned before, is the valley where the children of Israel camped while Moses was ascending and descending the mountain of God. As we proceeded through the valley, the holy men continually pointed out to us each place. At the very head of the valley, where we had camped and had seen the bush out of whose fire God spoke to the holy man Moses, we saw the place where he stood before the bush as God said to him: *Loosen the strap of your shoe, for the place on which you stand is holy ground.*

And as we set out from the bush, the guides began to show us all the other places. They pointed out first the place where the camp of the children of Israel stood in the days when Moses went up the mountain, and then the place where the calf was made, for a large stone is set there even today. As we went along, we saw at a distance the summit of the mountain which looks down over the whole valley; from that place the holy man Moses saw the children of Israel dancing in the days when they made the calf. Next they showed an enormous rock, at the very place where the holy man Moses came down from the mountain with Josue, the son of Nun; on this rock, Moses, in anger, broke the tables he was carrying. Then they showed how each and every one of them had had dwellings, the foundations of which are still visible today throughout the valley, and how they had been built in circular shape, out of stone. Then they showed the place where the holy man Moses, on his return from the mountain, ordered the children of Israel to run *from door to door.* Next they showed us where the calf which Aaron had built for them was burned at the command of the holy man Moses. Then they showed the torrent from which he gave drink to the children of Israel, as it is written in Exodus. Next we were shown the place where the seventy had received of the spirit of Moses, and then the place where the children of Israel had lusted for food. Moreover, they also showed us the place called The Burning, where a certain part of the camp had burned, and then the fire stopped because of the prayer of the holy man Moses. We were also shown where manna and quails had rained on them.

And so we were shown everything written in the holy books of Moses that was done there in that valley which lies below the mountain of God, the holy Mount Sinai. It was too much, however, to write down each one individually, because so many details could not be retained; besides, when Your Charity reads the holy books of Moses, she will perceive, carefully written, all that was done there. This is the valley where the Passover was celebrated, one year after the children of Israel had gone out of the land of Egypt, for they tarried in that valley for some time, while the holy man Moses twice climbed the mountain of God and came down again. Moreover, they also dwelt there long enough for the tabernacle to be made, and for all things shown on the mountain of God to be accomplished. Accordingly, we were shown the place where the tabernacle was first set up by Moses, and where everything was accomplished which God on the mountain had ordered Moses to bring about. We saw anew at the end of the valley the Graves of Lust, at the place where we once again returned to our route. It is here that on coming out of that large valley we took up the road by which we had come through those mountains about which I spoke earlier.

On the same day we also visited other very saintly monks, who, either because of age or because of infirmity, were unable to go up to the mountain of God for the offering of the sacrifice, but who, when we arrived, consented to receive us very hospitably in their cells. Once we had visited all the holy places we desired, especially the places the children of Israel touched on their journeying to and from the mountain of God, and after seeing the holy men who dwelt there, in the name of God, we returned to Pharan. Though I must always give thanks to God for all things, I shall not speak about the many favors which He deigned to confer upon me in spite of my unworthiness and lack of merit, in allowing me to travel through all these places, which I did not deserve. Yet I cannot sufficiently thank all those holy men who so willingly consented to receive my humble person in their cells and above all to guide me through all the places which I was forever seeking out, following Holy Scripture. Many of the holy men who dwelt on the mountain of God and around it, that is to say, those who were more robust in body, were kind enough to guide us as far as Pharan.

Once we had arrived at Pharan, which is thirty-five miles from Sinai, we had to stop there for two days in order to rest. On the third day, after an early morning departure, we arrived once again at the resting station which is in the desert of Pharan, where we had stopped on our journey down, as I mentioned earlier. Then, on the following day, after replenishing once again our water supply, we proceeded a short distance through the mountains and arrived at the resting station which was right above the sea. This is the spot where one comes out from among the mountains and once again begins to walk right beside the sea, so near the sea that at times the waves strike the animals' feet; yet at other times the route is through the desert at one hundred, two hundred, and sometimes as many as five hundred feet from the sea. There is no road there at all, only the sands of the desert all around. The Pharanites, who are accustomed to move about there with their camels, place markers for themselves here and there. It is by aiming for these markers that they travel by day. At night, however, the camels follow the markers. To be brief, from force of habit, the Pharanites move more skillfully and securely about this place at night than it is possible for other men to travel in places where there is an open road.

It was here on our return journey that we came out of the mountains, at the same spot where we had entered them on our way down. And once again we approached the sea. On their way back from Sinai, the children of Israel followed the route by which they had gone to the mountain of God as far as this same place, where we came out of the mountains and where we once again reached the Red Sea. From here on we now retraced the way by which we had come. From this place, however, the children of Israel went their own route, as it is written in the books of the holy man Moses. But we returned to Clysma by the same route and by the same resting stations by which we had come. When we arrived back at Clysma, we had to rest there once again, because we had travelled a very sandy route through the desert.

Chapters 22–23

After I had returned to Antioch, I remained there for a whole week, until whatever was necessary for our journey had been prepared. I then set out from Antioch and, after journeying for several days, arrived in the province called Cilicia, the capital city of which is Tarsus, the same Tarsus in which I had already been on my trip down to Jerusalem. Since the shrine of Saint Thecla is located a three-day journey from Tarsus, in Isauria, it was a great pleasure for me to go there, particularly since it was so near at hand.

I set out from Tarsus and I came to a certain city by the sea, still in Cilicia, called Pompeiopolis. From there I crossed over into the regions of Isauria, and I stayed at a city called Corycus. On the third day I arrived at a city called Seleucia of Isauria. On arriving there, I went to the bishop, a very holy man and a former monk. I also saw there in the same city a very beautiful church. Since it is around fifteen hundred feet from the city to the shrine of Saint Thecla, which lies beyond the city on a rather flat hill, I thought it best to go out there to make the overnight stop which I had to make.

At the holy church there is nothing but countless monastic cells for men and women. I met there a very dear friend of mine, and a person to whose way of life everyone in the East bears witness, the holy deaconess Marthana, whom I had met in Jerusalem, where she had come to pray. She governs these monastic cells of *aputactitae*, or virgins. Would I ever be able to describe how great was her joy and mine when she saw me? But to return to the subject: There are many cells all over the hill, and in the middle there is a large wall which encloses the church where the shrine is. It is a very beautiful shrine. The wall is set there to guard the church against the Isaurians, who are evil men, who frequently rob and who might try to do something against the monastery which is established there. Having arrived there in the name of God, a prayer was said at the shrine and the complete Acts of Saint Thecla was read. I then gave unceasing thanks to Christ our God, who granted to me, an unworthy woman and in no way deserving, the fulfillment of my desires in all things. And so, after spending two days there seeing the holy monks and the *aputactitae*, both men and women, who live there, and after praying and receiving Communion, I returned to Tarsus and to my journey.

I made a three-day stop before setting out on my journey from there, in the name of God. On the same day I arrived at the resting station called Mansocrenae, located at the base of Mount Tarsus, and I stopped there. The next day I climbed Mount Tarsus and travelled by a route, already known to me, through several provinces that I had already crossed on my journey down, that is, Cappadocia, Galatia, and Bithynia. Then I arrived at Chalcedon, where I stopped because of the very famous shrine of Saint Euphemia, already known to me from before. On the following day, after crossing the sea, I arrived in Constantinople, giving thanks to Christ our God who deigned to bestow such favor on me, an unworthy and undeserving person. Not only did He deign to fulfill my desire to go there, but He granted also the means of visiting what I desired to see, and of returning again to Constantinople.

After arriving there, I did not cease giving thanks to Jesus our God, who had deigned to bestow His grace upon me, in the various churches, that of the apostles and the numerous shrines that are here. As I send this letter to Your Charity and to you, reverend ladies, it is already my intention to go, in the name of Christ our God, to Asia, that is, to Ephesus, to pray at the shrine of the holy and blessed apostle John. If, after this, I am still living, I will either tell Your Charity in person—if God will deign to grant that—about whatever other places I shall have come to know, or certainly I will write you of it in letters, if there is anything else I have in mind. You, my sisters, my light, kindly remember me, whether I live or die.[53]

As these excerpts illustrate, Egeria's diary is a peculiar—if charming—document in many respects. On the one hand, it purports to be a narrative told in the first person to a specific audience (the "reverend sisters"), in which specific events of the author's journeys are described in detail. On the other hand, the account is so lacking in specificity beyond the description of the holy sites visited that the reader has very little idea of the narrator's views on anything besides her absolute belief in the validity of the Bible as confirmed by observation of the topographical features of the Old Testament narrative. Egeria's entire account of her travels seems to exist for no other purpose than to demonstrate to her audience the relationship between site and text. The narrator's "I" thus becomes subordinated to her central emphasis on validating—and almost reliving—biblical experience through visits to the very sites at which a particular event was reported to have occurred.

Besides its focus on the topography of the Bible (a feature that has made it invaluable to biblical archaeologists) the formulaic style of Egeria's narrative (mentioned previously) results in the visit to each new site being described in much the same way, including, for example, the reading of relevant biblical passages and praise of the local monks for their kindliness and their service as guides to the site. Coupled with this formulaic quality is a characteristic that Spitzer has identified as Egeria's "recapitulative" style, well exemplified in the excerpts presented above.[54] For example, in the description of the valley below Mt. Sinai (chapter 5), the story of the golden calf from Exodus 32:20 is alluded to three different times, each without reference to the other. Rather than subordinating the elements of her narrative, Egeria tends to repeat some item already mentioned and then to add further detail or to pivot from the repeated item to some new detail, thus moving through her narrative by recapitulation and expansion rather than by strictly logical progression.

While it is true that Egeria's style is formulaic and recapitulative—elements that lend the account a kind of epic tone—it may be going too far to speculate, as Spitzer does, that we are dealing here with an "idealized account of an ideal pilgrimage."[55] Despite its impersonal characteristics, we should perhaps not remove the diary so far from the realm of autobiography. It does seem, after all, to be a record of one woman's personal mission in life to visit sacred sites and to record that experience for her audience. Even in the few excerpts included above, one can easily note the recurrent theme of the personal fulfillment of the author's spiritual desire to set foot on sacred ground. She speaks repeatedly of her wish to visit the holy sites of the Old Testament and her satisfaction upon so doing. In chapter 5, for example, she expresses her gratitude to the monks "who so willingly consented to receive my humble person in their cells and above all to guide me through all the places which I was forever seeking out, following Holy Scripture." In chapter 23, in the context of her visit with the deaconess Marthana, she tells of her prayers of thanks to Jesus, "who granted me, an unworthy woman and in no way deserving, the fulfillment of my desires in all things." Coupled with her expression of fulfillment, we find here the motif of Christian humility, also a recurrent theme in the diary.

Another quality of the diary which suggests that we are dealing with autobiography—not idealization—is the implicit close relationship between author and audience. Despite the lack of concrete details about either in the extant portion of the manuscript, it is not difficult to detect a sense of intimacy between author and addressees. In the final paragraph of the excerpts above, for example, Egeria twice refers (in the Latin version, that is) to the "sisters" to whom she writes as "lumen meum" ("my light"), and it is clear throughout that her account is written expressly for them. As she concludes at the end of chapter 23, she will either recount her next adventures to the sisters in person upon her return, or she will report them in writing ("scriptis nuntiabo").

Given the limitation of her apparent purpose in writing the journal, we can still claim Egeria's pilgrimage narrative as the earliest surviving example of a diary that gives universal validation to an individual woman's personal experience. She does at least mention her friend Marthana by name, and she may have alluded to other contemporaries by name in the missing two-thirds of the text. Certainly her intrepid desire to undertake long, difficult, and at times dangerous trips in order to fulfil her spiritual needs comes through vividly in her account. (There is a reference to a protective escort of soldiers in chapter 9.) Her repeated addresses to her audience constantly remind us that the narrator is a woman speaking to other women. The fact that none of the male "actors" in the extant part of the account is mentioned by name—though their holiness and courteousness are certainly stressed—reduces their presence in the story simply to conduits for the validation of biblical experience through the narrator. In other words, it is the female "I" that experiences truth and transmits that truth to a female audience.

Barring the discovery of another, more complete copy of the manuscript of the so-called *Itinerarium Egeriae*, we will probably never know exactly who its author was or under what circumstances she was able to undertake her journeys through biblical lands in search of spiritual truth. But the fact remains that an account survives—albeit in incomplete form—of a fifth-century A.D. woman's lengthy travels to confirm the foundation on which her own religious beliefs rested, along with those of her female associates, whoever they may have been, perhaps nuns at a convent somewhere in Spain or France. Like women's diaries of later times that record literal and spiritual journeys, Egeria's travel diary adds a significant piece to the mosaic of female experience in a world that is still to this day defined largely from a male perspective.

Conclusion

The record recounted in this chapter shows that—at least on a limited scale, women in Rome wrote Latin elegiac poetry, oratory, and prose letters and memoirs. From the second century B.C., we have some (disputed) evidence of the letters of Cornelia, mother of the Gracchi; from the first century B.C., we know of the speech of Hortensia delivered in the Roman Forum to protest the war tax to be levied on her and her fellow aristocratic women. From the period of the end of the first century B.C. to after the turn of the century, we have six love poems in the elegiac tradition written by Sulpicia, whose directness of description (whether of happiness or separation or infidelity) gives her poems grace and charm. Among the successors of these Roman writers, we find women authors in the Christian-Latin tradition such as Proba (fourth century A.D.), whose cento based on Vergil tells of the life of Christ, and Egeria (fifth century A.D.), whose travelogue about the religious sites that she visited in Palestine represents the earliest woman's diary of which we know.

6 *Conclusion*

Even though the number of authors whom I have chronicled here is not large by modern standards, in many ways the record is astonishing. Far from having only one woman writer of antiquity—Sappho—as we might be led to believe by a typical modern account, we possess tangible evidence of several handfuls of women authors whose voices can still be heard or of whom there is at least some report.

A review of the genres represented by the women authors of ancient Greece and Rome makes clear that the medium of lyric and elegiac poetry was the one in which the most successful—or at least the most influential—women writers worked.[1] Egeria's prose is interesting for its Latinity and its historical value, but for real artistry and enduring literary qualities, we must look to Sappho or Nossis or Sulpicia. The flourishing of the female voice within the medium of lyric and elegiac poetry is not at all surprising, for these forms required no public support or participation by the author in public affairs. Given the social restrictions placed on women, we would hardly expect them to have produced, for example, Greek drama, which was written for large-scale public production in connection with state-sponsored religious festivals. Of course we need also to be aware of another factor that shapes our view of what women in antiquity wrote—the ease of preservation. Short verse is on the whole more likely to be quoted or anthologized than long treatises or other large-scale works. Still, even with allowances for such a likelihood, women writing in Greek, at any rate, seemed to favor the lyric and elegiac traditions.

An overview of the themes and subject matter treated by women writers of antiquity reveals a nearly total absence of some of the topics favored among so many of their male counterparts, especially battles and politics (historical or mythological). Instead, women writers tended to focus on such things as emotions, lovers, friendship, folk motifs, spiritual and ritualistic matters, various aspects of daily living, children, and pets. Sappho, for example, may call on Aphrodite to be her "comrade-in-arms" or talk about the superiority of what one loves over cavalry and infantry, but these are only occasional metaphors and analogies—actual battles have no place in her repertory of songs. By contrast, war is central in the poetry of some of her male counterparts from Archaic Greece—Alcaeus, Archilochus, and Tyrtaeus, to name a few. The closest we come to battle songs among any of our women writers are the two epigrams by Anyte in which she commemorates a fallen soldier, one epigram by her that is a dedicatory poem for a spear, and one epigram by Nossis dedicating captured armor.

The themes of love relationships and friendships recur in many of the writers I have discussed. Sappho, who speaks of "Eros, weaver of stories," is of course the poet of love par excellence. As we have seen, Nossis saw herself as a latter-day Sappho, and the indications are that Eros and Aphrodite are central to her poetry. Erinna, too, seems to focus on the close relationship (whether erotic or not) between the Erinna-narrator and her childhood friend, Baukis. Sulpicia, to judge from the six extant epigrams, also makes Eros her central theme, focusing on the relationship of the speaker of the poems with "Cerinthus." In Egeria's travel diary, I noted the importance of the female addressees (the "sisters," whoever they may have been) and the apparent close relationship between author and audience.

Although the standard classical mythological framework is evident in most of the authors I have discussed, these women writers tended to incorporate somewhat more folk material and local legends than did their male counterparts. Korinna is an obvious example, as contrasted with Pindar. She speaks in mythological terms of local mountains and rivers, whereas he tends to focus on panhellenic myths and to address a wider audience.

Women writers frequently stressed spiritual and ritualistic matters. Sappho, for example, describes the temple festivities conducted in honor of Aphrodite and elsewhere alludes to women standing around a moonlit altar; Proba urges her readers to celebrate Christian rites; and Egeria recounts her journey to the Holy Land in search of confirmation of biblical truth.

Not surprisingly, the realm of daily living, the household, and children often provided the women writers of Greece and Rome with their themes. We may recall Sappho's reference to a beautiful child more precious than all of Lydia, Anyte's description of a girl mourning for her pet grasshopper and cicada, Nossis' prayer to Artemis on behalf of a woman suffering the pangs of childbirth, and Myia's instructions on the correct method for the care and feeding of newborns. In a sense, the record of human experience preserved for us in the remains of these women's words parallels the archaeological record of antiquity in that it gives us a partial picture of the way people—including women and children—lived. Some literary "pots and pans" provide a useful counterbalance to the picture of the public and professional arenas recorded by male writers.

Dangerous though it is to generalize about matters of style, particularly in dealing with so many fragmentary works, straightforwardness and simplicity seem to be characteristic of many of the writers whom I have examined. Allusion, indirection, punning, and elaborate rhetorical figures are not present to the extent that we generally find them in the work of male writers of the ancient world. (A similar trend is revealed in a recent comparison of songs by male and female troubadours of the 13th century, in which the author points out that "the [women's] verse is rhymed, but there is less word play and less interest in the exercise of craft than in the men's poems; the women prefer the more straight-forward speech of conversation."[2])

Although again generalization is made difficult by the scattered and fragmentary nature of the evidence, one notably absent feature of the works I have examined is any sense of a pathological state of the woman as writer. By this I do not mean that the writers do not express suffering or anxiety, but rather that they do not seem to feel anxious about their role as writer in the way that later women authors do. To Amy Lowell's concern over the "strange, isolated little family" of women writers of the past whom she wishes she could speak with, we may add, to cite just one further example, May Sarton's reference in "My Sisters, O My Sisters" to "we who are writing women and strange monsters."[3] It would be interesting to know to what extent the sense of strangeness, peculiarity, or even monstrosity among modern women writers has been shaped by the critical context in which they do their work. As Alicia Ostriker has noted, "We seldom encounter, in praise of women poets, terms like *great, powerful, forceful, masterly, violent, large,* or *true.* The language used to express literary admiration in general presumes the masculinity of the author. . . ."[4] We have only to recall the ancient conception of the nine Muses, the female deities who inspire all the arts, along with the ancient evaluation of Sappho as the "tenth Muse," to see—by contrast—the inherently female nature of literary creativity according to the classical mode of thinking. We may speculate, at any rate, that the women writers of antiquity found certain genres in which they were comfortable expressing themselves, particularly lyric and elegiac poetry, and that they were supported in their efforts by a selected audience whom they addressed, whether Sappho's fellow aristocrats on Lesbos, Leontion's community within Epicurus' Garden in Athens, or the "sisters" to whom Egeria makes her report.

Despite the many voices of writing women of the classical world that have been irretrievably silenced, a surprising number of their traces allow for partial reconstruction of what has generally been overlooked altogether. Two contemporary writers, one a feminist theorist (Dale Spender) and the other a poet (Adrienne Rich), offer much that is worth pondering on the question of silence and the history of women:

Women's past is at least as rich as men's; that we do not know about it, that we encounter only interruptions and silence when we seek it, is part of our oppression. Unless and until we can reconstruct our past, draw on it, and *transmit it to the next generation*, our oppression persists.[5]

The entire history of women's struggle for self-determination has been muffled in silence over and over. One serious cultural obstacle encountered by any feminist writer is that each feminist work has tended to be received as if it emerged from nowhere; as if each of us had lived, thought, and worked without any historical past or contextual present. This is one of the ways in which women's work and thinking has been made to seem sporadic, errant, orphaned of any tradition of its own.[6]

I hope that this volume has lessened the sense of mutedness by pointing the way toward the origins of the tradition of women writers in the West. Certainly there is room for further study, both of the women discussed or mentioned in this book and of their successors in the Byzantine and medieval traditions.[7] Fortunately, studies of Renaissance and later women writers have now begun to appear with some regularity, and scholars are also turning their attention to the tradition of women writers in Japan and other non-Western countries.[8] Although it is difficult to reach back to earlier times and to cultures quite different from our own, it is important that we try to recover as much as we can. Faint though the voices of the women of Greek and Roman antiquity may be in some cases, their sound, if we listen carefully enough, can fill many of the gaps and silences of women's past.

Notes
Bibliography
Index

Notes

Chapter 1

1. Plato, *Anthologia Palatina* 9.506, in *The Greek Anthology*, ed. and trans. W. R. Paton (London: Heinemann, 1948). All translations in this chapter are my own. References to the original texts are given in the appropriate notes below.

2. For excellent studies of Archaic Greece, see T. J. Dunbabin, *The Greeks and Their Eastern Neighbors* (London: Society for the Promotion of Hellenic Studies, 1957) and Oswyn Murray, *Early Greece* (Atlantic Highlands, N.J.: Humanities Press, 1980).

3. P. N. Ure, "The Outer Greek World in the Sixth Century," in *Cambridge Ancient History* (Cambridge: Cambridge University Press, 1926), 4:99.

4. See Janet A. Fairweather, "Biographies of Ancient Writers," *Ancient Society* 5 (1974): 231–75 and Mary R. Lefkowitz, *The Lives of the Greek Poets* (Baltimore: Johns Hopkins University Press, 1981).

5. For summaries of the biographical tradition (and, in some cases, uncritical acceptance of it), see W. Aly, "Sappho," in *Real-Encyclopädie der Klassischen Altertumswissenschaft* and Wilhelm Schmid and Otto Stählin, *Geschichte der Griechischen Literatur* (Munich: Beck, 1929), 1:417–29.

6. Alcaeus, Z 61, in *Poetarum Lesbiorum Fragmenta*, ed. Edgar Lobel and Denys Page (Oxford: Clarendon Press, 1963). The adjective that I have translated as *holy* ("*agnos*") also carries the sense of "pure."

7. See Jane McIntosh Snyder, "The Web of Song: Weaving Imagery in Homer and the Lyric Poets," *Classical Journal* 76 (1981): 193–96 and Denys Page, *Sappho and Alcaeus* (Oxford: Clarendon Press, 1955), 296 n. 2.

8. My interpretation owes much to Gregory Nagy, "Phaethon, Sappho's Phaon, and the White Rocks of Leukas," *Harvard Studies in Classical Philology* 77 (1973): 137–77.

9. The motif of the bed of lettuce found in the Aphrodite-Phaon story also appears in some versions of the Aphrodite-Adonis story. See Marcel Detienne, *The Gardens of Adonis: Spices in Greek Mythology* (Sussex: Har-

vester, 1977) 67–71, who points out that the Greeks connected lettuce with impotence.

10. There is some evidence that Sappho did mention Phaon; cf. fragment 211, in *Poetarum Lesbiorum Fragmenta*, ed. Edgar Lobel and Denys Page (Oxford: Clarendon Press, 1963).

11. Menander, fragment 258K, in *Menandri . . . quae supersunt*, ed. A. Koerte (Leipzig: Teubner, 1957).

12. Ovid, *Heroides* 15.47–50, *P. Ovidius Naso*, ed. Rudolf Ehwald (Leipzig: Teubner, 1915–24).

13. Howard Jacobson, *Ovid's Heroides* (Princeton: Princeton University Press, 1974), 297. As he notes (277–78), the authenticity of the Sappho epistle has been the subject of fierce debate.

14. On the musical instrument most commonly associated with Sappho, see Jane McIntosh Snyder, "The *Barbitos* in the Classical Period," *Classical Journal* 67 (1972): 331–40. For a list of ancient representations of Sappho, see Gisela M. A. Richter, *The Portraits of the Greeks* (London: Phaidon Press, 1965), 1:70–72. Besides the museum numbers, these vases are here identified by the page numbers on which they appear in John D. Beazley, *Attic Red-Figure Vase-Painters*, 2d ed. (Oxford: Clarendon Press, 1963), abbreviated ARV², and *Paralipomena* (Oxford: Clarendon Press, 1971), abbreviated Para.

15. Cicero, *In Verrem* 2.4.126, *Marcus Tullius Cicero: Scripta Quae Manserunt Omnia*, ed. F. Mark et al. (Leipzig: Teubner, 1914–38).

16. Adrienne Rich, "Vesuvius at Home: The Power of Emily Dickinson," in *On Lies, Secrets, and Silence: Selected Prose 1966–1978* (New York: Norton, 1979), 163. See also Mary R. Lefkowitz, "Critical Stereotypes and the Poetry of Sappho," *Greek, Roman, and Byzantine Studies* 14 (1973): 113–23.

17. Aelianus *apud Stobaeus Anthologion*, 3.29.58, *Ioannis Stobaei Anthologium*, ed. C. Wachsmuth and O. Hense (Berlin: Weidmann, 1884–1912); cf. Valerius Maximus, 8.7,14, *Valerii Maximi Factorum et Dictorum Memorabilium Libri Novem*, ed. C. Kempf (Stuttgart: Teubner, 1966).

18. Herodotus, 2.134–35, *Herodoti Historiae*, ed. C. Hude (Oxford: Clarendon Press, 1908).

19. John M. Edmonds, ed. *The Fragments of Attic Comedy* (Leiden: E. J. Brill, 1957–61), 2:263; for other examples see Edmonds, *Fragments*, 1:483; 2:161, 327, 623; 3:133.

20. Edmonds, *Fragments*, 2:350.

21. Edmonds, *Fragments*, 3:133. Although it is difficult to generalize on the basis of such fragments, it seems quite likely that the comic derision of Sappho in the fourth century may have been the basis for much of the later criticism of her moral character. For an appraisal of the scholarship of F. G. Welcker in this area, see William M. Calder III, "F. G. Welcker's *Sapphobild* and its Reception in Wilamowitz," *Hermes* 49 (1986): 131–56.

22. Aristotle, *Rhetorica* 1398 b 12, *Aristotelis Opera*, ed. I. Bekker (Oxford: Oxford University Press, 1837).

23. Antipater of Thessaloniki, *Anthologia Palatina* 9.26, in *The Greek Anthology*, ed. and trans. W. R. Paton (London: Heinemann, 1948). For other examples from the Roman period, see David M. Robinson, *Sappho and Her Influence* (1924; reprint, New York: Cooper Square, 1963,) 119–33.

24. Tatianus, *Ad Graecos* 53A, *Tatianus: Oratio ad Graecos*, ed. J. K. T. Otto (Wiesbaden: M. Sändig, 1969).

25. Lucian, *Dialogi Meretricii* 5, *Luciani Opera*, ed. M. D. MacLeod (Oxford: Clarendon Press, 1972).

26. "Sappho" in *Suidae Lexicon*, ed. Ada Adler (Leipzig: Teubner, 1928–1938); cf. Aly, "Sappho." Much of the supposedly biographical information summarized above is derived from the *Suda*.

27. L. D. Reynolds and N. G. Wilson, *Scribes and Scholars: A Guide to the Transmission of Greek and Latin Literature* (Oxford: Clarendon Press, 1974), 44.

28. John Lyly, *Sapho and Phao, The Complete Works of John Lyly*, ed. R. Warwick Bond (Oxford: Clarendon Press, 1967), (1.2).

29. Examples are collected by Henry Thornton Wharton, ed., *Sappho: Memoir, Text, Selected Renderings, and a Literal Translation* (1898; reprint, Amsterdam: Liberac, 1974), 51–64.

30. Maurice Thompson, "The Sapphic Secret," *Atlantic Monthly* 73 (1894): 371–72.

31. Mary Mills Patrick, *Sappho and the Island of Lesbos* (Boston: Houghton Mifflin, 1912), 100. Along the same lines, she imagines that "it was part of Sappho's profession, as the head of her school, to write poetry and to teach her pupils how to compose, and such poems were perhaps intended to serve as models in giving a concrete expression to the deeper emotions" (111). An updated version of essentially the same view is presented by Judith Hallett, "Sappho and Her Social Context: Sense and Sensuality," *Signs* 4 (1979): 447–64; she presents Sappho as a sort of professor of "sensual awareness and sexual self-esteem" (450), qualities which she supposedly instilled in young brides-to-be. For a more general study of women's poetry (and poetry written for female choruses) as *paideia*, see Claude Calame, *Les Choeurs de jeunes filles en Grèce archaïque* (Rome: Edizioni dell' Ateneo & Bizzarri, 1977), 2 vols.

32. Ulrich von Wilamowitz-Moellendorff, *Sappho und Simonides: Untersuchungen über griechische Lyriker* (Berlin: Weidmann, 1913), 17–78. On Wilamowitz' attitude of "romantic chivalry" toward Sappho, see Richard Jenkyns, *Three Classical Poets: Sappho, Catullus, and Juvenal* (London: Duckworth, 1982), 1–5.

33. J. B. Bury, ed., *Greek Literature from the Eighth Century to the Persian*

Wars, vol. 4 of *Cambridge Ancient History* (Cambridge: Cambridge University Press, 1926), 498.

34. Page, 144.

35. David M. Robinson, 44.

36. Dolores Klaich, *Woman + Woman: Attitudes toward Lesbianism* (New York: William Morrow, 1974), 160.

37. For a comprehensive survey of the scholarship on Sappho since the seventeenth century, see Helmut Saake, *Sapphostudien* (Munich: F. Schöningh, 1972), 13–36.

38. My translations of Sappho throughout this chapter are based on the Greek text in a standard edition, *Poetarum Lesbiorum Fragmenta*, ed. Edgar Lobel and Denys Page (Oxford: Clarendon Press, 1963). The translations are numbered according to this edition as well. I use ellipses to indicate where gaps in the text occur and square brackets to show where I have added words to fill out the sense. For excellent summaries of recent scholarly articles on Sappho's poetry, see Douglas E. Gerber, "Studies in Greek Lyric Poetry: 1967–1975," *Classical World* 70 (1976): 106–15. On the importance of recognizing the fragmentary nature of most Greek lyric, see W. R. Johnson, *The Idea of Lyric* (Berkeley: University of California Press, 1982), 24–26.

39. For the former view, see Paul Friedrich, *The Meaning of Aphrodite* (Chicago: University of Chicago Press, 1978) 108; for the latter, Page 16. Tilmar Krischer ("Sapphos Ode an Aphrodite," *Hermes* 96 [1968]: 1–14) rightly concludes that Aphrodite is presented as offering real—if more psychological than pragmatic—help.

40. Herodotus, 2.134–35.

41. Alcaeus, G1 129.

42. [Longinus], *De Sublimitate* 10, *ta symbainonta tais erotikais maniais pathemata*, ed. D. A. Russell (Oxford: Clarendon Press), 1968.

43. Wilamowitz-Moellendorff, 58–59.

44. Page 30–33.

45. Max Treu, *Sappho* (Munich: Ernst Heimeran, 1954), 178–79; Hermann Frankel, *Early Greek Poetry and Philosophy*, trans. Moses Hadas and James Willis (New York: Harcourt Brace Jovanovich, 1973), 176; Thomas McEvilley, "Sappho, Fragment Thirty-One: The Face Behind the Mask," *Phoenix* 32 (1978): 1–18.

46. Odysseus Tsagarakis, *Self-Expression in Early Greek Lyric, Elegiac, and Iambic Poetry* (Wiesbaden: Franz Steiner, 1977), 75–76.

47. George Devereux, "The Nature of Sappho's Seizure in Fr. 31 LP as Evidence of Her Inversion," *Classical Quarterly* 20 (1970): 27–34; for opposing views, see M. Marcovich, "Sappho: Fr. 31: Anxiety Attack or Love Declaration?," *Classical Quarterly* 22 (1972): 19–32 and G. L. Koniaris, "On Sappho, Fr. 31 (L.-P.)," *Philologus* 112 (1968): 173–86. The interpretation presented here owes much to Mary R. Lefkowitz, "Critical Stereotypes."

48. On the association of love and death in Sappho, see D. D. Boedeker, "Sappho and Acheron," in *Arktouros: Hellenic Studies Presented to Bernard M. W. Knox*, ed. Glen W. Bowersock, Walter Burkert, and Michael C. J. Putnam (Berlin: Walter de Gruyter, 1979), 40–52. On *chloros*, see Eleanor Irwin, *Colour Terms in Greek Poetry* (Toronto: Hakkert, 1974), 31–78.

49. See William H. Race, *The Classical Priamel from Homer to Boethius*, *Mnemosyne*. suppl. 74 (Leiden: E. J. Brill, 1982).

50. Page, 57.

51. See, for example, Gary Wills, "The Sapphic 'Umvertung aller Werte,' " *American Journal of Philology* 88 (1967): 434–42. Cf. Page, 53: "The sequence of thought might have been clearer." In the view of Jack Winkler, "there is a charming parody of logical argumentation in these stanzas" ("Gardens of Nymphs: Public and Private in Sappho's Lyrics," *Women's Studies* 8 [1981]: 74).

52. On Sappho's emphasis on the active choices made by Helen, see Page DuBois, "Sappho and Helen," *Arethusa* 11 (1978): 89–99.

53. Wilamowitz-Moellendorff, 51.

54. Page, 83.

55. Anne Burnett, "Desire and Memory (Sappho Frag. 94)," *Classical Philology* 74 (1979): 25; she notes (26 n. 37) that "it is hard to avoid the conclusion that the scholarly determination to discover a miserable woman behind Sappho's poems is connected with the scholarly recognition of the nature of the love she refers to. The unexpressed reasoning seems to be unnatural, therefore unhappy." Burnett expands her ideas on the role of memory in Sappho's songs in general in *Three Archaic Poets* (Cambridge: Harvard University Press, 1983), 277–313. On the importance of the memory of past intimacies in fragment 94, see also Eva Stehle Stigers, "Sappho's Private World," *Women's Studies* 8 (1981): 54–56.

56. Thomas McEvilley, "Sapphic Imagery and Frag. 96," *Hermes* 101 (1973): 274. See also Rebecca Hague, "Sappho's Consolation to Atthis, fr. 96 LP," *American Journal of Philology* 105 (1984): 29–36.

57. For a summary of what is known of the contents of each of the nine books, see Page 112–16; Book 1 alone contained 1320 lines.

58. Aristophanes, *Peace* 1352–53, *Aristophanis Comoediae*, ed. F. W. Hall, 2 vols. (Oxford: Clarendon Press, 1906–07).

59. On Greek attitudes towards lesbianism, see Kenneth J. Dover, *Greek Homosexuality* (Cambridge: Harvard University Press, 1978), 171–84.

60. Readers who know some Greek will find the Greek text along with excellent translations in Willis Barnstone, trans., *Sappho* (New York: New York University Press, 1965). There is a very useful collection of all the ancient *testimonia* and the fragments (in Greek with English translation) in Sappho, *Greek Lyric*, trans. David A. Campbell, vol. 1, Loeb Classical Library (Cambridge: Harvard University Press, 1982). Also recommended is Mary Barnard, trans., *Sappho: A New Translation* (Berkeley: University

of California Press, 1958). Other versions include Guy Davenport, trans., *Sappho: Poems and Fragments* (Ann Arbor: University of Michigan Press, 1965) and Suzy Q. Groden, trans., *Sappho* (Indianapolis: Bobbs-Merrill, 1966); see also Guy Davenport, trans., *Archilochos, Sappho, Alkman: Three Lyric Poets of the Late Greek Bronze Age* (Berkeley: University of California Press, 1980).

61. Algernon Charles Swinburne, "Anactoria," in *Poems* (London: Chatto and Windus, 1904), 1:58.

62. See Pierre Louÿs, *Collected Works*, trans. Mitchell S. Buck et al. (New York: Boni and Liveright, 1926).

63. Wilamowitz-Moellendorff, 63. For a more balanced appraisal of Louÿs' literary output, see H. P. Clive, *Pierre Louÿs (1870–1925): A Biography* (Oxford: Clarendon Press, 1978).

64. Cf. William Pratt, ed., *The Imagist Poem* (New York: Dutton, 1963), 17–19.

65. Hilda Doolittle, *Collected Poems of H.D.* (New York: Boni and Liveright, 1925), 191–92; see also Thomas B. Swann, *The Classical World of H.D.* (Lincoln: University of Nebraska Press, 1962), 109–21.

66. Olga Broumas, "Demeter," in *Beginning with O* (New Haven: Yale University Press, 1977), 21. For a more detailed analysis of the relationship between Sappho and various twentieth-century poets, particularly Renée Vivien and H.D., see Susan Gubar, "Sapphistries," *Signs* 10 (1984): 43–62. See also Judy Grahn, *The Highest Apple: Sappho and the Lesbian Poetic Tradition* (San Francisco: Spinsters, Ink, 1985).

67. Amy Lowell, "The Sisters," in *The Complete Poetical Works* (Boston: Houghton Mifflin, 1955), 459.

Chapter 2

1. Even more shadowy than Megalostrata are two women poets who may have lived in the late Archaic period, Kleobulina and Charixena, about whom practically nothing is known. On the former, cf. Schmid and Stählin, 1:372 n. 3 and F. A. Wright, "The Women Poets of Greece," *Fortnightly Review* ns 113 (1923): 326.

2. For a good general description of Spartan life and culture, see L. F. Fitzhardinge, *The Spartans* (London: Thames and Hudson, 1980).

3. Alkman, 59(b), in *Poetae Melici Graeci*, ed. Denys Page (Oxford: Clarendon Press, 1962). All translations in this chapter are my own. References to the original texts are given in the appropriate notes below.

4. Athenaeus, 13. 600D, *Athenaeus: Dipnosophistarum Libri XV*, ed. G. Kaibel, 3 vols. (Leipzig: Teubner, 1887–90).

5. For basic information about the nature and structure of such odes, as well as detailed discussion of six of them, see Mary R. Lefkowitz, *The*

Victory Ode: An Introduction (Park Ridge, N.J.: Noyes Press, 1976). An excellent general introduction may also be found in Frank J. Nisetich, *Pindar's Victory Songs* (Baltimore: Johns Hopkins University Press, 1980), 1–77.

6. On the dubious significance of stories about literary "pupils," see Lefkowitz, *Lives,* especially 63–65. On the statue A. Kalkmann ("Tatians Nachrichten über Kunstwerke," *Rheinisches Museum* 42 [1887]: 489–524) points out that of the statues of women poets named by Tatian, only one (Silanion's statue) is known to us from other sources. He attempts to discredit Tatian's credibility and claims that his list of statues is worthless to the history of art, a view not necessarily shared by art historians (e.g., A. Allen and J. Frel, "A Date for Corinna," *Classical Journal* 68 [1972]: 26–30).

7. Plutarch, *Quaestiones Graecae* 40, *Plutarch's Moralia,* ed. and trans. F. C. Babbitt, 16 vols. (London: Heinemann, 1938–63).

8. See Fairweather, n. 6.

9. Pausanias, 9.22.2, *Pausanias's Description of Greece,* ed. J. G. Frazer, 6 vols. (New York: Biblo and Tannen, 1965).

10. Pausanias, 9.22.2.

11. Aelian, *Varia Historia* 13.25, *Claudius Aelianus: Varia Historia,* ed. Mervin R. Dilts (Leipzig: Teubner, 1974). On the misreading see H. J. Rose, "Pindar and Korinna," *Classical Review* 48 (1934): 8.

12. Plutarch, *De gloria Atheniensium* 347F; cf. scholiast on Aristophanes, *Acharnenses* 720, *Scholia in Aristophanem,* ed. W. J. W. Koster, 4 vols. (Groningen: J. B. Wolters, 1960–64).

13. E. Lobel, "Corinna," *Hermes* 65 (1930): 356–65.

14. Scholarship favoring the early date includes *Frühgriechische Lyriker,* ed. Zoltan Franyó and Bruno Snell (Berlin: Akademie Verlag, 1976), 3:13; Allen and Frel; Kurt Latte, "Die Lebenzeit der Korinna," *Eranos* 54 (1956): 57–67; *Euterpe,* ed. Douglas E. Gerber (Amsterdam: Hakkert, 1970), 394–95; Umbertina Lisi, *Poetesse Greche* (Catania: Studio Editoriale Moderno, 1933) 110; and C. M. Bowra, "The Date of Corinna," *Classical Review* 45 (1931): 4–5. Scholarship arguing for (or at least tending to favor) a post-fifth-century date includes M. L. West, "Corinna," *Classical Quarterly* 20 (1970): 277–87; Pierre Guillon, "Corinne et les Oracles Béotiens: La Consultation d'Asopos," *Bulletin de Correspondance Hellénique* 82 (1958): 47–60; and *Corinna,* ed. Denys Page (London: Society for the Promotion of Hellenic Studies, 1953), 65–84.

15. Tatianus, *Ad Graecos* 52B. See Allen and Frel, n. 13.

16. In my translations of the poems throughout this chapter, words that appear within square brackets have been added to fill out the sense of the fragments. The Greek text for Korinna, Praxilla, and Telesilla is in *Poetae Melici Graeci* [*PMG*], ed. Denys Page (Oxford: Clarendon Press, 1962),

the numbering system of which I have used throughout. A more detailed study of the fragments of Korinna may be found in Jane McIntosh Snyder, "Korinna's 'Glorious Songs of Heroes,' " *Eranos* 82 (1984): 1–10.

17. Scholiast on Euripides, *Phoenissae* 26, *Scholia in Euripidem*, ed. E. Schwartz, 2 vols. (Berlin: G. Reimer, 1887–91).

18. Pseudo-Plutarch, *De musica* 14.

19. Homer, *Iliad* 21.212ff, *Homeri Ilias*, ed. Thomas W. Allen (Oxford: Clarendon Press, 1931).

20. Lisi, 112 n.7.

21. This point is made by Lisi, 117.

22. Lisi, 122.

23. West, "Corinna," 280.

24. *Frühgriechische Lyriker*, 3:133. It should be noted that there is some doubt about the spelling and etymology of the term; see Pierre Chantraine, ed., *Dictionnaire Étymologique de la Langue Grecque* (Paris: Klincksieck, 1968), 1:217 and H. G. Liddell et al., eds., *Greek-English Lexicon: Supplement* (Oxford: Clarendon Press, 1968), s.v. [ϝ]εροῖα. See also Dee Lesser Clayman, "The Meaning of Corinna's ϝεροῖα," *Classical Quarterly* 28 (1978): 396–97, who argues convincingly for the reading ϝεροῖα and translates the term as "The Narratives."

25. Schmid-Stählin, 444.

26. Propertius, 2.3.22 *Sexti Properti Carmina*, ed. E. A. Barber (Oxford: Clarendon Press, 1953). For a discussion of the difficulties in the Latin text here, see L. Richardson, Jr., *Propertius: Elegies I–IV* (Norman: University of Oklahoma Press, 1977), 220–21.

27. Statius, *Silvae* 5.3.156–58, *P. Papini Stati Silvae*, ed. I. Phillimore (Oxford: Clarendon Press, 1904).

28. For translation of *tenuis* as "meagre," see J. H. Mozley, ed. and trans., *Statius* (London: Heinemann, 1967), 1:316.

29. Tatianus, *Ad Graecos* 52B. For a study of the art and history of the city, see Audrey Griffin, *Sikyon* (Oxford: Clarendon Press, 1982).

30. Athenaeus, 15.694A.

31. For a thorough discussion of the whole group of *skolia*, see Richard Reitzenstein, *Epigramm und Skolion* (1893; reprint, Hildesheim: G. Olms, 1970), 3–44.

32. Scholiast on Aristophanes, *Wasps* 1238, *PMG*, 388.

33. Scholiast on Aristophanes, *Thesmophoriazusae* 528, cited in *PMG*, 388.

34. Athenaeus 15.695D.

35. Wilamowitz' view is summarized in the 1912 edition of Schmid and Stählin, 1:204. The 1929 edition retracts this supposition.

36. Lisi prefers the latter (140).

37. W. Aly, "Praxilla von Sikyon," in *Real-Encyclopädie der Klassischen Altertumswissenschaft*.

38. Zenobius, 4.21, *Corpus Paroemiographorum Graecorum*, ed. E. L. von Leutsch and F. G. Schneidewin, 2 vols. (Hildesheim: G. Olms, 1958).

39. For the interpretation here, see Lisi, 140 and Aly, "Praxilla." Their views contradict those of Schmid and Stählin, who speak of the fragment's "comic coloration" (451).

40. Herodotus, 5.67.

41. For a discussion of the topography, cf. R. A. Tomlinson, *Argos and the Argolid* (Ithaca, N.Y.: Cornell University Press, 1972), 15–28.

42. Herodotus, 3.131.

43. Pausanias, 2.19.3.

44. Pausanias, 2.20.8. For discussion of this prophecy within the context of other Delphic responses, see Joseph Fontenrose, *The Delphic Oracle* (Berkeley: University of California Press, 1978), 71, 169.

45. Plutarch, *De mulierum virtutibus* 245C. J. G. Frazer (ed., *Pausanias's Description of Greece* [New York: Biblo and Tannen, 1965]) cites other examples of this sort of exchange of costume; in his view, "the story of the defence of Argos by Telesilla may have been invented to explain this festival" (3:197). See also Pierre Vidal-Naquet, "Slavery and the Rule of Women," in *Myth, Religion, and Society*, ed. Raymond L. Gordon (Cambridge: Cambridge University Press, 1981), 191–93.

46. Maximus Tyrius, 37.5, *Maximi Tyrii Philosophumena*, ed. H. Hobein (Leipzig: Teubner, 1910). Cf. Lisi, 135. Tyrtaeus of Sparta provides a good example of the tendency to derive biographical material from the author's works. Because he wrote martial poetry, he was supposed to have been an Athenian (who but Athenians could be poets?) who became a Spartan general. Cf. Lefkowitz, *Lives*, 38–39.

47. Tomlinson, 94; see also 209.

48. For a romantic interpretation of Telesilla as love poet and soldier, see "Telesila" [*sic*] in Doolittle, 272–75.

49. Marilyn B. Skinner, "Corinna of Tanagra and Her Audience," *Tulsa Studies in Women's Literature* 2 (1983): 10. For a different view, see Nancy Demand, *Thebes in the Fifth Century* (London: Routledge and Kegan Paul, 1982), who believes that Korinna's choral poetry for girls may represent "a Boeotian parallel for Sappho's circle" (98).

Chapter 3

1. For a convenient summary, see F. W. Walbank, *The Hellenistic World* (Cambridge: Harvard University Press, 1982), especially 176–97. See also Michael Grant, *From Alexander to Cleopatra: The Hellenistic World* (New York: Scribner, 1982).

2. See Cornelius Vermeule, *Greek Art: Sokrates to Sulla* (Boston: Museum of Fine Arts, 1980), 55–60.

3. Meleager, *Anthologia Palatina* 4.1, in *The Greek Anthology: Hellenistic Epigrams*, ed. A. S. F. Gow and D. L. Page, 2 vols. (Cambridge: Cambridge University Press, 1965). All translations in this chapter are my own. References to the original texts are given in the appropriate notes below.

4. On the question of authorship, see A. S. F. Gow and D. L. Page, eds., *The Greek Anthology: Hellenistic Epigrams* (Cambridge: Cambridge University Press, 1965), 2:91.

5. Pollux 5.48, in *Pollucis Onomasticon*, ed. E. Bethe, 3 vols. (Leipzig: Teubner, 1900–1937).

6. Gow and Page summarize the evidence for her date (90).

7. Georg Luck, "Die Dichterinnen der griechischen Anthologie," *Museum Helveticum* 11 (1954): 181.

8. Pausanias, 10.38.13. See Sylvia Barnard, "Hellenistic Women Poets," *Classical Journal* 73 (1978): 208–10, who notes parallels with the miracles connected with the poet-kitharode Arion. See Gow and Page, 2:89 for a summary of opinions regarding Pausanias' description of Anyte as "ten poiesasan ta epe" ("the one who wrote verse").

9. For parallels in the pseudobiography of other Hellenistic poets, see Lefkowitz, *Lives*, 117–35.

10. Except for the hexameter lines of Moero and "The Distaff" and two hexameter lines of Erinna (see below), the Greek text of the poems on which I have based my translations throughout this chapter is *The Greek Anthology: Hellenistic Epigrams*, ed. A. S. F. Gow and D. L. Page (Cambridge: Cambridge University Press, 1965), vol. 1. The numbers assigned to the epigrams of Anyte, Nossis, Moero, and Erinna are for convenience in discussing them; the numbers cited in parentheses refer to the traditional numbering within the *Anthologia Palatina* (*Anth. Pal.*) and the *Anthologia Planudea* (*Anth. Plan.*), which together constitute what is today called *The Greek Anthology*. An exception is Anyte's poem 9, which is preserved in Pollux. The edition of *The Greek Anthology* by Gow and Page is restricted chronologically to the Hellenistic period; for the complete collection, see *The Greek Anthology*, ed. and trans. W. R. Paton (London: Heinemann, 1948). Useful overviews of the authors discussed in this chapter and in chapter 2 (as well as of two more obscure figures, Hedyle and Melinno) will be forthcoming in articles by Marilyn B. Skinner in the *Dictionary of Continental Women Writers*.

11. There is uncertainty about the authorship of 6 and 7; see Gow and Page, 2:102–4. I have omitted two further epitaphs sometimes attributed to Anyte which are almost certainly not by her (*Anth. Pal.* 7.236, 7.492).

12. On such incriptions see G. Herrlinger, *Totenklage um Tiere in der antiken Dichtung* (Stuttgart: W. Kohlhammer, 1930), 39.

13. Marcus Argentarius, *Anthologia Palatina* 7.364, in *The Greek Anthology: Hellenistic Epigrams*, ed. A. S. F. Gow and D. L. Page, 2 vols. (Cambridge: Cambridge University Press).

14. Pausanias, 8.45.5.

15. W. W. Tarn, *Hellenistic Civilisation* (Cleveland: World Publishing, 1961), 276. For the range of more recent views, cf. Peter Jay, ed. and trans. (*The Greek Anthology and Other Ancient Epigrams* [London: Allen Lane, 1973]), who says that "Anyte introduced the pastoral element into the epigram" (13); Grant, who states that "in a limited sense" Anyte may have been a forerunner of Theocritus' pastoral style (267); and Robert Coleman, ed., *Vergil: Eclogues* (Cambridge: Cambridge University Press, 1977), who argues that the "pastoral motifs" in Anyte's work are merely a common feature of Hellenistic epigrams in general (2). For an early attempt to demonstrate the existence of pastoral poetry in Arcadia before Theocritus, see Reitzenstein, 121–36.

16. T. B. L. Webster, *Hellenistic Poetry and Art* (New York: Barnes and Noble, 1964), 3.

17. Richard Aldington, *Medallions in Clay* (New York: Alfred A. Knopf, 1921), preface. For Aldington's connections with Ezra Pound and other imagists, see Janice S. Robinson, *H.D.: The Life and Work of an American Poet* (Boston: Houghton Mifflin, 1982), 29–61 *passim*.

18. Wright, 328. For a new critical edition of Anyte's poems (with commentary in English), see *The Epigrams: Anyte*, ed. D. Geoghagan (Rome: Edizioni dell' Ateneo & Bizzarri, 1979).

19. Polybius, 12.5.9, *Polybii Historiae*, ed. L. Dindorf, 5 vols. (Stuttgart: Teubner, 1962–63).

20. On the question of Nossis' dates, see Gow and Page, 2:437. For a detailed study of the apparently woman-centered character of Nossis' epigrams, see Marilyn B. Skinner, "Nossis *Thelyglossos*: Lesbian Author and Male Audience," in a collection of papers, edited by Sarah B. Pomeroy, from the 1987 Berkshire Conference of Women Historians, Wellesley College (Chapel Hill: University of North Carolina Press, forthcoming).

21. Meleager, *Anthologia Palatina* 4.1.9–10.

22. Heather White, *Essays in Hellenistic Poetry* (Amsterdam: J. C. Gieben, 1980), 19–20. Cf. Pherecrates 108.29 in Edmonds, 1:248 for *rhoda* as *pudenda muliebra*. For various other attempts to interpret the lines, see Gow and Page, 2:435–36.

23. See Reitzenstein, 139.

24. See, however, Marilyn B. Skinner, "Greek Women and the Metronymic: A Note on an Epigram by Nossis," *Ancient History Bulletin* 1 (1987): 39–42, who argues persuasively that Greek women may have regularly addressed each other using the mother's name rather than the patronymic and thus that Nossis' epigram illustrates a "gender-specific speech trait," not a cultural phenomenon of Locri.

25. Livy, 24.3.3, *Titi Livi Ab Urbe Condita*, ed. Robert S. Conway and C. F. Walters, 4 vols. (Oxford: Clarendon Press, 1914–34).

26. Athenaeus 13.572F.

27. See Gow and Page, 2:441–42.

28. For examples of the vase paintings, see Arthur D. Trendall and T. B. L. Webster, *Illustrations of Greek Drama* (London: Phaidon, 1971), 117–44.

29. "Homeric Hymn to Apollo" 3.16, *The Homeric Hymns*, ed. T. W. Allen, W. R. Halliday, and E. E. Sikes (Oxford: Clarendon Press, 1936).

30. Doolittle, "Nossis," 230–31. For a discussion of other poems relating to H.D.'s view of poetry, see Vincent Quinn, *Hilda Doolittle* (New York: Twayne, 1967), 40.

31. Meleager, *Anthologia Palatina* 4.1.5.

32. Tatianus, *Ad Graecos* 33. For Moero's probable dates, see Gow and Page, 2:414; cf. Reitzenstein 135n.

33. Moero in Athenaeus, 11.491B.

34. Udo W. Scholz, "Erinna," *Antike und Abendland* 18 (1973): 15–40. See also Crusius, "Erinna," in *Real-Encyclopädie der Klassischen Altertumswissenschaft*: "Es ist sehr fraglich, ob diese Suidasnotizen als selbständige Überlieferung neben den Epigrammen angesehen werden dürfen" ("It is highly questionable whether these notes in the *Suda* should be regarded as representing a tradition independent of the epigrams").

35. On Asclepiades' dates, see Gow and Page, 2:115; on Erinna's dates, 2:281. Donald N. Levin, "Quaestiones Erinneanae" (*Harvard Studies in Classical Philology* 66 [1962]: 194) argues for Erinna's dates as approximately 400–350 B.C. See also Luck, "Die Dichterinnen," 170, who regards Erinna as earlier than Anyte, Moero, and Nossis.

36. Gow and Page, 2:32.

37. On the textual difficulty in lines 5–6, see Giuseppe Giangrande, "An Epigram of Erinna," *Classical Review* ns 19 (1969): 1–3.

38. Erinna in Athenaeus, 7.283 D.

39. Reitzenstein, 143; cf. Gow and Page, 2:282. They also point out that four anonymous hexameter lines attributed by Blass to Erinna could be from "The Distaff." The lines concern girls' celebration of Demeter; cf. Erinna, in *Collectanea Alexandrina*, ed. J. U. Powell (Oxford: Clarendon Press, 1925), 186.

40. Levin, 193.

41. Erinna, "The Distaff," in M. L. West, "Erinna," *Zeitschrift für Papyrologie und Epigraphik* 25 (1977): 95–119. The numbers at the left refer to the line numbers of the fragment in the edition by M. L. West. See also Erinna, in *Supplementum Hellenisticum*, ed. Hugh Lloyd-Jones and Peter Parsons (Berlin: Walter de Gruyter, 1983), 186–92.

42. For the former view, cf. C. M. Bowra, "Erinna's *Lament for Baucis*," in *Greek Poetry and Life: Essays Presented to Gilbert Murray* (Oxford: Clarendon Press, 1936), 341; for the latter, M. L. West, "Erinna," *Zeitschrift für Papyrologie und Epigraphik* 25 (1977): 118–19.

43. Bowra, "Erinna's Lament," 339–40; but see Averil Cameron and Alan Cameron, "Erinna's Distaff," *Classical Quarterly* ns 19 (1969): 285–88, who argue that *elakate* would have been an appropriate original title.

44. Bowra, "Erinna's Lament," 328; cf. Pollux 9.125.

45. Marylin B. Arthur, "The Tortoise and the Mirror: Erinna PSI 1090," *Classical World* 74 (1980): 53–65.

46. For a nearly contemporary reference (third century B.C.) to both Erinna and Nossis making the latter the daughter of Erinna and associating them both with lesbianism, see Herodas 6.20 and the commentary by I. C. Cunningham, ed., *Herodas Mimiambi* (Oxford: Clarendon Press, 1971), 164.

47. For these three theories, see Bowra, "Erinna's Lament," 334; West, "Erinna," 108–9; and Marilyn B. Skinner, "Briseis, the Trojan Women, and Erinna," *Classical World* 75 (1982): 268.

48. Sarah B. Pomeroy, "Supplementary Notes on Erinna," *Zeitschrift für Epigraphik* 32 (1978): 17–21.

49. Arthur, 56–57; Skinner, "Briseis," 265 n. 2.

50. Sylvia Barnard, 208.

51. Meleager, *Anthologia Palatina* 4.1.32.

52. *Inscriptiones Graecae* (Berlin: G. Reimer, 1873–), 9.2.62. Cf. Sarah B. Pomeroy, *Goddesses, Whores, Wives, and Slaves* (New York: Schocken, 1975), 126 and "*Technikai kai Mousikai*," *American Journal of Ancient History* 2 (1977): 54–55.

53. Athenaeus 7.297B.

54. For a recent study of the Greek *oikos* (house) from an anthropological point of view, see Sally C. Humphreys, *The Family, Women and Death: Comparative Studies* (London: Routledge and Kegan Paul, 1983), 16–21.

55. For an exception, cf. Theocritus, *Idylls* 28, in *Bucolici Graeci*, ed. A. S. F. Gow (Oxford: Clarendon Press, 1952). See also Snyder, "The Web of Song," 193–96.

56. For some much later epigrams, written in Aeolic Greek by a woman named Julia Balbilla while she was on a tour of Egypt with the emperor Hadrian (second century A.D.), see *Corpus Inscriptionum Graecarum* (Berlin: G. Reimer, 1828–77), 3, numbers 4725–30 and the edition by A. and E. Bernand, eds. *Les Inscriptions grecques et latines du Colosse de Memnon* (Cairo: Institut français d'archéologie orientale, 1960). The poems were inscribed as graffiti on the feet and legs of a colossal statue of Memnon near Thebes.

Chapter 4

1. The Latin text was reprinted in 1830, but Ménage's work lay largely ignored until 1984, when it was again translated into English, this time in a complete edition which provides full documentation of Ménage's sources;

see Gilles Ménage, *The History of Women Philosophers*, trans. Beatrice H. Zedler (Lanham, Maryland: University Press of America, 1984).

2. For a brief survey of women connected with the Garden, see Jane McIntosh Snyder, "Lucretius and the Status of Women," *Classical Bulletin* 53 (1976): 17–20.

3. For a list of ancient references to Leontion, see Fritz Geyer, "Leontion," in *Real-Encyclopädie der Klassischen Altertumswissenschaft*.

4. Cicero, *Natura Deorum* 1.93. All translations in this chapter are my own. References to the original texts are given in the appropriate notes below.

5. Pliny, *Naturalis Historia, praefatio* 29, in *Plinius Secundus: Natural History*, ed. H. Rackham, 10 vols. (London: Heinemann, 1938–63).

6. Diogenes Laertius, 10.4, 10.5, 10.6, 10.7, 10.23, in *Lives of Eminent Philosophers*, ed. R. D. Hicks, 2 vols. (Cambridge: Harvard University Press, 1950). Cf. Athenaeus, 13.588b, who says that Leontion was Epicurus' mistress, and that "even when she began to be a philosopher, she did not stop being a *hetaira*, but openly consorted with all the Epicureans in the Garden, even in front of Epicurus."

7. Diogenes Laertius, 10.5.

8. The text has been heavily restored, including all but three letters of Leontion's name; see Christian Jensen, "Ein neuer Brief Epikurs," *Abhandlungen der Gesellschaft der Wissenschaften zu Göttingen*, Philologisch-Historische Klasse, III 5 (1933): 1–94, especially 17, 45–47.

9. On the appearance of several of these names in contemporary inscriptions, see Catherine J. Castner, "Epicurean *Hetairai* as Dedicants to Healing Deities?," *Greek, Roman, and Byzantine Studies* 23 (1982): 51–57. Cf. L. Robert, "Inscriptions de Julia Gordos et du Nord-Est de la Lydie," *Hellenica* 6 (1948): 90.

10. Cicero, *De Finibus* 2.21.68. He criticizes the Epicureans as pleasure seekers who never mention such heroic figures as Solon, Miltiades, Themistokles, etc.: "Wouldn't it be better to say something about such heroes than in so many tomes to speak about Themista?"

11. My account of Cynicism follows the conclusions drawn by Donald R. Dudley, *A History of Cynicism* (London: Methuen, 1937), especially 34–36, 42–53.

12. A somewhat more lurid follow-up is preserved in Apuleius, 2.49, *Apulei Platonici: Florida*, ed. Rudolf Helm (Leipzig: Teubner, 1959) according to which Krates took Hipparchia off to a public portico, where the two of them engaged in sexual intercourse in broad daylight.

13. Diogenes Laertius, 6.96–98.

14. "Hipparchia," in *Suidae Lexicon*.

15. Menander, *Didumi*, fragment 117K, in *Menandri . . . quae supersunt*, ed. A. Koerte (Leipzig: Teubner, 1957).

16. Antipater of Sidon, *Anthologia Palatina* 7.413, in *The Greek Anthology:*

Hellenistic Epigrams, ed. A. S. F. Gow and D. L. Page, 2 vols. (Cambridge: Cambridge University Press, 1965).

17. Ovid, *Metamorphoses* 10.560–707.

18. For a useful summary and evaluation of the sources for Pythagoras' life and philosophy, see Peter Gorman, *Pythagoras: A Life* (London: Routledge and Kegan Paul, 1979). A more skeptical approach may be found in Walter Burkert, *Lore and Science in Ancient Pythagoreanism*, trans. Edwin L. Minar, Jr. (Cambridge: Harvard University Press, 1972), who does point out, however, that "though many sources may be late and not very reliable, more must lie behind them all than a simple zero."

19. See Gorman, 153–70.

20. Diogenes Laertius, 8.42–43.

21. Iamblichus, *Iamblichi De Vita Pythagorica Liber*, ed. L. Deubner (Leipzig: Teubner, 1937).

22. Nancy Demand, 132–33.

23. Sarah Pomeroy, *Goddesses*, 133–34. An argument for the authenticity of the letters may be found in Mary Ellen Waith, "Authenticating the Fragments and Letters," in *A History of Women Philosophers*, ed. Mary Ellen Waith (Dordrecht: Nijhoff, 1987), 1:59–74.

24. For another example, a letter attributed to Periktione on the subject of "harmony" as applied to women, see Pomeroy, *Goddesses*, 134–36. The letter advises marital fidelity, moderation in diet and dress, and toleration of a husband's drunkenness, infidelity, etc. A French translation of Periktione's letter and several others not included in the present chapter may be found in Clarisse Bader, *La Femme Grecque* (Paris: Librairie Academique, 1873), 2:404–29. For an alphabetical listing of all of these authors and their contemporaries, along with a very brief summary of the contents of their work, see Holger Thesleff, ed., *An Introduction to the Pythagorean Writings of the Hellenistic Period*, Acta Academiae Aboensis, vol. 24.3 (Åbo: Åbo Akademi, 1961), 7–29.

25. "Theano," in *Suidae Lexicon*.

26. The aulos, a wind instrument similar to an oboe, was particularly associated with drinking parties and with paid female entertainers, including prostitutes. Cf. Plato, *Symposium* 176e, *Platonis Opera*, ed. I. Burnet, 5 vols. (Oxford: Clarendon Press, 1901).

27. Theano, in *The Pythagorean Texts of the Hellenistic Period*, ed. Holger Thesleff, Acta Academiae Aboensis, ser. A, (Åbo: Åbo Akademi, 1965), 30:197.

28. Myia, in *The Pythagorean Texts of the Hellenistic Period*, ed. Holger Thesleff, Acta Academiae Aboensis, ser. A, (Åbo: Åbo Akademi, 1965), 30:123.

29. Theano, 30:200.

30. Sarah Pomeroy, *Women in Hellenistic Egypt* (New York: Schocken, 1984), 68.

31. Charles Kingsley, *Hypatia, or New Foes with an Old Face* (New York: Thomas Crowell, 1897), 127.

32. Margaret Alic, *Hypatia's Heritage: A History of Women in Science from Antiquity through the Nineteenth Century* (Boston: Beacon Press, 1986), 41.

33. Photius, *Bibliotheca* 242.38 in *Photius: Bibliothèque*, ed. and trans. R. Henry, 3 vols. (Paris: Société d'édition "Les belles lettres," 1959–62).

34. See Karl Praechter, "Hypatia," *Real-Encyclopädie der Klassischen Altertumswissenschaft*.

35. Marilyn Bailey Ogilvie, *Women in Science: Antiquity through the Nineteenth Century* (Cambridge: MIT Press, 1986), 104.

36. "Hypatia," in *Suidae Lexicon*.

37. Sokrates, *Historia Ecclesiastica* 7.15, in *Patrologiae, Patrum Graecorum Traditio Catholica*, ed. J.-P. Migne (Paris: 1864).

38. Mary R. Lefkowitz, *Women in Greek Myth* (London: Duckworth, 1986), 107.

39. For an excellent discussion of Gibbon's account in particular and of Hypatia's philosophical interests in general, see J. M. Rist, "Hypatia," *Phoenix* 19 (1965): 214–25. A very detailed study of the ancient and Byzantine sources may be found in R. Hoche, "Hypatia, die Tochter Theons," *Philologus* 15 (1860): 435–74.

40. "Hypatia," in *Suidae Lexicon*.

41. Synesios, epistle 10, in *Epistolographi Graeci*, ed. R. Hercher (Paris: Didot, 1871), 638–739. For Synesios' letters in the context of early Christianity and the classical background, see Stanley K. Stowers, *Letter Writing in Greco-Roman Antiquity* (Philadelphia: Westminster Press, 1986).

42. Synesios, epistle 81.

43. E.g., see Charles C. Gillispie, ed., *Dictionary of Scientific Biography* (New York: Scribner, 1972), 615–16. For a diagram of the hydroscope, see Morris R. Cohen and I. E. Drabkin, *A Source Book in Greek Science* (Cambridge: Harvard University Press, 1958), 240.

44. Synesios, epistle 15.

45. On the succession, see R. T. Wallis, *Neoplatonism* (London: Duckworth, 1972), 138–78.

46. Palladas, *Anthologia Palatina* 9.400, in *The Greek Anthology*, ed. and trans. W. R. Paton, 5 vols. (London: Heinemann, 1948).

47. Georg Luck, "Palladas—Christian or Pagan?," *Harvard Studies in Classical Philology* 63 (1958): 455–71 points out that "oikos" in line 2 cannot mean "constellation." He argues, however, that Palladas is not the author of the poem and that the Hypatia referred to is not our Hypatia.

48. Clement of Alexandria, *Stromateis* 4.14, in *Clemens, Titus Flavius: Les Stromates*, ed. C. Mondesert et al., 2 vols. (Paris: Cerf, 1951). Clement, a second-century A.D. convert to Christianity, quotes Theano on the subject of the soul's immortality: "Theano the Pythagorean writes, 'For those who

have acted wickedly, life would indeed be a feast of evils and death a great boon, when they die, unless the soul were immortal' " (*Stromateis* 4.7). Cf. Theano, 201.

Chapter 5

1. Eve Cantarella, *Pandora's Daughters: The Role and Status of Women in Greek and Roman Antiquity*, trans. Maureen B. Fant (Baltimore: Johns Hopkins University Press, 1987), 178.

2. See, for example, Peter Dronke, *Women Writers of the Middle Ages: A Critical Study of Texts from Perpetua to Marguerite Porete* (Cambridge: Cambridge University Press, 1984), 19–21.

3. Quintilian, *Institutio Oratoria*, 1.1.6, in *Marcus Fabius Quintilianus: Institutionis Oratoriae Libri XII*, ed. L. Radermacher, 2 vols. (Leipzig: Teubner, 1965). With the exception of the excerpt from Egeria's diary (see below), all translations in this chapter are my own. References to the original texts are given in the appropriate notes below.

4. On Laelia, see Cicero, *Brutus* 211.

5. F. Münzer, "Cornelia," in *Real-Encyclopädie der Klassischen Altertumswissenschaft*.

6. Cicero, *Brutus* 211.

7. For the Latin text of the fragments, see Cornelia, *Cornelii Nepotis Vitae cum Fragmentis*, ed. Peter K. Marshall (Leipzig: Teubner, 1977). For a summary listing of bibliography on both sides of the issue of authenticity, see E. von Stern, "Zur Beurteilung der politischen Wirksamkeit des Tiberius und Gaius Gracchus," *Hermes* 56 (1921): 273 n. 1. The case has been reexamined by Hans Ulrich Instinsky, "Zur Echtheitsfrage der Brieffragmente der Cornelia," *Chiron* 1 (1971): 177–89, who concludes that the letters are fictional, perhaps by someone nearly contemporary with the Gracchi.

8. Appian, *Bellum Civile* 4.32-33, in *Appian's Roman History*, ed. and trans. Horace White, 4 vols. (London: Heinemann, 1912–13).

9. Valerius Maximus, 8.3.

10. Tacitus, 4.53.2, in *P. Cornelius Tacitus: Annales*, ed. H. Heubner (Stuttgart: Teubner, 1983).

11. Sallust, *Cataline* 25, in *C. Sallustius Crispus: Catalina, Iugurtha, Fragmenta Ampliora*, ed. A. Kurfess (Leipzig: Teubner, 1968).

12. Propertius, 1.2.27, 2.3.21.

13. Ovid, *Tristia* 3.7.

14. Martial, 10.35, 38 in *M. Valerii Martialis Epigrammaton Libri*, ed. W. Heraeus (Leipzig: Teubner, 1976). Seventy hexameter lines about the expulsion of the philosophers during the reign of Domitian are sometimes attributed to this Sulpicia (a contemporary of Martial); see Sulpicia, *Poetae Latini Minores*, ed. A. Baehrens (Leipzig: Teubner, 1888), 5:93–97.

15. M. Haupt, "Varia," *Hermes* 5 (1871): 32–34.

16. Matthew Santirocco, "Sulpicia Reconsidered," *Classical Journal* 74 (1979): 229–39. My interpretation owes much to this well-reasoned analysis.

17. Ezra Pound, "Horace," *The Criterion* 9 (1929–30); *Arion* 9 (1970): 187.

18. Cf. L. Herrmann, "Reconstruction du livret de Sulpicia," *Latomus* 9 (1950): 35–47.

19. Sulpicia, Tibullus 3.13, in *Tibulli Aliorumque Carminum Libri Tres*, ed. J. P. Postgate (Oxford: Clarendon Press, 1906).

20. See Kirby Flower Smith (ed., *The Elegies of Albius Tibullus* [1913; reprint, New York: American Book, 1979]), who says of her poems that "it seems evident that none of them was ever intended for publication" (79).

21. Smith, 81.

22. Sulpicia, Tibullus 3.14.

23. Reading "suo" rather than "tuo."

24. Sulpicia, Tibullus 3.15.

25. Santirocco, 232.

26. Sulpicia, Tibullus 3.16.

27. Sulpicia, Tibullus 3.17.

28. Sulpicia, Tibullus 3.18.

29. Georg Luck, *The Latin Love Elegy* (New York: Barnes and Noble, 1960), 102.

30. Luck, 101.

31. Santirocco, 237.

32. On the relationship between paganism and Christianity, see R. A. Markus, "Paganism, Christianity and the Latin Classics in the Fourth Century," in *Latin Literature of the Fourth Century*, ed. J. W. Binns (London: Routledge and Kegan Paul, 1974), 1–21.

33. See P. Courcelle, "Les exégèses Chrétiennes de la quatrième églogue," *Revue des Études Anciennes* 59 (1957): 294–319. On centos, see F. Raby, *Christian-Latin Poetry* (Oxford: Clarendon Press, 1927), 16 and Domenico Comparetti, *Vergil in the Middle Ages*, trans. E. F. M. Benecke (1908; reprint, Hamden, Conn.: Archon Books, 1966), 53–54.

34. Maria R. Cacioli, "Adattamenti semantici e Sintattici nel Centone Virgiliano di Proba," *Studi Italiani Filologia Classica* 41 (1969): 188–246.

35. Vergil, *Aeneid* 9.583, 3.426, in *P. Vergili Maronis Opera*, ed. R. A. B. Mynors (Oxford: Clarendon Press, 1969).

36. A recent comprehensive study of the poem may be found in Elizabeth A. Clark and Diane F. Hatch, *The Golden Bough, The Oaken Cross: The Virgilian Cento of Faltonia Betitia Proba* (Chico, Calif.: Scholars Press, 1981). Their study includes the Latin text and a translation (to which I am indebted for the interpretation of a few problematic phrases), several essays, and an extensive bibliography.

37. Proba, line 23, in *Poetae Christiani Minores*, ed. C. Schenkl, vol. 16 of *Corpus Scriptorum Ecclesiasticorum Latinorum* (Vindobonae [Vienna]: F. Tempsky, 1888).

38. Proba, lines 1–55.

39. Vergil, *Aeneid* 1.279.

40. Vergil, *Aeneid* 6.851.

41. Vergil, *Aeneid* 2.777.

42. Proba, lines 693–94.

43. See Markus, 13 and A. Momigliano, "Popular Religious Beliefs and the Late Roman Historians," *Studies in Church History* 8 (1972): 14–15.

44. Isidore of Seville, 5, in *Isidore: De Viris Illustribus*, ed. Carmen C. Merino (Salamanca: Consejo Superior de Investigaciones Científicas, 1964). Cf. Cacioli, 246 n. 1.

45. See Arthur Ludwich, "Eudokia, die Gattin des Kaisers Theodosius II, als Dichterin," *Rheinisches Museum* 37 (1882): 206–25. For the Greek text of her poetry, see Eudocia, *Eudocia Augusta, Proclus Lycius, Claudianus*, ed. Arthur Ludwich (Leipzig: Teubner, 1897). On the new fragment, see Judith Green and Yoram Tsafrir, "Greek Inscriptions from Hammat Gader: A Poem by the Empress Eudocia and Two Building Inscriptions," *Israel Exploration Journal* 32 (1982): 78–91. On Eudocia as a historical figure, see Kenneth G. Holum, *Theodosian Empresses: Women and Imperial Dominion in Late Antiquity* (Berkeley: University of California Press, 1982).

46. For a translation, see Green and Tsafrir, 80.

47. For a study of one other woman author who converted to Christianity, Vibia Perpetua of third-century A.D. Carthage, see Mary R. Lefkowitz, "The Motivation for St. Perpetua's Martyrdom," *Journal of the American Academy of Religion* 44 (1976): 417–21. The account of her execution contains an extended quotation claimed by the (anonymous) narrator to be from her memoirs, including an account of her days in prison and the visions that she had; for the Latin text (with English translation), see Perpetua, 8.2, in *Acts of the Christian Martyrs*, ed. Herbert Musurillo (Oxford: Oxford University Press, 1972).

48. See, for example, Cynthia Huff, *British Women's Diaries* (New York: AMS Press, 1985); of the diaries included in this descriptive bibliography of nineteenth-century manuscripts, fifteen are travel diaries. See also Mary Jane Moffat and Charlotte Painter, eds., *Revelations: Diaries of Women* (New York: Random House, 1974).

49. George E. Gingras, ed. and trans., *Egeria: Diary of a Pilgrimage* (New York: Newman Press, 1970), 7. The following discussion owes much to his lucid introduction. For a listing of bibliography on Egeria, see M. Starowieyski, "Bibliographia Egeriana," *Augustinianum* 19 (1979): 297–317 and Thomas P. Halton and Robert D. Sider, "A Decade of Patristic Scholarship 1970–1979," *Classical World* 76 (1983): 381–82. For a study of later pilgrimage narratives, see Christian K. Zacher, *Curiosity and Pilgrimage*:

The Literature of Discovery in Fourteenth-Century England (Baltimore: Johns Hopkins University Press, 1974).

50. Gingras, 8. For a reexamination of the identity of Egeria, see Hagith S. Sivan, "Piety and Pilgrimage in the Age of Gratian: Who was Egeria?" *Harvard Theological Review* 81 (1988): forthcoming. Egeria's presumed Spanish origins have been questioned by Clifford Weber, "Egeria's Norman Homeland," *Harvard Studies in Classical Philology* 92 (1988): forthcoming, who (on the basis of the word *tumba*) argues persuasively that her homeland must have been France.

51. Gingras, 43; see also J. Ziegler, "Die *Peregrinatio Aetheriae* und das *Onomastikon* des Eusebius," *Biblica* 12 (1931): 70–84.

52. K. P. Harrington, ed., *Medieval Latin* (Chicago: University of Chicago Press, 1962), 1. A short excerpt from Egeria's diary is the first selection in his anthology.

53. Egeria, *Egeria: Diary of a Pilgrimage*, ed. and trans. George E. Gingras (New York: Newman Press, 1970), 51–53, 56–60, 86–89. The translation quoted here is by Gingras.

54. Leo Spitzer, "The Epic Style of the Pilgrim Aetheria," *Comparative Literature* 1 (1949): 225–58.

55. Spitzer, 249.

Chapter 6

1. See Elaine Fantham, "Women in Antiquity: A Selective (and Subjective) Survey 1979–84," *Echos du Monde Classique* 30 ns 5 (1986): 21 n. 22.

2. Meg Bogin, *The Women Troubadours* (New York: Norton, 1980), 13.

3. Lowell, 459; May Sarton, "My Sisters, O My Sisters," in *Collected Poems: 1930–1973* (New York: Norton, 1974), 74–75.

4. Alicia Suskin Ostriker, *Stealing the Language: The Emergence of Women's Poetry in America* (Boston: Beacon Press, 1986), 3.

5. Dale Spender, *Women of Ideas and What Men Have Done to Them* (London: Routledge and Kegan Paul, 1982), 12.

6. Adrienne Rich, "Foreword: On History, Illiteracy, Passivity, Violence, and Women's Culture," in *On Lies, Secrets, and Silence: Selected Prose 1966–1978* (New York: Norton, 1979), 11.

7. One recent study is Katharina M. Wilson, ed., *Medieval Women Writers* (Athens: University of Georgia Press, 1984), which includes (among others) Hrotsvit, Marie de France, and Christine de Pizan. See also chapter 5, n. 2.

8. See, for example, Sandra M. Gilbert and Susan Gubar, eds., *Shakespeare's Sisters: Feminist Essays on Women Poets* (Bloomington: Indiana University Press, 1979); by the same authors, *The Madwoman in the Attic: The Woman Writer and the Nineteenth-Century Literary Imagination* (New Haven: Yale University Press, 1979) and *No Man's Land: The Place of the*

Woman Writer in the Twentieth Century, vol. 1 of *The War of the Words* (New Haven: Yale University Press, 1987). On women writers of song in Japan, see Yung-Hee Kwon, "The Female Entertainment Tradition in Medieval Japan: The Case of the *Asobi*," *Theatre Journal* 40 (1988): 205–16.

Bibliography

Primary Sources

Classical texts in Greek and Latin are included under Primary Sources. For English translations other than Loeb Classical Texts (which include both the original text and a translation), see Secondary Sources.

Aelian. *Claudius Aelianus: Varia Historia*. Edited by Mervin R. Dilts. Leipzig: Teubner, 1974.

Alcaeus. In *Poetarum Lesbiorum Fragmenta*, edited by Edgar Lobel and Denys Page. Oxford: Clarendon Press, 1963.

Alkman. In *Poetae Melici Graeci*, edited by Denys Page. Oxford: Clarendon Press, 1962.

Antipater of Sidon. In *The Greek Anthology: Hellenistic Epigrams*, edited by A. S. F. Gow and D. L. Page. 2 vols. Cambridge: Cambridge University Press, 1965.

Antipater of Thessaloniki. In *The Greek Anthology*, edited and translated by W. R. Paton. 5 vols. London: Heinemann, 1948.

Antiphanes. In *The Greek Anthology: Hellenistic Epigrams*, edited by A. S. F. Gow and D. L. Page. 2 vols. Cambridge: Cambridge University Press, 1965.

Anyte. *The Epigrams: Anyte*. Edited by D. Geoghagan. Rome: Edizioni dell' Ateneo & Bizzari, 1979.

————. In *The Greek Anthology: Hellenistic Epigrams*, edited by A. S. F. Gow and D. L. Page. 2 vols. Cambridge: Cambridge University Press, 1965.

Appian. *Appian's Roman History*. Edited and translated by Horace White. 4 vols. London: Heinemann, 1912–13.

Apuleius. *Apulei Platonici: Florida*. Edited by Rudolf Helm. Leipzig: Teubner, 1959.

Aristophanes. *Aristophanis Comoediae*. Edited by F. W. Hall. 2 vols. Oxford: Clarendon Press, 1906–1907.

Aristotle. *Aristotelis Opera.* Edited by I. Bekker. II vols. Oxford: Oxford University Press, 1837.

Asclepiades. In *The Greek Anthology: Hellenistic Epigrams,* edited by A. S. F. Gow and D. L. Page. 2 vols. Cambridge: Cambridge University Press, 1965.

Athenaeus. *Athenaeus: Dipnosophistarum Libri XV.* Edited by G. Kaibel. 3 vols. Leipzig: Teubner, 1887–90.

Broumas, Olga. *Beginning with O.* New Haven: Yale University Press, 1977.

Catullus. *Catullus: A Commentary.* Edited by C. J. Fordyce. Oxford: Clarendon Press, 1961.

Cicero. *Marcus Tullius Cicero: Scripta Quae Manserunt Omnia.* Edited by F. Mark et al. 40 vols. Leipzig: Teubner, 1914–38.

Clement of Alexandria. *Clemens, Titus Flavius: Les Stromates.* Edited by C. Mondesert, et al. 2 vols. Paris: Cerf, 1951.

Corinna. See Korinna.

Cornelia. *Cornelii Nepotis Vitae cum Fragmentis.* Edited by Peter K. Marshall. Leipzig: Teubner, 1977.

Corpus Inscriptionum Graecarum. Edited by A. Boeckh et al. Berlin: G. Reimer, 1828–77.

Diogenes Laertius. *Lives of Eminent Philosophers.* Edited and translated by R. D. Hicks. 2 vols. Cambridge: Harvard University Press, 1950.

Doolittle, Hilda. *Collected Poems of H.D.* New York: Boni and Liveright, 1925.

Egeria. *Itinerarium Egeriae (Peregrinatio Aetheriae).* Edited by O. Prinz. Vol. 5 of Sammlung Vulgärlateinischer Texte. Heidelberg: Carl Winter, 1960.

Erinna. In Athenaeus, *Athenaeus: Dipnosophistarum Libri XV,* edited by G. Kaibel. 3 vols. Leipzig: Teubner, 1887–90.

———. In *Collectanea Alexandrina,* edited by J. U. Powell. Oxford: Clarendon Press, 1925.

———. In *The Greek Anthology: Hellenistic Epigrams,* edited by A. S. F. Gow and D. L. Page. 2 vols. Cambridge: Cambridge University Press, 1965.

———. In *Supplementum Hellenisticum.* Edited by Hugh Lloyd-Jones and Peter Parsons. Berlin: Walter de Gruyter, 1983.

———. "The Distaff." In M. L. West. "Erinna." *Zeitschrift für Papyrologie und Epigraphik* 25 (1977): 95–119.

Eudocia. *Eudocia Augusta, Proclus Lycius, Claudianus.* Edited by Arthur Ludwich. Leipzig: Teubner, 1897.

Euripides. *Euripidis Fabulae.* Edited by J. Diggle. 2 vols. Oxford: Clarendon Press, 1981.

Herodas. *Herodas Mimiambi.* Edited by I. C. Cunningham. Oxford: Clarendon Press, 1971.

Herodotus. *Herodoti Historiae*. Edited by C. Hude. Oxford: Clarendon Press, 1908.

Homer. *Homeri Ilias*. Edited by Thomas W. Allen. Oxford: Clarendon Press, 1931.

The Homeric Hymns. Edited by T. W. Allen, W. R. Halliday, and E. E. Sikes. Oxford: Clarendon Press, 1936.

Iamblichus. *Iamblichi De Vita Pythagorica Liber*. Edited by L. Deubner. Leipzig: Teubner, 1937.

Inscriptiones Graecae. Berlin: G. Reimer, 1873–.

Isidore of Seville. *Isidore: De Viris Illustribus*. Edited by Carmen C. Merino. Salamanca: Consejo Superior de Investigaciones Cientificas, 1964.

Kingsley, Charles. *Hypatia, or New Foes With an Old Face*. New York: Thomas Crowell, 1897.

Korinna. *Corinna*. Edited by Denys Page. London: Society for the Promotion of Hellenic Studies, 1953.

————. In *Euterpe*, edited by Douglas Gerber. Amsterdam: Hakkert, 1970.

————. In *Frühgriechische Lyriker*, edited by Zoltan Franyó and Bruno Snell. 4 vols. Berlin: Akademie Verlag, 1976.

————. In *Poetae Melici Graeci*, edited by Denys Page. Oxford: Clarendon Press, 1962.

Livy. *Titi Livi Ab Urbe Condita*. Edited by Robert S. Conway and C. F. Walters. 4 vols. Oxford: Clarendon Press, 1914–34.

[Longinus.] *De Sublimitate*. Edited by D. A. Russell. Oxford: Clarendon Press, 1968.

Lowell, Amy. "The Sisters." In *The Complete Poetical Works*. Boston: Houghton Mifflin, 1955.

Lucian. *Luciani Opera*. Edited by M. D. MacLeod. 2 vols. Oxford: Clarendon Press, 1972.

Lyly, John. *The Complete Works of John Lyly*. Edited by R. Warwick Bond. 3 vols. Oxford: Clarendon Press, 1967.

Marcus Argentarius. In *The Greek Anthology: Hellenistic Epigrams*, edited by A. S. F. Gow and D. L. Page. 2 vols. Cambridge: Cambridge University Press, 1965.

Martial. *M. Valerii Martialis Epigrammaton Libri*. Edited by W. Heraeus. Leipzig: Teubner, 1976.

Maximus Tyrius. *Maximi Tyrii Philosophumena*. Edited by H. Hobein. Leipzig: Teubner, 1910.

Meleager. In *The Greek Anthology: Hellenistic Epigrams*, edited by A. S. F. Gow and D. L. Page. 2 vols. Cambridge: Cambridge University Press, 1965.

Menander. *Menandri . . . quae supersunt*. Edited by A. Koerte. Leipzig: Teubner, 1957.

————. *Menandri Reliquiae Selectae*. Edited by F. H. Sandbach. Oxford: Clarendon Press, 1972.

Moero. In Athenaeus, *Athenaeus: Dipnosophistarum Libri XV*, edited by G. Kaibel. 3 vols. Leipzig: Teubner, 1887–90.

——. In *The Greek Anthology: Hellenistic Epigrams*, edited by A. S. F. Gow and D. L. Page. 2 vols. Cambridge: Cambridge University Press, 1965.

Myia. In *The Pythagorean Texts of the Hellenistic Period*, edited by Holger Thesleff. Acta Academiae Aboensis, ser. A. Vol. 30. Åbo: Åbo Akademi, 1965.

Nossis. In *The Greek Anthology: Hellenistic Epigrams*, edited by A. S. F. Gow and D. L. Page. 2 vols. Cambridge: Cambridge University Press, 1965.

Ovid. *P. Ovidius Naso*. Edited by Rudolf Ehwald. 3 vols. Leipzig: Teubner, 1915–24.

Palladas. In *The Greek Anthology*, edited and translated by W. R. Paton. 5 vols. London: Heinemann, 1948.

Pausanias. *Pausanias's Description of Greece*. Edited by J. G. Frazer. 6 vols. New York: Biblo and Tannen, 1965.

Perpetua. In *Acts of the Christian Martyrs*, edited by Herbert Musurillo. Oxford: Oxford University Press, 1972.

Photius. *Photius: Bibliotheque*. Edited and translated by R. Henry. 3 vols. Paris: Société d'édition "Les belles lettres," 1959–62.

Plato. In *The Greek Anthology*. Edited and translated by W. R. Paton. 5 vols. London: Heinemann, 1948.

——. *Platonis Opera*. Edited by I. Burnet. 5 vols. Oxford: Clarendon Press, 1901.

Pliny the Elder. *Plinius Secundus: Natural History*. Edited and translated by H. Rackham. 10 vols. London: Heinemann, 1938–63.

Plutarch. *Plutarch's Moralia*. Edited and translated by F. C. Babbitt. 16 vols. London: Heinemann, 1938–63.

Pollux. *Pollucis Onomasticon*. Edited by E. Bethe. 3 vols. Leipzig: Teubner, 1900–1937.

Polybius. *Polybii Historiae*. Edited by L. Dindorf. 5 vols. Stuttgart: Teubner, 1962–63.

Praxilla. In *Poetae Melici Graeci*, edited by Denys Page. Oxford: Clarendon Press, 1962.

Proba. In *Poetae Christiani Minores*, edited by C. Schenkl. Vol. 16 of *Corpus Scriptorum Ecclesiasticorum Latinorum*, Vindobonae (Vienna): F. Tempsky, 1888.

Propertius. *Sexti Properti Carmina*. Edited by E. A. Barber. Oxford: Clarendon Press, 1953.

Quintilian. *Marcus Fabius Quintilianus: Institutionis Oratoriae Libri XII*. Edited by L. Radermacher. 2 vols. Leipzig: Teubner, 1965.

Sallust. *C. Sallustius Crispus: Catalina, Iugurtha, Fragmenta Ampliora*. Edited by A. Kurfess. Leipzig: Teubner, 1968.

Sappho. In *Euterpe*, edited by Douglas Gerber. Amsterdam: Hakkert, 1970.

———. In *Frühgriechische Lyriker*, edited by Zoltan Franyó and Bruno Snell. 4 vols. Berlin: Akademie Verlag, 1976.

———. In *Greek Lyric*, translated by David A. Campbell. Vol. 1. Loeb Classical Library. Cambridge: Harvard University Press, 1982.

———. In *Poetarum Lesbiorum Fragmenta*, edited by Edgar Lobel and Denys Page. Oxford: Clarendon Press, 1963.

Sarton, May. "My Sisters, O My Sisters." In *Collected Poems: 1930–1973*. New York: Norton, 1974.

Scholiast on Aristophanes. *Scholia in Aristophanem*. Edited by W. J. W. Koster. 4 vols. Groningen: J. B. Wolters, 1960–64.

Scholiast on Euripides. *Scholia in Euripidem*. Edited by E. Schwartz. 2 vols. Berlin: G. Reimer, 1887–91.

Sokrates. In *Patrologiae, Patrum Graecorum Traditio Catholica*, edited by J.-P. Migne. Paris, 1864.

———. *Sokrates Scholasticus: Historia Ecclesiastica Tripartita*. Edited by W. Jacob. Vol. 71 of *Corpus Scriptorum Ecclesiasticorum Latinorum*. Vindobonae (Vienna): Hoelder-Pichler-Tempsky, 1952.

Statius. *P. Papini Stati Silvae*. Edited by I. Phillimore. Oxford: Clarendon Press, 1904.

Stobaeus. *Ioannis Stobaei Anthologium*. Edited by C. Wachsmuth and O. Hense. Berlin: Weidmann, 1884–1912.

Suidae Lexicon. Edited by Ada Adler. 5 vols. Leipzig: Teubner, 1928–38.

Sulpicia. In *Poetae Latini Minores*, edited by A. Baehrens. 6 vols. Leipzig: Teubner, 1888.

———. In *Tibulli Aliorumque Carminum Libri Tres*, edited by J. P. Postgate. Oxford: Clarendon Press, 1906.

Swinburne, Algernon Charles. *Poems*. 6 vols. London: Chatto and Windus, 1904.

Synesios. In *Epistolographi Graeci*, edited by R. Hercher. Paris: Didot, 1871.

Tacitus. *P. Cornelius Tacitus: Annales*. Edited by H. Heubner. Stuttgart: Teubner, 1983.

Tatian. *Tatianus: Oratio ad Graecos*. Edited by J. K. T. Otto. Wiesbaden: M. Sändig, 1969.

Telesilla. In *Poetae Melici Graeci*, edited by Denys Page. Oxford: Clarendon Press, 1962.

Theano. In *The Pythagorean Texts of the Hellenistic Period*, edited by Holger Thesleff. Acta Academiae Aboensis, ser. A, vol. 30. Åbo: Åbo Akademi, 1965.

Theocritus. In *Bucolici Graeci*, edited by A. S. F. Gow. Oxford: Clarendon Press, 1952.

Valerius Maximus. *Valerii Maximi Factorum et Dictorum Memorabilium Libri Novem*. Edited by C. Kempf. Stuttgart: Teubner, 1966.

Vergil. *P. Vergili Maronis Opera.* Edited by R. A. B. Mynors. Oxford: Clarendon Press, 1969.

Zenobius. In *Corpus Paroemiographorum Graecorum*, edited by E. L. von Leutsch and F. G. Schneidewin. 2 vols. and supplement. Hildesheim: G. Olms, 1958.

Secondary Sources

Aldington, Richard. *Medallions in Clay.* New York: Alfred A. Knopf, 1921.

Alic, Margaret. *Hypatia's Heritage: A History of Women in Science from Antiquity through the Nineteenth Century.* Boston: Beacon Press, 1986.

Aly, W. "Praxilla von Sikyon." In *Real-Encyclopädie der Klassischen Altertumswissenschaft.*

————. "Sappho." In *Real-Encyclopädie der Klassischen Altertumswissenschaft.*

Allen, A., and J. Frel. "A Date for Corinna." *Classical Journal* 68 (1972): 26–30.

Arthur, Marylin B. "The Tortoise and the Mirror: Erinna PSI 1090." *Classical World* 74 (1980): 53–65.

Bader, Clarisse. *La Femme Grecque.* Vol. 2. Paris: Librairie Academique, 1873.

Barnard, Mary, trans. *Sappho: A New Translation.* Berkeley: University of California Press, 1958.

Barnard, Sylvia. "Hellenistic Women Poets." *Classical Journal* 73 (1978): 208–10.

Barnstone, Willis, trans. *Sappho.* New York: New York University Press, 1965.

Beazley, John D. *Attic Red-Figure Vase-Painters.* 2d ed. 3 vols. Oxford: Clarendon Press, 1963.

————. *Paralipomena.* Oxford: Clarendon Press, 1971.

Bernand, A., and E. Bernand, eds. *Les Inscriptions grecques et latines du Colosse de Memnon.* Cairo: Institut français d'archéologie orientale, 1960.

Boedeker, D. D. "Sappho and Acheron." In *Arktouros: Hellenic Studies presented to Bernard M. W. Knox*, edited by Glen W. Bowersock, Walter Burkert, and Michael C. J. Putnam, 40–52. Berlin: Walter de Gruyter, 1979.

Bogin, Meg. *The Women Troubadours.* New York: Norton, 1980.

Bowra, C. M. "The Date of Corinna." *Classical Review* 45 (1931): 4–5.

————. "Erinna's *Lament for Baucis.*" In *Greek Poetry and Life: Essays Presented to Gilbert Murray.* Oxford: Clarendon Press, 1936.

Burkert, Walter. *Lore and Science in Ancient Pythagoreanism.* Translated by Edwin L. Minar, Jr. Cambridge: Harvard University Press, 1972.

Burnett, Anne. "Desire and Memory (Sappho Frag. 94)." *Classical Philology* 74 (1979): 16–27.

———. *Three Archaic Poets*. Cambridge: Harvard University Press, 1983.

Bury, J. B., ed. *Greek Literature from the Eighth Century to the Persian Wars*. Vol. 4 of *Cambridge Ancient History*. Cambridge: Cambridge University Press, 1926.

Cacioli, Maria R. "Adattamenti Semantici e Sintattici nel Centone Virgiliano di Proba." *Studi Italiani Filologia Classica* 41 (1969): 188–246.

Calame, Claude. *Les Choeurs de jeunes filles en Grèce archaïque*. 2 vols. Rome: Edizioni dell' Ateneo & Bizzarri, 1977.

Calder, William M., III. "F. G. Welcker's *Sapphobild* and its Reception in Wilamowitz." *Hermes* 49 (1986): 131–56.

Cameron, Averil, and Alan Cameron. "Erinna's Distaff." *Classical Quarterly* ns 19 (1969): 285–88.

Cantarella, Eve. *Pandora's Daughters: The Role and Status of Women in Greek and Roman Antiquity*. Translated by Maureen B. Fant. Baltimore: Johns Hopkins University Press, 1987.

Castner, Catherine J. "Epicurean *Hetairai* as Dedicants to Healing Deities?" *Greek, Roman, and Byzantine Studies* 23 (1982): 51–57.

Chantraine, Pierre, ed. *Dictionaire Étymologique de la Langue Grecque*. 4 vols. Paris: Klincksieck, 1968.

Clark, Elizabeth A., and Diane F. Hatch. *The Golden Bough, The Oaken Cross: The Virgilian Cento of Faltonia Betitia Proba*. Chico, Calif.: Scholars Press, 1981.

Clayman, Dee Lesser. "The Meaning of Corinna's. ϝεροῖα" *Classical Quarterly* 28 (1978): 396–97.

Clive, H. P. *Pierre Louÿs (1870–1925): A Biography*. Oxford: Clarendon Press, 1978.

Cohen, Morris R., and I. E. Drabkin. *A Source Book in Greek Science*. Cambridge: Harvard University Press, 1958.

Coleman, Robert, ed. *Vergil: Eclogues*. Cambridge: Cambridge University Press, 1977.

Comparetti, Domenico. *Vergil in the Middle Ages*. Translated by E. F. M. Benecke. 1908. Reprint. Hamden, Conn.: Archon Books, 1966.

Courcelle, P. "Les exégèses Chrétiennes de la quatrième églogue." *Revue des Études Anciennes* 59 (1957): 294–319.

Crusius. "Erinna." In *Real-Encyclopädie der Klassischen Altertumswissenschaft*.

Davenport, Guy, trans. *Archilochos, Sappho, Alkman: Three Lyric Poets of the Late Greek Bronze Age*. Berkeley: University of California Press, 1980.

———, trans. *Sappho: Poems and Fragments*. Ann Arbor: University of Michigan Press, 1965.

Demand, Nancy. *Thebes in the Fifth Century*. London: Routledge and Kegan Paul, 1982.

Detienne, Marcel. *The Garden of Adonis: Spices in Greek Mythology*. Sussex: Harvester Press, 1977.

Deuel, Leo. "Pearls from Rubbish Heaps: Grenfell and Hunt." In *Testa-*

ments of Time: The Search for the Lost Manuscripts and Records, 132–49. New York: Alfred A. Knopf, 1965.

Devereux, George. "The Nature of Sappho's Seizure in Fr. 31 LP as Evidence of Her Inversion." *Classical Quarterly* 20 (1970): 17–34.

Dover, Kenneth J. *Greek Homosexuality.* Cambridge: Harvard University Press, 1978.

Dronke, Peter. *Women Writers of the Middle Ages: A Critical Study of Texts from Perpetua to Marguerite Porete.* Cambridge: Cambridge University Press, 1984.

DuBois, Page. "Sappho and Helen." *Arethusa* 11 (1978): 89–99.

Dudley, Donald R. *A History of Cynicism.* London: Methuen, 1937.

Dunbabin, T. J. *The Greeks and their Eastern Neighbors.* London: Society for the Promotion of Hellenic Studies, 1957.

Edmonds, John M., ed. *The Fragments of Attic Comedy.* 3 vols. Leiden: E. J. Brill, 1957–61.

Fairweather, Janet A. "Biographies of Ancient Writers." *Ancient Society* 5 (1974): 231–75.

Fantham, Elaine. "Women in Antiquity: A Selective (and Subjective) Survey 1979–84." *Echos du Monde Classique* 30 ns 5 (1986): 1–24.

Fitzhardinge, L. F. *The Spartans.* London: Thames and Hudson, 1980.

Fontenrose, Joseph. *The Delphic Oracle.* Berkeley: University of California Press, 1978.

Frankel, Hermann. *Early Greek Poetry and Philosophy.* Translated by Moses Hadas and James Willis. New York: Harcourt Brace Jovanovich, 1973.

Frazer, J. G., ed. *Pausanias's Description of Greece.* 6 vols. New York: Biblo and Tannen, 1965.

Friedrich, Paul. *The Meaning of Aphrodite.* Chicago: University of Chicago Press, 1978.

Gerber, Douglas E. "Studies in Greek Lyric Poetry: 1967–1975." *Classical World* 70 (1976): 106–15.

Geyer, Fritz. "Leontion." In *Real-Encyclopädie der Klassischen Altertumswissenschaft.*

Giangrande, Giuseppe. "An Epigram of Erinna." *Classical Review* ns 19 (1969): 1–3.

Gilbert, Sandra, M., and Susan Gubar. *The Madwoman in the Attic: The Woman Writer and the Nineteenth-Century Literary Imagination.* New Haven: Yale University Press, 1979.

———. *No Man's Land: The Place of the Woman Writer in the Twentieth Century.* Vol. 1 of *The War of the Words.* New Haven: Yale University Press, 1987.

———. eds. *Shakespeare's Sisters: Feminist Essays on Women Poets.* Bloomington: Indiana University Press, 1979.

Gillispie, Charles C., ed. *Dictionary of Scientific Biography.* New York: Scribner, 1972.

Gingras, George E., ed. and trans. *Egeria: Diary of a Pilgrimage.* New York: Newman Press, 1970.

Goodwater, Leanna. *Women in Antiquity: An Annotated Bibliography.* Metuchen, N.J.: Scarecrow Press, 1975.

Gorman, Peter. *Pythagoras: A Life.* London: Routledge and Kegan Paul, 1979.

Gow, A. S. F., and D. L. Page, eds. *The Greek Anthology: Hellenistic Epigrams.* 2 vols. Cambridge: Cambridge University Press, 1965.

Grahn, Judy. *The Highest Apple: Sappho and the Lesbian Poetic Tradition.* San Francisco: Spinsters, Ink, 1985.

Grant, Michael. *From Alexander to Cleopatra: The Hellenistic World.* New York: Scribner, 1982.

Green, Judith, and Yoram Tsafrir. "Greek Inscriptions from Hammat Gader: A Poem by the Empress Eudocia and Two Building Inscriptions." *Israel Exploration Journal* 32 (1982): 78–91.

Griffin, Audrey. *Sikyon.* Oxford: Clarendon Press, 1982.

Groden, Suzy Q., trans. *The Poems of Sappho.* Indianapolis: Bobbs-Merrill, 1966.

Guillon, Pierre. "Corinne et les Oracles Béotiens: La Consultation d'Asopos." *Bulletin de Correspondance Hellénique* 82 (1958): 47–60.

Gubar, Susan. "Sapphistries." *Signs* 10 (1984): 43–62.

Hague, Rebecca. "Sappho's Consolation to Atthis, fr. 96 LP." *American Journal of Philology* 105 (1984): 29–36.

Hallett, Judith. "Sappho and Her Social Context: Sense and Sensuality." *Signs* 4 (1979): 447–64.

Halton, Thomas P., and Robert D. Sider. "A Decade of Patristic Scholarship 1970–1979." *Classical World* 76 (1983): 381–82.

Harrington, K. P., ed. *Medieval Latin.* Chicago: University of Chicago Press, 1962.

Haupt, M. "Varia." *Hermes* 5 (1871): 21–47.

Herrmann, L. "Reconstruction du livret de Sulpicia." *Latomus* 9 (1950): 35–47.

Herrlinger, G. *Totenklage um Tiere in der antiken Dichtung.* Stuttgart: W. Kohlhammer, 1930.

Hoche, R. "Hypatia, die Tochter Theons." *Philologus* 15 (1860): 435–74.

Holum, Kenneth G. *Theodosian Empresses: Women and Imperial Dominion in Late Antiquity.* Berkeley: University of California Press, 1982.

Huff, Cynthia. *British Women's Diaries.* New York: AMS Press, 1985.

Humphreys, Sally C. *The Family, Women and Death: Comparative Studies.* London: Routledge and Kegan Paul, 1983.

Instinsky, Hans Ulrich. "Zur Echtheitsfrage der Brieffragmente der Cornelia." *Chiron* 1 (1971): 177–89.

Irwin, Eleanor. *Colour Terms in Greek Poetry.* Toronto: Hakkert, 1974.

Jacobson, Howard. *Ovid's Heroides*. Princeton: Princeton University Press, 1974.

Jay, Peter, ed. and trans. *The Greek Anthology and Other Ancient Epigrams*. London: Allen Lane, 1973.

Jenkyns, Richard. *Three Classical Poets: Sappho, Catullus, and Juvenal*. London: Duckworth, 1982.

Jensen, Christian. "Ein neuer Brief Epikurs." *Abhandlungen der Gesellschaft der Wissenschaften zu Göttingen*, Philologisch-Historische Klasse, III 5 (1933): 1–94.

Johnson, W. R. *The Idea of Lyric*. Berkeley: University of California Press, 1982.

Kalkmann, A. "Tatians Nachrichten über Kunstwerke." *Rheinisches Museum* 42 (1887): 489–524.

Klaich, Dolores. *Woman + Woman: Attitudes toward Lesbianism*. New York: William Morrow, 1974.

Koniaris, G. L. "On Sappho, Fr. 31 (L.-P.)." *Philologus* 112 (1968): 173–86.

Krischer, Tilmar. "Sapphos Ode an Aphrodite." *Hermes* 96 (1968): 1–14.

Kwon, Yung-Hee. "The Female Entertainment Tradition in Medieval Japan: The Case of the *Asobi*." *Theatre Journal* 40 (1988): 205–16.

Latte, Kurt. "Die Lebenzeit der Korinna." *Eranos* 54 (1956): 57–67.

Lefkowitz, Mary R. "Critical Stereotypes and the Poetry of Sappho." *Greek, Roman, and Byzantine Studies* 14 (1973): 113–23.

———. *The Lives of the Greek Poets*. Baltimore: Johns Hopkins University Press, 1981.

———. "The Motivation for St. Perpetua's Martyrdom." *Journal of the American Academy of Religion* 44 (1976): 417–21.

———. *The Victory Odes: An Introduction*. Park Ridge, N. J.: Noyes Press, 1976.

———. *Women in Greek Myth*. London: Duckworth, 1986.

Levin, Donald N. "Quaestiones Erinneanae." *Harvard Studies in Classical Philology* 66 (1962): 193–204.

Liddell, H. G., et al., eds. *Greek-English Lexicon: Supplement*. Oxford: Clarendon Press, 1968.

Lisi, Umbertina. *Poetesse Greche*. Catania: Studio Editoriale Moderno, 1933.

Lobel, E. "Corinna." *Hermes* 65 (1930): 356–65.

Louÿs, Pierre. *Collected Works*. Translated by Mitchell S. Buck. New York: Boni and Liveright, 1926.

Luck, Georg. "Die Dichterinnen der griechischen Anthologie." *Museum Helveticum* 11 (1954): 170–87.

———. *The Latin Love Elegy*. New York: Barnes and Noble, 1960.

———. "Palladas—Christian or Pagan?" *Harvard Studies in Classical Philology* 63 (1958): 455–71.

Ludwich, Arthur. "Eudokia, die Gattin des Kaisers Theodosius II, als Dichterin." *Rheinisches Museum* 37 (1882): 206–25.

McEvilley, Thomas. "Sapphic Imagery and Frag. 96." *Hermes* 101 (1973): 257–78.

———. "Sappho, Fragment Thirty-One: The Face Behind the Mask." *Phoenix* 32 (1978): 1–18.

Marcovich, M. "Sappho: Fr. 31: Anxiety Attack or Love Declaration?" *Classical Quarterly* 22 (1972): 19–32.

Markus, R. A. "Paganism, Christianity and the Latin Classics in the Fourth Century." In *Latin Literature of the Fourth Century*, ed. J. W. Binns. London: Routledge and Kegan Paul, 1974.

Ménage, Gilles. *The History of Women Philosophers*. Translated by Beatrice H. Zedler. Lanham, Maryland: University Press of America, 1984.

Moffat, Mary Jane, and Charlotte Painter, eds. *Revelations: Diaries of Women*. New York: Random House, 1974.

Momigliano, A. "Popular Religious Beliefs and the Late Roman Historians." *Studies in Church History* 8 (1972): 14–15.

Mozley, J. H., ed. and trans. *Statius*. Vol. 1. London: Heinemann, 1967.

Münzer, F. "Cornelia." In *Real-Encyclopädie der Klassischen Altertumswissenschaft*.

Murray, Oswyn. *Early Greece*. Atlantic Highlands, N. J.: Humanities Press, 1980.

Nagy, Gregory. "Phaethon, Sappho's Phaon, and the White Rocks of Leukas." *Harvard Studies in Classical Philology* 77 (1973): 137–77.

Nisetich, Frank J., trans. *Pindar's Victory Songs*. Baltimore: Johns Hopkins Press, 1980.

Ogilvie, Marilyn Bailey. *Women in Science: Antiquity through the Nineteenth Century*. Cambridge: MIT Press, 1986.

Ostriker, Alicia Suskin. *Stealing the Language: The Emergence of Women's Poetry in America*. Boston: Beacon Press, 1986.

Oxford Classical Dictionary. Edited by N. G. L. Hammond and H. H. Scullard. Oxford: Clarendon Press, 1970.

Page, Denys, ed. and trans. *Sappho and Alcaeus*. Oxford: Clarendon Press, 1955.

Patrick, Mary Mills. *Sappho and the Island of Lesbos*. Boston: Houghton Mifflin, 1912.

Pomeroy, Sarah B. *Goddesses, Whores, Wives, and Slaves*. New York: Schocken, 1975.

———. "Supplementary Notes on Erinna." *Zeitschrift für Epigraphik* 32 (1978): 17–22.

———. "Technikai kai Mousikai." *American Journal of Ancient History* 2 (1977): 51–68.

———. *Women in Hellenistic Egypt*. New York: Schocken, 1984.

Pound, Ezra. "Horace." *The Criterion* 9 (1929–30); *Arion* 9 (1970): 178–87.

Praechter, Karl. "Hypatia." In *Real-Encyclopädie der Klassischen Altertumswissenschaft.*

Pratt, William, ed. *The Imagist Poem.* New York: Dutton, 1963.

Quinn, Vincent. *Hilda Doolittle.* New York: Twayne, 1967.

Raby, F. *Christian-Latin Poetry.* Oxford: Clarendon Press, 1927.

Race, William H. *The Classical Priamel from Homer to Boethius. Mnemosyne,* suppl. 74. Leiden: E. J. Brill, 1982.

Reitzenstein, Richard. *Epigramm und Skolion.* 1893. Reprint. Hildesheim: G. Olms, 1970.

Reynolds, L. D., and N. G. Wilson. *Scribes and Scholars: A Guide to the Transmission of Greek and Latin Literature.* Oxford: Clarendon Press, 1974.

Rich, Adrienne. "Foreword: On History, Illiteracy, Passivity, Violence, and Women's Culture." In *On Lies, Secrets, and Silence: Selected Prose 1966–1978.* New York: Norton, 1979.

———. "Vesuvius at Home: The Power of Emily Dickinson." In *On Lies, Secrets, and Silence: Selected Prose 1966–1978.* New York: Norton, 1979.

Richardson, L., Jr. *Propertius: Elegies I–IV.* Norman: University of Oklahoma Press, 1977.

Richter, Gisela M. A. *The Portraits of the Greeks.* 4 vols. London: Phaidon Press, 1965.

Rist, J. M. "Hypatia." *Phoenix* 19 (1965): 214–25.

Robert, L. "Inscriptions de Julia Gordos et du Nord-Est de la Lydie." *Hellenica* 6 (1948): 89–104.

Robinson, David M. *Sappho and Her Influence.* 1924. Reprint. New York: Cooper Square, 1963.

Robinson, Janice S. *H.D.: The Life and Work of an American Poet.* Boston: Houghton Mifflin, 1982.

Roller, Duane W. "Tanagra Survey Project 1985: Preliminary Report." *Echos du Monde Classique* 30 ns 5 (1986): 160–72.

Rose, H. J. "Pindar and Korinna." *Classical Review* 48 (1934): 8.

Saake, Helmut. *Sapphostudien.* Munich: F. Schöningh, 1972.

Santirocco, Matthew. "Sulpicia Reconsidered." *Classical Journal* 74 (1979): 229–39.

Schmid, Wilhelm, and Otto Stählin, eds. *Geschichte der Griechischen Literatur.* 5 vols. Munich: Beck, 1929.

Scholz, Udo W. "Erinna." *Antike und Abendland* 18 (1973): 15–40.

Sivan, Hagith S. "Piety and Pilgrimage in the Age of Gratian: Who Was Egeria?" *Harvard Theological Review* 81 (1988): forthcoming.

Skinner, Marilyn B. "Briseis, the Trojan Women, and Erinna." *Classical World* 75 (1982): 265–69.

———. "Corinna of Tanagra and Her Audience." *Tulsa Studies in Women's Literature* 2 (1983): 9–20.

————. "Greek Women and the Metronymic: A Note on an Epigram by Nossis." *Ancient History Bulletin* 1 (1987): 39–42.

————. "Nossis Thelyglossos: Lesbian Author and Male Audience." In volume edited by Sarah B. Pomeroy. Chapel Hill: University of North Carolina Press, forthcoming.

Smith, Kirby Flower, ed. *The Elegies of Albius Tibullus.* 1913. Reprint. New York: American Book, 1979.

Snyder, Jane McIntosh. "The *Barbitos* in the Classical Period." *Classical Journal* 67 (1972): 331–40.

————. "Korinna's 'Glorious Songs of Heroes.'" *Eranos* 82 (1984): 1–10.

————. "Lucretius and the Status of Women." *Classical Bulletin* 53 (1976): 17–20.

————. "The Web of Song: Weaving Imagery in Homer and the Lyric Poets." *Classical Journal* 76 (1981): 193–96.

Spender, Dale. *Women of Ideas and What Men Have Done to Them.* London: Routledge and Kegan Paul, 1982.

Spitzer, Leo. "The Epic Style of the Pilgrim Aetheria." *Comparative Literature* 1 (1949): 225–58.

Starowieyski, M. "Bibliographia Egeriana." *Augustinianum* 19 (1979): 297–317.

Stern, E. von. "Zur Beurteilung der politischen Wirksamkeit des Tiberius und Gaius Gracchus." *Hermes* 56 (1921): 229–301.

Stigers, Eva Stehle. "Sappho's Private World." *Women's Studies* 8 (1981): 54–56.

Stowers, Stanley K. *Letter Writing in Greco-Roman Antiquity.* Philadelphia: Westminster Press, 1986.

Swann, Thomas B. *The Classical World of H.D.* Lincoln: University of Nebraska Press, 1962.

Tarn, W. W. *Hellenistic Civilisation.* Cleveland: World Publishing, 1961.

Thesleff, Holger. *An Introduction to the Pythagorean Writings of the Hellenistic Period.* Acta Academiae Aboensis, vol. 24.3. Åbo: Åbo Akademi, 1961.

Thesleff, Holger, ed. *The Pythagorean Texts of the Hellenistic Period.* Acta Academiae Aboensis, ser. A, vol. 30. Åbo: Åbo Akademi, 1965.

Thompson, Maurice. "The Sapphic Secret." *Atlantic Monthly* 73 (1894): 365–72.

Tomlinson, R. A. *Argos and the Argolid.* Ithaca, N.Y.: Cornell University Press, 1972.

Trendall, Arthur D., and T. B. L. Webster. *Illustrations of Greek Drama.* London: Phaidon, 1971.

Treu, Max. *Sappho.* Munich: Ernst Heimeran, 1954.

Tsagarakis, Odysseus. *Self-Expression in Early Greek Lyric, Elegiac, and Iambic Poetry.* Wiesbaden: Franz Steiner, 1977.

Ure, P. N. "The Outer Greek World in the Sixth Century." In *Cambridge Ancient History*. Cambridge: Cambridge University Press, 1926.

Vermeule, Cornelius. *Greek Art: Sokrates to Sulla*. Boston: Museum of Fine Arts, 1980.

Vidal-Naquet, Pierre. "Slavery and the Rule of Women." In *Myth, Religion, and Society*, edited by Raymond L. Gordon. Cambridge: Cambridge University Press, 1981.

Waith, Mary Ellen. "Authenticating the Fragments and Letters." In *A History of Women Philosophers*, edited by Mary Ellen Waith. Vol. 1. Dordrecht: Nijhoff, 1987.

Walbank, F. W. *The Hellenistic World*. Cambridge: Harvard University Press, 1982.

Wallis, R. T. *Neoplatonism*. London: Duckworth, 1972.

Weber, Clifford. "Egeria's Norman Homeland." *Harvard Studies in Classical Philology* 92 (1988): forthcoming.

Webster, T. B. L. *Hellenistic Poetry and Art*. New York: Barnes and Noble, 1964.

West, M. L. "Corinna." *Classical Quarterly* 20 (1970): 277–87.

———. "Erinna." *Zeitschrift für Papyrologie und Epigraphik* 25 (1977): 95–119.

Wharton, Henry Thorton, ed. and trans. *Sappho: Memoir, Text Selected Renderings, and a Literal Translation*. 1898. Reprint. Amsterdam: Liberac, 1974.

White, Heather. *Essays in Hellenistic Poetry*. Amsterdam: J. C. Gieben, 1980.

Wilamowitz-Moellendorff, Ulrich von. *Sappho und Simonides: Untersuchungen über griechische Lyriker*. Berlin: Weidmann, 1913.

Wills, Gary. "The Sapphic 'Umvertung aller Werte.'" *American Journal of Philology* 88 (1967): 434–42.

Wilson, Katharina M., ed. *Medieval Women Writers*. Athens: University of Georgia Press, 1984.

Winkler, Jack. "Gardens of Nymphs: Public and Private in Sappho's Lyrics." *Women's Studies* 8 (1981): 65–91.

Wright, Frederick A. "The Women Poets of Greece." *Fortnightly Review* ns 113 (1923): 323–33.

Zacher, Christian K. *Curiosity and Pilgrimage: The Literature of Discovery in Fourteenth-Century England*. Baltimore: Johns Hopkins University Press, 1974.

Ziegler, J. "Die *Peregrinatio Aetheriae* und das *Onomastikon* des Eusebius." *Biblica* 12 (1931): 70–84.

Index

Jane McIntosh Snyder was born in 1943 in Champaign, Illinois and was educated at Wellesley College and the University of North Carolina at Chapel Hill, from which she received her Ph.D. in Classics in 1969. Since 1968 she has taught at The Ohio State University, where she has served as associate dean of the College of Humanities. At present she is chair of the Department of Classics. Her publications include articles and books on Lucretius, women in antiquity, Greek lyric poetry, and ancient Greek musical instruments. A professional violinist in her spare time, she plays with the Pro Musica Chamber Orchestra of Columbus.